Mass Market
Medieval

Mass Market Medieval

Essays on the Middle Ages in Popular Culture

Edited by David W. Marshall

McFarland & Company, Inc., Publishers
Jefferson, North Carolina, and London

LIBRARY OF CONGRESS CATALOGUING-IN-PUBLICATION DATA

Mass market medieval : essays on the Middle Ages in popular
  culture / edited by David W. Marshall.
      p.   cm.
  Includes bibliographical references and index.

  ISBN-13: 978-0-7864-2922-6
  (softcover : 50# alkaline paper) ∞

  1. Medievalism.   2. Medievalism—Social aspects.
  3. Medievalism—Political aspects.   4. Popular culture.
  5. Commercial products—Social aspects.   6. Middle Ages in art.
  7. Middle Ages in literature.   8. Middle Ages in motion pictures.
  9. Rock music—Social aspects.   10. Culture in motion pictures.
  I. Marshall, David W., 1970–
  CB353.M37   2007
  909.07—dc22   2007001362

British Library cataloguing data are available

Cover image ©2007 Photodisc

Manufactured in the United States of America

*McFarland & Company, Inc., Publishers
  Box 611, Jefferson, North Carolina 28640
  www.mcfarlandpub.com*

For my parents,
who introduced me to the Middle Ages
with a fox named Robin Hood

Acknowledgments

Without the labor, patience, and diligence of the contributors, this collection would not be. My gratitude goes to them for enabling me to draw a composite picture of the medievalism of popular culture so that others may become equally distracted by it. Kevin J. Harty's generosity with valuable time, sage advice, and needed encouragement leave an indelible mark on this collection and its editor. Thank you, Kevin. Thanks, too, to Jackie Jenkins and Katherine Lewis for prompting me to see the series of sessions I organized at the International Congress on the Middle Ages as not just a pleasant intellectual enterprise, but a means of compiling a book that explored a topic with which I have been preoccupied for several years. Finally, thanks to my wife, whom I bored with one bad medieval movie after another, irritated with a series of "medievally" games, exasperated with recounting the plots of fantasy novels, and generally drove mad with my obsession. Thanks, too, to my sons, for letting me play with their toy knights, Vikings, and castles.

Table of Contents

Introduction:
The Medievalism
of Popular Culture

DAVID W. MARSHALL

S ince its publication in 2003 and film adaptation in 2006, Dan Brown's *The Da Vinci Code* has drawn an audience of millions into a mysterious labyrinth that traces its way back in time to a Middle Ages marked by warrior monks and church secrets. Led by symbologist Robert Langdon, cryptologist Sophie Neveu, and the occasional albino flagellant monk, readers race from Chartres Cathedral to the Temple Church in London, where reclining Templar effigies watch passively over clues available only to those who know how to decipher them. While the novel spins back in time to the first century A.D. and forward up to the modern day, Brown centers *The Da Vinci Code* on the Middle Ages and the 1099 founding of the Priory of Sion, and in doing so, sets the medieval as the point of origin for the covert ecclesiastical structures that his mystery uncovers. This centering of the plot, however, also draws the medieval forward in time and gives it a sense of immediate relevance that suggests the medieval past still communicates through its symbols and images to (post-)modern people like Robert Langdon and Sophie Neveu. Beyond this notion of the past speaking to the present, Brown offers readers an opportunity to see the possibility not just of seeing meaning, but also of creating meaning from the past. Our albino flagellant monk evokes an aura of difference in his devotion to mortification. That difference becomes for Brown a means of making meaning. The flagellant's thought, "pain is good," and his adjusting his spiked belt strikes readers as alien and fanatical. Brown's use of extreme elements of the medieval past makes a distorted version of the Middle Ages (existing in the present) by isolating and exaggerating them. One might go further to suggest that

Brown's entire novel creates a medieval past that never was by fixating on a small set of iconic images—in particular the Templars as the proto–secret society—to build a fictional Middle Ages devoid of peasants, primogeniture, or pesky details that have no bearing on the desired trajectory of the plot. All of this twisting and pulling of the past amounts to what may be the most commercially successful example of medievalism in recent history.

As a field of study, medievalism interrogates how different groups, individuals, or eras for various reasons, often distortedly, remember the Middle Ages. This interest in how the medieval is remembered distinguishes medievalism from medieval studies, which maintains an interest in what the Middle Ages actually were, how they looked and worked in their reality. Medievalism, on the other hand, prompts scholars to ask how the Middle Ages are invoked in their myriad incarnations and for what purpose in relation to the historical context of any given expression of them. For example, from Spenser's *Faerie Queene* (1596) to Walpole's *Castle of Otronto* (1765) to Scott's *Ivanhoe* (1791) and Kingsley's less than notable *Hereward the Wake* (1865–66), scholars have examined literary medievalism. Outside of literary medievalism, academics have explored the ways in which moderns have attempted to revive medieval practices and philosophies such as those of William Morris and the British Arts and Crafts movement or the Pre-Raphaelite Brotherhood, even looking at quirkier expressions like the 1839 Eglinton Tournament, in which members of the British aristocracy attempted a medieval joust before rain set their plans back. In American history, the idealization or demonization of the Middle Ages has been taken up by political historians in studies of early political tracts such as those produced by Thomas Jefferson and Thomas Paine that used the period for its potential as either a positive or a negative model of social order, respectively. Additionally, studies of nineteenth century European nationalism are very much indebted to analyses of histories that extend national identities back into the Middle Ages, such as Macaulay's four-volume history of Britain (1849), as an organizing idea. What has been absent from these now accepted types of studies are manifestations of the medieval as popular culture.

Over the last thirty years or so, mainstream medievalism has emerged from its "reputation as an aberration" (Simmons 1) to become a significant element of medieval studies—a reputation that the medievalism of popular culture has yet to shed. The legitimizing of medievalism in general is largely due to three bursts of activity. Much of the credit goes to Leslie Workman, who, in the first burst in 1976, began publishing the journal *Studies in Medievalism*. Workman's journal allowed scholars to begin taking up the subject and publishing articles in the field of medievalism. The second burst occurred in 1991, with Norman Cantor's study *Inventing the Middle Ages*, which examines the ways that postwar scholars figured and refigured the Middle Ages by grafting unconsidered assumptions onto their descriptions of the period. The number of published scholarly books and articles on medievalism grew exponentially from 1991, as Cantor seems to have brought Workman's underappreciated journal and its subject into the mainstream.

It makes sense that this growth of medievalism coincided with the emergence of a school of historical thought that positions history as a constructed interplay of past events and ideologically motivated interpretation. This movement within historical study found its capstone in 1975 with the publication of Hayden White's *Metahistory*, in which White concludes that "there are no grounds on which one [historical account] is more 'realistic.' This means that one being held as more 'truthful' than the others can only be seen as biases of the related establishment or author" (xi). White, drawing together the work of historians in the 1960s, managed to show that histories conceal the past with present concerns—a governing idea in both Workman's creation of *Studies in Medievalism* a year later and in Cantor's *Inventing the Middle Ages*. Because White claims historiography is historically contingent and dependant upon the ideological situation of the historian, medievalists have been required to pay greater attention to the formative influences of medieval studies and the present concerns that color our views of that past. Hayden White solidified, if not forced, the adoption of medievalism as an important field of study by suggesting that uncertainty in the interpretation of the past leads to choices of representation that are predetermined by conventional models in the historian's mind. Medievalism as an area of study offers a solution to White's disturbance, because in this field of inquiry, researchers begin to differentiate between what we know of the Middle Ages and what we have made the Middle Ages to be. Medievalism asks scholars to approach the period as one of those old European castles that has been augmented and modified over the years. The task is to create a genealogy of sorts, to locate what parts of the castle are not original in order to better reveal the true edifice—as Workman did in establishing his journal and as Cantor did in *Inventing the Middle Ages*.

The third burst of activity signals what appears to be a splintering in the trajectory of the field and the pairing of popular culture and medievalism. This shift begins in the late 1980s with a smattering of articles and books that took up the topic of the Middle Ages as represented in film, including studies such as Martin B. Schichtman's "Hollywood's New Weston: The Grail Myth in Francis Ford Coppola's *Apocalypse Now* and John Boorman's *Excalibur*" (1984), François Amy de la Bretèque's edited issue of *Cahiers de la cinémathèque* titled *Le Moyen Age au Cinéma* (1985), Linda Tarte Holly's "Medievalism in Film: The Matter of Arthur, a Filmography" (1988), Norris J. Lacy's "Arthurian Film and the Tyranny of Tradition" (1989), and David Turner's *Robin of the Movies* (1989).[1] As part of these early stages of studying the medievalism of popular culture, in 1987 Kevin J. Harty began a process of legitimizing the field with his articles "Cinema Arthuriana: A Filmography," which took steps to define the corpus, and "Cinema Arthuriana: Translations of the Arthurian Legend to the Screen," followed in 1989 by "Cinema Arthuriana: A Bibliography of Selected Secondary Materials," which drew together the scholarly work done on medieval movies. That work was followed in 1990 by David Williams' article "Medieval Movies," which extended the scope of Harty's work. Harty's collection of essays *Cinema Arthuriana* in 1991 continued to draw critical attention to the burgeoning field, followed in 1999 by *King Arthur on Film*. But perhaps no work did more to bring attention to medieval movies as a field of study than Harty's extensive 1999 filmography *The Reel Middle Ages*, which has given other scholars an in-road to the subject by supplying an exhaustive survey of the corpus of medieval movies. Harty's work has caused a blossoming of scholarship on filmic representations of the Middle Ages that include *A Knight at the Movies* and *The Medieval Hero on Film*, amongst other titles. What Harty popularized is the scholarly study of contemporary cultural products that invoke the Middle Ages in popular forms.

This new trajectory for medievalism can be distinguished from what might be described as genealogical medievalism by its affinity not with the concerns of historical production and the interpretation of the past that is genealogical medievalism's goal, but rather with media production and representation of the past. Genealogical medievalism addresses the accumulative production of an idea of the Middle Ages that continually sets the parameters for understanding what that period was. Pop cultural medievalism, thus, has less to do with meta-history and the building of a scholarly genealogy and more to do with the cultural studies movement that emerged in the 1970s and that gained momentum in the 1980s. Cultural studies originally concerned itself with the culture of the masses, particularly in British cultural studies, which brought critical attention to objects normally deemed low culture. This brand of medievalism approaches the products of mass-culture—in Harty's work, film—with a mind, on the one hand, to define the cultural mores and values particular uses of the medieval embody, and on the other, to attempt to answer the question: what do the Middle Ages mean to any given group? To that extent, the medievalism of popular culture is an area that shares aspects with genealogical medievalism, but diverges in its attention to current concerns. But outside of film, to which plenty of attention is given, other popular forms have gone largely unstudied.

The reasons the medievalism of popular culture has been relatively neglected are not difficult to divine. Generally speaking, popular manifestations of medievalism can fall more within the realm of cultural studies programs than medieval studies—an area focused on investigation of the "actual" Middle Ages. Within cultural studies programs, there is an emphasis on scholarship which treats culture after the 1970s, and there are rarely scholars well-versed enough in the specifics of the Middle Ages to feel comfortable dissecting the various formulations of medieval tropes or images against a baseline of what might be considered normative in the period itself. Within medieval studies, there seems to be a confluence of factors directing attention away from contemporary popular media. Given pop-cultural medievalism's relation to cultural studies, it suffers from the same high-cultural stigma under which cultural studies programs labored for years. Under this stigma, examining pop cultural appropriations of the medieval is reduced to analysis of simulacra, which in Frederic Jameson's thinking leaves the scholar studying a pastiche, a hodge-podge representation that has neither a real connection to the past nor any clear bearing on the present. In this way, the high-culture/low-culture divide becomes redefined in terms of chronology. In one version of this model, the Middle Ages stands in for high culture, while pop cultural uses of it are positioned as low, and hence unworthy of serious examination on an academic level. Analysis of popular piety in the Middle Ages, for example, is appropriate subject matter, but the use of medieval tropes in contemporary popular religion is not. In another version of this model, studies of what might be considered popular materials are permissible, provided they are well-removed from the present moment. Thus, numerous studies have been done on Sir Walter Scott's medievalism, but they can be folded into either genealogical medievalism or Victorian studies, which has been a repository for studies of appropriation of the medieval. Contemporary popular manifestations lack that legitimating home.

Despite this lack, some scholars are working on medievalism in popular culture, and the focus on film is beginning to give way to other media in which the phenomenon appears. Donald L. Hoffman and Elizabeth S. Sklar have edited a collection of essays, *King Arthur in Popular Culture*, that covers uses and representations of Arthuriana in film, print, games, and commercial culture. Susan Aronstein has written on both the contemporary men's movement that arose in the '90s and (with Nancy Coiner) on that castle of glitz and glamour, the Excalibur casino. Additionally, some of the contributors to this collection are raising the profile of the area. Daniel T. Kline works with the group MEMO to examine the various means by which the medieval is transported into electronic media such as video games or Web sites, and in the last couple years, Carl Grindley has taken the initiative to start a society for the study of medievalism in popular culture. So, despite the relatively minimal attention given to the subject, it is a field ripe for picking, and harvesters are beginning to reap the crop.

But this is a bumper crop, making it a shame that the mounting area of popular culture in medieval studies continues to sit in a marginal position—again, with the exception of film. In his observation that the twentieth century media are those now rediscovering the Middle Ages, Umberto Eco has committed something of an understatement. The use of medieval images and tropes in popular culture has seen an explosion in recent years. The boom in the production of medievalist objects can be attributed to two interrelated developments. First, the economic policies of the Reagan-Thatcher years that shifted Western economies from manufacturing to service and consumer goods produced a culture of hyper-consumerism. As Jameson observes of this economy, "the frantic economic urgency of producing fresh waves of ever more novel-seeming goods (from clothing to airplanes), at ever greater rates of turnover, now assigns an increasingly essential structural function and position to aesthetic innovation and experimentation" (4). Innovation, however, does not require pushing towards the future, but allows for turning to the past. Thereby, the Middle Ages becomes a source of design inspiration in the promulgation of kitsch culture. The second cause spins off of this market explanation. Technological progress, namely the development of new media such as commercial cable television, the creation of the home video industry, and the rapid progress in electronic games and media, enables consumers to indulge in the medieval to what most would call an excess. These shifts in the market and in the technological advances related to it ultimately produce commodification across time and space such that the European Middle Ages are packaged into easily consumable nuggets in a process that we might think of as shrink-wrapping time.

For example, I can sit on a wooden monks' bench in my living room decorated with faux-ruined medieval arches and tapestries—all available from Design Toscano—while I watch a documentary about knights and tournaments or the latest cable-release movie about King Arthur, taking a break only to eat some Dak ham, branded with the Viking profile. Or perhaps I might rather enjoy spending several hours forming alliances and waging war against weak vassals in a computer strategy game (with a computer gargoyle perched on my monitor, again courtesy of Design Toscano) while I listen to some of Man-o-War's greatest hits—a stack of medieval comic books or medieval mysteries awaiting me should I need a break. If I need to leave the house, there is always Medieval Times for dinner and a show, or my annual Renaissance fair (which revels more in iconic images of the Middle Ages than in the Renaissance). The kitsch-filled consumer culture so lamented by Jameson has created a vast field for exploring an ongoing passion for the Middle Ages in contemporary culture. If medieval is what you want, medieval is what you can get.

Contrary to Jameson's lament that these examples of pastiche are meaningless "blank parody," however, Linda Hutcheon might lead us to say that medieval kitsch is a site of cultural conversations in which producers and consumers connect with a period marked in our understanding of it by rigid categories of gender, religion, and class (to name just a few).[2] Those rigid categories offer opportunities to invoke conservative political positions or alternatively to resist those same positions. For example, in his 1977 novel *Eaters of the Dead*, Michael Crichton offers a rewriting of *Beowulf* that positions women as both the sexual playthings for admirable barbarians and a primitive female priestess/queen, represented by female fertility statues with bulging breasts and bellies, who must be destroyed by the hyper-masculine Beowulf corollary. The book might be read as a reaction to second-wave feminism by neutralizing the threat posed by women who do not fit into the typical role.[3] The Sister Frevisse mysteries, such as *The Maiden's Tale*, however, present the portrait of nun who manages to work on the boundaries of her proper role to solve murders. The series offers the possibility of working outside the limits of normal social roles in a form of literary liberation. The Crichton example provides perhaps the best reason for taking up the task of exploring pop cultural medievalism.

One thing we have learned from genealogical medievalism is that the Middle Ages have been a source of material for justifying all manner of political and social positions. One story, for example, goes that Hitler requested that a genealogy be written for him that would trace his lineage back to Woden, just as so many of the early Germanic kings had. But the forms of medievalism in popular culture also have problematic aspects. The popular computer game "Age of Empires" is one such case insofar as it might read as naturalizing imperial aspirations. The difficulty here is in the subtlety with which it happens. Because "Age of Empires" can be written off as just another silly computer game, the potential influence goes unnoticed. In such a reading, millions of game-players internalize a rhetoric of global influence and control that might occlude the problems with neo-colonial endeavors. The study of pop cultural medievalism thus becomes a means of locating the ways in which the Middle Ages continue to be used to justify or naturalize socio-political agendas, or at least to desensitize us to them.

Furthermore, popular contemporary medievalism can be a barometer for cultural shifts occurring around us. Locating the connectedness of various representations of the medieval points to less individual, more broadly cultural desires for the medieval and what they might signify at any given time, and in so doing, facilitates a means of offering a particular relevance for the medievalist to debates about social affairs by translating the medieval signs used to communicate communal desires and fears. Returning to the example of Crichton's *Eaters of the Dead*, we might use the film version, *The Thirteenth Warrior*, made some twenty-five years later, to suggest that despite the persistence of anti-feminist ideas, the lack of box-office success indicates an abatement of the reactionary invective. The serious treatment of medievalism in popular culture opens avenues for medievalists to further engage in the social debates that occupy other areas of academic inquiry. This reason should be particularly appealing to medievalists, since scholars of the Middle Ages sometimes find themselves feeling marginalized in the larger academic setting and as if medieval studies must explain their usefulness in ways that studies of other periods do not.

There is a strange irony in the marginal position of pop-cultural medievalism. As Eco has (by now, famously) observed, "People seem to like the Middle Ages." And as Louise Fradenberg would point out, a group included in that broad term *people* is medievalists. She writes, "Our enjoyment of the signifier is at the heart of our practice in literary and cultural studies, but we have permitted our explicit attention to the issue of enjoyment to flag somewhat" (206). As Fradenburg suggests, medievalists study the Middle Ages because of an initial enjoyment of the period, an enjoyment she claims becomes ignored in study and teaching. Popular representations of the period are frequently the first introduction to medieval studies. So, truth be told, while Eco points out the popular appeal of the medieval, medievalists seem to like pop culture. It can be instructive to inquire why we like the period. Identifying the source of appeal can be a means of locating the cultural resonance that the Middle Ages continues to have with twenty-first century people. To that end, enjoyment is not just a lure, but an in-road. Pleasure, in other words, is a valid reason to pursue the field. If popular representations or uses of medieval forms were the initial draw into medieval studies, it seems relevant to study the sources of that enjoyment. But unlike the *people* in Eco's statement who continually discover and enjoy the Middle Ages, medieval studies seem to maintain an impression that medievalists outgrow that initial draw of popular forms of the medieval for more intellectually heady materials.

We might also study the medievalism of popular culture because it aids the institutional work of genealogical medievalism. By undertaking study of what Eco describes as the continual rediscovery of the Middle Ages, medievalists construct an archive that documents the uses and abuses, the representations and misrepresentations, or the dreams and nightmares of the Middle Ages that continue to influence understandings of the period and perpetuate myths and agendas. While genealogical medievalism has focused largely on constructions of the medieval such as the aforementioned history of Macaulay, paintings of the Pre-Raphaelites, and Sir Walter Scott's novels, current popular culture perpetuates the distortions of earlier periods insofar as twenty-first century writers and artists find inspiration in Scott or the pre–Raphaelites. Moreover, those writers and artists find new ways of twisting the medieval in the service of twenty-first century interests. The essays in this collection, for example, add to the growing repository of studies that explore the ways that these new producers of culture are offering up the Middle Ages for consumption. To that end, analyses of popular media including those in this volume become a valuable means of sharing the labors of genealogical medievalists by building a contemporary archive of the distortions of the Middle Ages in various media.

The study of pop-cultural medievalism can also better prepare medievalists to teach their subject. This may seem a strange contention given the notion that it is expertise in our area that facilitates good teaching of the subject. But exploring the scope of pop-cultural uses of the medieval brings educators into close contact with students by offering a view of the Middle Ages from the students' perspective. Most of our students encounter the medieval via popular media, be it video games, the trappings of Goth culture, children's novels, Tolkien's recent resurgence, or, of course, film. A brief survey, therefore, gives teachers of the Middle Ages a clearer sense of what (mis)conceptions of the period students carry on medieval subjects. But teachers of the Middle Ages can go beyond simply being acquainted with students' illusions about the medieval. Those forms of popular media can become tools for teaching. For example, as Daniel T. Kline described at the 38th International Congress on Medieval Studies, "Age of Empires" can be used to draw attention to social structures in the Middle Ages. The game positions players as rulers who command serfs to harvest raw materials and produce buildings and weapons. In the classroom, the game can be used to draw attention to the labor force, or third estate, within the medieval social structure and to open up a discussion of modes of production for the icons of medieval culture, like castles, cathedrals, and city walls. Pastiche thereby becomes productive and educational. Granted, there are some theoretical problems with this, if we consider Hayden White's arguments about history. Using the game to spark a conversation about medieval labor assumes knowledge of a "real Middle Ages," which White suggests is unknowable. But despite White's claims about the unknowability of a real period of history, there are certainly knowable elements. A mass labor force, which was referred to by some as the third estate, is a knowable aspect of the Middle Ages, even if that knowledge of the third estate is mediated through Gower or the Chessbook or one of the many other sources that discuss the lower classes as such.

The present collection is offered as an introduction into the medievalism of popular culture. All the contributors share an interest in popular media, though individual and theoretical perspectives are diverse. The rationale for such a broad survey is both to provide readers with a general scope of the types of media in use in recent medievalism as well as to demonstrate the array of approaches being taken to the subject. Because each essay could be categorized in multiple ways, there is no rigid structuring principle to this collection. Rather, essays are arranged in a continuum of affiliations, grouped loosely around five functions of the medieval within popular culture. The first few essays explore ways that study of the medieval in popular culture exposes social concerns of recent times. The social uses segue into the political with several contributions that examine the use of the medieval in recent political contexts. Those treatments of political medievalism transition into studies of historiographical medievalism with a set of essays addressing how medieval history is offered up for consumption. Essays on how the Middle Ages are taught (or can teach) shift the historiographical into the pedagogical uses of the medieval. The collection concludes with essays that consider the extent to which medieval forms structure products of popular culture. As a collection, these examinations of the medievalism of popular culture offer inroads into studying appropriations of the medieval into mainstream culture—and perhaps into enjoying those appropriations as well.

Notes

My thanks to Paul Gutjahr, Purnima Bose, Bailey McDaniel, Judy Nitsch, and Bryan Rasmussen for reading this introduction in its various stages.

1. A limited amount of work was done on medievalism in film prior to the development of the area as a recognized field of study. See Behlmer, "Robin Hood on the Screen"; Richards, *Swordsmen of the Screen from Douglas Fairbanks to Michael York*, Barthélemy, *Le Mythe de Tristan et Yseult au cinema*; Durand, "La Chevalerie à l'écran."

2. Jameson and Hutcheon have engaged in this debate via their respective books. Jameson's *Postmodernism: The Cultural Logic of Late Capitalism* is addressed directly by Hutcheon in her *Politics of Postmodernism*.

3. I am beginning work on a book that will take up the myriad ways that *Beowulf* has been appropriated in the twentieth century, addressing the Crichton book alongside Gardner's *Grendel* in one chapter, with other chapters devoted to the range of comic books, musical adaptations, films, games, and translations.

Works Cited

Agrawal, R.R. *The Medieval Revival and Its Influence on the Romantic Movement*. New Delhi: Abhinav Publications, 1990.

Baines, Paul. "'All of the House of Forgery': Walpole, Chatterton, and Antiquarian Commerce." *Poetica: An International Journal of Linguistic and Literary Studies* 39–40 (1994): 45–72.

Banham, Joanna, and Jennifer Harris. *William Morris and the Middle Ages: A Collection of Essays.* Manchester: Manchester University Press, 1984.

Barclay, David E. "Medievalism and Nationalism in Nineteenth-Century Germany." In *Medievalism in Europe*, edited by Leslie J. Workman. Studies in Medievalism, vol. 5. Cambridge: D.S. Brewer, 1993. 5–22.

Barczewski, Stephanie L. *Myth and National Identity in Nineteenth Century Britain: The Legends of King Arthur and Robin Hood.* Oxford; New York: Oxford University Press, 2000.

Barthélemy, Armengual. *Le Mythe de Tristan et Yseult au cinema.* Algiers: Travail et culture, 1952.

Beckett, Ruth. "Past and Present: Carlyle and Ruskin on Scott and Victorian Medievalism; Selected Papers from 4th International Scott Conference, Edinburgh, 1991." In *Scot in Carnival*, edited by J.H. Alexander and David Hewitt. Aberdeen: Association for Scottish Literary Studies, 1993. 512–22.

Behlmer, Rudy. "Robin Hood on the Screen." *Films in Review* 16 (1965): 91–102.

Bonnel, Roland. "Medieval Nostalgia in France, 1750–1789: The Gothic Imaginary at the End of the Old Regime." In *Medievalism in Europe*, edited by Leslie J. Workman. Studies in Medievalism, vol. 5. Cambridge: D.S. Brewer, 1993. 139–63.

Boos, Florence S. "Alternative Victorian Futures: Historicism, Past and Present and a Dream of John Ball." In *History and Community: Essays in Victorian Medievalism*, edited by Florence S. Boos. New York: Garland, 1992. 3–37.

_____. "The Medieval Tales of William Morris' The Earthly Paradise." *Studies in Medievalism* 1.1 (1979): 45–54.

de la Bretèque, Amy, ed. *Le Moyen Age au Cinéma. Cahiers de la cinémathèque* 42–43 (summer 1985): 1–188. (Special issue.)

Brown, Dan. *The DaVinci Code.* New York: Doubleday, 2003.

Burke, John J., Jr. "The Romantic Window and the Postmodern Mirror: The Medieval Worlds of Sir Walter Scott and Umberto Eco." In *Scot in Carnival*, edited by J.H. Alexander and David Hewitt. Aberdeen: Association for Scottish Literary Studies, 1993. 556–68.

Cantor, Norman F. *Inventing the Middle Ages.* New York: Harper Perennial, 1993.

Cheney, Liana De Girolami. "The Fair Lady and the Virgin in Pre-Raphaelite Art: The Evolution of a Societal Myth." In *Pre-Raphaelitism and Medievalism in the Arts*, edited by Linda Cheney De Girolami. Lewinston, N.Y.: Mellen, 1992. 241–80.

Cochran, Rebecca. "Swinburne's 'Lancelot' and Pre-Raphaelite Medievalism." *Victorian Newsletter* 74 (fall 1988): 58–62.

Crichton, Michael. *Eaters of the Dead.* New York: Ballantine Books, 1993.

Durand, Jacques. "La Chevalerie à l'écran." *Avant-scène du cinema* 221 (1979): 29–40.

Eco, Umberto. *Travels in Hyperreality.* Trans. William Weaver. San Diego: Harvest Books, 1983.

Fradenburg, Louise Olga. "'So That We May Speak of Them': Enjoying the Middle Ages." *New Literary History* 28.2 (spring 1997), 205–230.

Frazer, Margaret. *The Maiden's Tale.* New York: Berkeley, 1998.

Fuwa, Yuri. "Malory's Morte Darthur in Tennyson's Library." In *Medievalism in England*, edited by Leslie J. Workman. Studies in Medievalism, vol. 4. Cambridge: D.S. Brewer, 1994. 161–69.

Gebhard, Caroline. "Agnes of Sorrento: Harriet Beecher Stowe's Medieval Correction to Nathaniel Hawthorne's The Marble Faun." In *Reinventing the Middle Ages and the Renaissance: Constructions of the Medieval and Early Modern Periods*, edited by William F. Gentrup. Turnhout: Brepols, 1998. 167–186.

Harty, Kevin J. "Cinema Arthuriana: a Filmography." *Quondam et Futurus* 7 (spring 1987): 5–8; 7 (summer 1987): 18.

_____. "Cinema Arthuriana: Translations of the Arthurian Legend to the Screen." *Arthurian Interpretations* 2 (fall 1987): 95–113.

_____. "Cinema Arthuriana: A Bibliography of Selected Secondary Materials." *Arthurian Interpretations* 3 (spring 1989): 119–37.
_____, ed. *Cinema Arthuriana: Essays on Arthurian Film.* New York: Garland, 1991.
_____. *The Reel Middle Ages: Films About Medieval Europe.* Jefferson, N.C.: McFarland, 1999.
Hoffman, Donald, and Elizabeth Sklar, eds. *King Arthur in Popular Culture.* Jefferson, N.C.: McFarland, 2002.
Holly, Linda Tarte. "Medievalism in Film: The Matter of Arthur, a Filmography." In *Mittelalter-Rezeption* III, ed. Jürgen Kühnel. Göppingen: Kümmerle, 1988.
Hughes, Linda K. "Skirmishes at the Periphery: Edward Howard, Eglinton, and Aristocratic Chivalry in Metropolitan Magazine." In *The Arthurian Revival: Essays on Form, Tradition, and Transformation,* ed. Debra N. Mancoff. New York: Garland, 1992. 3–30.
Hutcheon, Linda. *Politics of Postmodernism.* New York: Routledge, 2002.
Jameson, Frederic. *Postmodernism, Or, the Cultural Logic of Late Capitalism.* Durham: Duke University Press, 1992.
Kenney, Alice P. "Yankees in Camelot: The Democratization of Chivalry in James Russell Lowell, Mark Twain and Edwin Arlington Robinson." *Studies in Medievalism* 1.2 (spring 1982): 73–78.
Kenney, Alice P. "The Necessity of Invention: Medievalism in America." *Literary Review: An International Journal of Contemporary Writing* 23 (1980): 559–75.
Krier, Theresa M., ed. *Refiguring Chaucer in the Renaissance.* Gainesville: University Press of Florida, 1998.
Lacy, Norris. "Arthurian Film and the Tyranny of Tradition." *Arthurian Interpretations* 4 (fall 1989): 75–85.
Richards, Jeffrey. *Swordsmen of the Screen from Douglas Fairbanks to Michael York.* London: Routledge, 1977.
Schichtman, Martin B. "Hollywood's New Weston: The Grail Myth in Francis Ford Coppola's Apocalypse Now and John Boorman's Excalibur." *Post Script* 4 (autumn 1984): 35–49.
Schoenfield, Mark. "Waging Battle: Ashford vs. Thornton, Ivanhoe, and Legal Violence." In *Medievalism and the Quest for the "Real" Middle Ages,* ed. Clare Simmons. London; Portland: Frank Cass, 2001. 61–86.
Simmons, Clare A. Introduction to *Medievalism and the Quest for the "Real" Middle Ages,* ed. Clare Simmons. London: Frank Cass, 2001.
Summers, David A. *Spenser's Arthur: The British Arthurian Tradition and the Faerie Queene.* Lanham, Md.: University Press of America, 1997.
Turner, David. *Robin of the Movies.* Kingswinford, England: Yeoman Press, 1989.
White, Hayden. *Metahistory: The Historical Imagination in Nineteenth-Century Europe.* Baltimore: Johns Hopkins University Press, 1975.
Williams, David. "Medieval Movies." *Yearbook of English Studies* 20 (1990): 1–32.
Wood, Roger. "'The History Is Concisely This': Thomas Paine's Account of the Peasants' Revolt." In *Medievalism in North America,* ed. Kathleen Verduin. Studies in Medievalism, vol. 6. Cambridge: D.S. Brewer, 1994. 5–20.

1 Chaucer for a New Millennium
The BBC Canterbury Tales*

KEVIN J. HARTY

In memory of John Christopher Kleis.

W hile Chaucer's place in the academy remains secure, he has failed to capture the popular imagination in the same way in which, say, both Dante and Boccaccio have.[1] This failure is especially apparent in terms of film, and by extension television. Chaucer's lack of popular appeal is not easily explained, though it may be that he has proven too easily and singularly associated with Roman Catholicism to be embraced by successive ages of dissent and doubt.[2] The BBC's decision to commission a series of telefilms presenting new versions of selected *Canterbury Tales* for the twenty-first century is, therefore, all the more remarkable: "[T]he series aims to do in the 21st century what Chaucer did in the 14th and hold a mirror up to society and produce a story with strong characters and an even stronger moral code. 'Each tale has been updated to reflect Britain today,' says producer Kate Bartlett, 'with themes like the cult of celebrity, the obsession with youth and bigotry shown towards asylum seekers'" (Hamilton 20).

The Miller's Tale

The BBC series begins with what may well be—for a variety of reasons—Chaucer's most well-known tale, that of the Miller.[3] In Chaucer, the tale of the Miller follows that of the Knight as a kind of commentary on it. The Knight's tale is a high-minded romance with a strong

13

philosophical undercurrent speculating on the nature of fortune and free will in a fallen world. The Miller's tale is a fabliau, a ribald tale, which in many ways apes the world view of the Knight's tale by turning it upside down. There is no known direct source for the Miller's tale, but Chaucer weaves together a narrative about a *senex amans*, a jealous older husband married to a much younger wife, with three common enough folk tale motifs: a fear of a second Deluge, a misdirected kiss, and a branding with a hot poker.[4]

Chaucer's tale is set in Oxford, where an old carpenter, John, who has wed a much younger wife, Alison, has taken in an extremely "handy" (in all senses of the word) student, Nicholas, as a lodger. Nicholas sets into motion an elaborate scheme to cuckold John, which begins to unravel when Alison's other would-be suitor, Absolon, the effeminate and overly fastidious local parish clerk, shows up outside her cottage late at night to woo her.

In the BBC version, the action moves to a karaoke pub *cum* B&B in Kent, owned by the volatile, older, and extremely jealous John Crosby. The pub's principal singer is John's much younger wife, Alison, who often performs duos with the also young Danny Absolon, the local barber and Alison's at times less-than-secret admirer. Enter Nick Zakian, a grifter in a stolen flashy red sports car that has inconveniently run out of gas on the village green. One glimpse of Alison sets Nick's hormones in motion as he tries, with great success eventually, to convince everyone in the village that he is a well-connected record producer and all-around nice guy, who also—seemingly out of the goodness of his heart—defends the elderly and defenseless from the village rowdies and hooligans.

John quickly falls for Nick's promise of wealth beyond his imagination, Danny is left to hang out to dry, and a number of the villagers suddenly give Nick free access to their savings in light of promises he makes to enrich them or to improve their lives. As slick as he is amoral, Nick soon enough also beds Alison almost—thanks to some drug-laced cookies her husband unknowingly gobbles up—right under John's eyes, when he turns up at a fake recording system to watch Alison cut a demo. At the same time, Nick runs up thousands and thousands of pounds in charges on John's credit card, which he has conveniently nicked, and bilks Jean Smallwood, an overly trusting aged widow, out of her life's savings and Malcolm Wickens, an almost as old and equally trusting tobacconist, out of his store's entire stock. In the telefilm's last scene, a flustered Alison stands on the motorway under a flyover in the pouring rain as a bus on the London-Canterbury route speeds by. Inside the coach, comfortably warm and dry, Nick sits down next to a newly-engaged couple whom he tries to convince to take part in a reality-show about the newly engaged, which he claims that he is promoting.

Chaucer's tale concludes with the three male principals getting what they deserve in the end—in one case quite literally. In a bow to chivalry, Alison escapes more-or-less unscathed. John ends up with a broken arm and becomes the laughing stock of Oxford. Nicholas and Absolon suffer even more ignominious punishments, and Chaucer's tale has at least a sense of poetic justice about it, a sense recognized by John's fellow villagers and by Chaucer's other story-telling pilgrims who, with the exception of the Reeve, think that the Miller's tale is indeed "nyce" (funny).

The conclusion of the BBC version of the Miller's tale has no such moral niceties. While Nick does indeed suffer a bit of heated posterior retribution from Danny, Alison quickly applies a healing ointment to the affected area, and Nick soon seems no worse for wear. Indeed, Nick triumphs in the end, leaving bewildered villagers—John, Alison, Danny and others—and baffled police in his wake. Chaucer's tale does not spare the foolish and the overly clever, but, in the BBC version of the tale, deceit wins out, and Nick the grifter escapes ready to prey upon others with yet another scheme.

The Wife of Bath's Tale

The second BBC tale is that of the Wife of Bath. In Chaucer, the Wife of Bath gives a virtuoso performance, first in a lengthy self-revelatory prologue and then in a shorter tale. The portrait that Chaucer allows the Wife to paint of herself in her prologue is heavily indebted to more general traditions concerning the so-called "old bawd" in medieval literature as well as to a series of individual antifeminist works—if not diatribes—from ancient, patristic, and medieval writers.

Chaucer's portrait of the Wife does not so much support this antifeminist attitude as reduce it to its extremes to create a character more sinned against than sinner. The Wife's tale is a sort of anti-romance, in which a knight rapes rather than rescues a damsel, and as punishment must answer the riddle of what it is that women desire most. The particular tale, that of an enchanted loathly lady, is known in various forms in medieval literature. In the Wife's telling, the theme of sovereignty in marriage is the foremost concern, a concern that has informed the multiple marriages that the Wife herself has endured, as she details in her prologue. The Wife's tale has a kind of fairy tale ending in which youth, beauty, and rightful sovereignty prevail, even if such an ending escapes the Wife herself in her own life.[5]

In the BBC version, the wife becomes Beth Craddock, an aging soap opera star—she admits to being fifty or so. In a clever conflation, the BBC version incorporates narrative elements and details from both the Wife's original prologue and her subsequent tale. Framing Beth's story are parts of a tell-all television interview that she gives to her publicist, Jessica, to plug her already popular television show, now in its sixth season.

"Married," as she readily admits, "more times than you've had hot dinners," Beth is still incredibly attractive despite her age—thanks to vitamins and nutritional supplements, exercise, and the odd injection of Botox. One day, she returns home from the day's shoot on the set to James, her dentist husband of sixteen years, who announces he is leaving her because his mistress has had a baby—five years ago, he adds *sotto voce*. Beth consoles herself by beginning an affair with her twenty-something-year-old co-star, Jerome, an affair that is replicated in the script of the soap opera in which they both star.

While it is clear that Jerome really does love Beth, her motives are more complex. When she and Jerome marry—to the horror of his parents, but the seeming approval of her friends—Beth's drunken wedding toast nods a bit too obviously toward the faux Chaucerian: "Who am I to begrudge my chamber of Venus?" But the connubial bliss is short-lived, as the popularity of the soap opera is suddenly in jeopardy when focus groups register a profound disapproval of her relationship with Jerome both on and off the screen. "No one bats an eyelid," Beth vainly protests, "when some old, bald sixty-year old man is shagging some bimbo, but when you turn it around the other way, it becomes something horrific." But the show must go on, and Beth agrees to having Jerome written out of the soap.

Only Beth does not tell Jerome that he has been written out of the show. She instead convinces him to quite the soap opera, so as not to get typecast, and to pursue other opportunities. When Jerome eventually finds out the truth, an ugly scene follows in which he strikes Beth. Eventually, they are reconciled, if only briefly, but only after we are at first led to believe that Jerome has seriously injured Beth. The camera zooms in on a shot of Beth's seemingly horribly battered and bruised face. After several painful minutes during which Jerome thinks that he has somehow been the cause of the swollen and bruised condition of her face, Beth confesses that she has just undergone some plastic surgery further to retain her youthful looks. The scene fades to Beth concluding the interview that frames the BBC tale. She and Jerome have now divorced, and Beth is clearly on the lookout for another husband.

Both Chaucer's Wife and Beth share a dilemma: they seem unable to live with or without men. Chaucer's Wife is, however, more sympathetic. She is, as I indicated above, more sinned against than sinner. As E. Talbot Donaldson once commented, Chaucer's satiric portrait of the Wife has a double edge. Those who defend the antifeminist tradition, which she seems to validate, are satirized because her character is "a monstrous perversion of what experience shows; but women are satirized too, because in many of her characteristics, inextricably interwoven with the monstrosities, the Wife of Bath is precisely what experience teaches" (1076).

Beth is not nearly so sympathetic a character. If Chaucer's Wife is profoundly human, mixing weakness with fortitude as she goes about fictional daily life in the fourteenth century (see Donaldson 1076), Beth seems more venal. Jerome's love for Beth is genuine. As Peter Nicholls, the actor playing Jerome, indicated in a promotional piece for the telefilm: "'When we first meet Jerome, he's the baby of the show. He's got fame and money and an excessive lifestyle. He wears designer labels and has an expensive haircut—the whole works.... He's sown so many wild oats that now he's beginning to realise he just can't go on like that. He's just using these girls for sex, just like they are using him—and an excess of anything gets boring'" (*BBC TV* 6–7).

Unlike Beth, Jerome seems content to settle down. But, like her Chaucerian counterpart, Beth wants to be in charge, both of her life and her career—and unfortunately of Jerome's as well. Their breakup is caused not by spousal infidelity, as had been true of her marriage to James, but by her lying to Jerome. If Chaucer's Wife pleads her case for understanding to her own advantage, the same cannot quite be said of Beth.

The Knight's Tale

In Chaucer, the Knight begins the game of storytelling that is the meta-narrative of *The Canterbury Tales*, thereby setting a lofty tone and style that his fellow pilgrims are invited to imitate or abandon. Freely adapting his story from Boccaccio, Chaucer's Knight tells a tale of love and war set in ancient Athens, then under the rule of Theseus, the city's lord and governor. Early in the tale, Theseus imprisons Palamon and Arcite, two knights among the few surviving soldiers in the army of Creon the Tyrant of Thebes, whom Theseus has defeated in battle. Time passes, and the prisoner knights spy from their cell window Emily, Theseus's sister-in-law, with whom they both immediately fall in love. The two vow that all's fair in love and war, and Arcite's release from jail but subsequent exile from Athens leads Chaucer's Knight to pose a philosophical conundrum to his fellow pilgrims and by extension to readers of the tale: which of the two equally worthy lovers is better off, Arcite in exile and separated from his beloved or Palamon in prison but still able to steal glimpses of Emily?

In the long tale that ensues, the Knight pulls out all the narrative stops—it is good to remember that the Canterbury pilgrims are vying for

a prize to be awarded to whoever among them tells the best tale: Palamon manages to escape from prison; Arcite, so disfigured by grief at
being separated from Emily, is able to return to Theseus's court unrec-
ognized; Arcite and Palamon fight each other only to have Theseus inter-
vene and order a formal tournament to settle who will win Emily's hand;
each knight recruits a host of worthies to support his cause; Palamon
invokes Venus that he might win Emily's hand; Arcite invokes Mars that
he might win the battle; Emily invokes Diana—in vain—that she might
not have to marry either of the two; and, in the subsequent lists, thanks
to the intervention of Saturn, the god of chaos, both Palamon and Arcite
get what they ask for, when Arcite's horse bolts after he has won the joust
with Palamon, topples over onto him, and crushes him to death. The tale
then ends with a meditation, deeply indebted to Boethius, on the roles
of Fortune and free will in human life.[6]

The BBC version of the Knight's tale is decidedly much narrower in
scope. Chaucer's complex tale with its grand sweep and earthly and heav-
enly cast of thousands is reduced to a simple love triangle set initially in
a minimum security prison. Boyhood friends Paul and Ace find themselves
happily sharing the same prison cell, although Ace's sentence is up sooner
than Paul's because he will shortly be eligible for parole. Both men are
intent upon bettering themselves while in prison, even more so when the
pretty Emily arrives at the prison to teach a course in creative writing.
Indeed, they are the first to enroll in the course, and both are instantly
smitten with Emily. But when Paul writes a letter to Emily expressing his
feelings for her, the two longtime friends come to blows. Their friendship now a thing of the past, the rivalry between Paul and Ace intensifies.

That rivalry continues once Ace is sent home on probation, with
each man equally jealous of the other and possessive of Emily, whom we
learn is caught in an abusive relationship with her current boyfriend.
Freedom comes, Paul finds, with a price tag: he must wear an ankle monitor and adhere to a strict curfew, and he finds nothing and no one to
connect with on the outside. In an attempt to reconnect with Emily, he
enrolls in a course at her college. One day, he manages to snap a photograph of Emily and himself, which he promptly sends to Paul in prison,
further to antagonize him. Paul in turn approaches Emily during class,
expressing his love for her, and revealing his jealousy and possessiveness.

Alarmed by the obviously budding relationship between a prisoner
and a prison employee, Theo, the warden, has Paul transferred to another
prison. En route, Paul manages to escape, and Emily and a reluctant Ace
try to find him. Both Paul and Ace have unrealistic perceptions about
Emily's feelings towards them, and in a moment of confrontation, Paul
douses all three of them with gasoline and threatens to strike a match.
Emily defuses the situation at first, but a freak accident ignites the

gasoline, and Ace is consumed in flames. Paul subsequently returns to prison to serve out his sentence. The tale ends with Paul and Emily furtively holding hands during visitors' day at the prison.

The BBC episode follows Chaucer in having Emily wooed by two equally worthy (or unworthy) would-be suitors, who both believe that all is fair in love and war. And the resolution of the love triangle in the BBC version is no less unsatisfying than that in Chaucer's tale, where one of the lessons seems to be that you should be careful about what you pray or ask for. But, while in Chaucer this resolution is clearly, thanks to the intervention of Saturn, an example of the seeming chaos of a fallen world, in the BBC version the resolution, like the story it concludes, is somehow less grand, the result of a freak accident rather than the caprice of the gods.

A lack of love of any kind unhinges both Ace and Paul. Deprived of the mutual bond of their friendship, which had previously sustained them, they invest all their emotions in Emily, never for a minute stopping to consider if she reciprocates either of their affections. Emily, however, is a stronger protagonist in the BBC version of the tale. In Chaucer, her wishes do not count. The world in which she lives is a world governed by the will of men, earthly and divine. In contrast, the BBC's Emily has agency. She first frees herself from an abusive relationship with her boyfriend and then freely chooses a relationship with Paul.

The Shipman's (Sea Captain's) Tale

Scholars are fairly unanimous in their view that the Shipman's tale was originally intended for the Wife of Bath. The manuscripts of the prologue retain feminine pronouns, and there is a lack of connection between the tale and its teller based on his portrait in the General Prologue. The Shipman's tale, like that of the Miller, is a fabliau, but one without the good-natured humor of the earlier tale. Here, in a story based on a folk tale known as "the lover's gift regained," cleverness is the key, and one can easily be too clever by half. A rich merchant keeps a luxurious house, which a monk, Don John, often visits. The merchant and monk though not really blood relations claim a kinship, which both eagerly embrace. They even call each other "cousin." The merchant's wife, who is a spendthrift, enlists the monk's aid to pay off debts that she has accumulated. The monk agrees on the promise of a sexual reward from the wife.

As the merchant prepares to set out on a business trip, the monk asks to borrow a hundred francs from him, the exact amount the wife owes. The merchant freely agrees to the loan; the monk in turn gives the hundred francs to the wife, who in turn beds him. The monk subsequently tells the merchant that he has repaid the debt to the wife. The merchant confronts his wife, who says that she has spent the money on clothes so that she can look the part of a prosperous merchant's wife, and the slightly exasperated merchant resigns himself to his situation.[7]

The BBC tale, renamed the Sea Captain's tale, is set in the Indian émigré community in present day Gravesend. Jetender, a rich older godfather-like figure in the community, has been married for a year to the much younger Meena. Despite the many gifts Jetender lavishes on his wife, she is in debt to the tune of £10,000 to a local jeweler. Jetender has taken under his wing a new member of the émigré community, the much younger Pushpinder, who has recently arrived from India, where rumor has it he was a drug dealer, to open a Hindu health food store and bar and Internet cafe in Gravesend.

Desperate for money to pay what she owes the jeweler before he approaches Jetender for the amount, Meena seduces Pushpinder and convinces him to lend her the money, which he first borrows from Jetender. As in Chaucer, Pushpinder tells Jetender that he has repaid the money to Meena. Both Meena and the wife in Chaucer's tale are clearly wily women who manipulate both their husbands and their paramours. The wife in Chaucer's tale tells Don John—in a comment worthy of the Wife of Bath—that women all desire the same six things: husbands who are vigorous, wise, rich, generous, obedient, and good in bed.[8] Meena, if a drunken Jetender is to be believed, has had a long history of manipulating men for money and gifts.

In Chaucer's tale, marital infidelity and clerical malfeasance go hand in hand. In the BBC version of the tale, Pushpinder is an unwitting dupe of the more experienced and clever Meena. At one point, he claims that she is the first woman with whom he has had sex, and his overly romantic view of their affair is part of his undoing. Pushpinder seems not to know what hit him when she seduces him first in an alley, then in a hotel room, her bedroom, and his bedroom. A line that both she and Jetender use to complain about how their relationship is different now from the time when they were first married—"we had sex everywhere at first—even in the airing cupboard"—establishes Meena's sexual pedigree and prowess.

The monk in Chaucer's tale escapes scot-free. Pushpinder, whose shop Meena destroys with a polo mallet, is almost killed by an enraged Jetender, when he finds out about the adultery, and is sent packing back to India clearly a broken and chastened man. Jetender in turn is less smug than Chaucer's merchant. If he has a failing, it is in marrying a younger wife, although the Indian community among whom the tale is set is clearly tradition-bound, and an arranged marriage between Meena and Jetender would seem to be fairly common if not expected. Meena is, however, more than simply the clever wife of an older smug, prosperous merchant. She is selfish, spoiled, and seemingly innately deceptive—at one point in the telefilm she even passes off take away Indian food as a home-cooked meal. Jetender's final moment of reconciliation with her may simply underscore a common enough theme, medieval or modern: there is no fool like an old fool.

The Pardoner's Tale

Chaucer's Pardoner is one of the true rascals among the Canterbury pilgrims. An able representative of an ignoble profession, itself a classic example of one of the worst kinds of clerical abuse in medieval times, the Pardoner is, as Chaucer suggests in the General Prologue, a eunuch, his lack of physical manliness mirroring his spiritual impotency and serving as a warning to all of the inefficacy of whatever he says or does.

Like the Wife of Bath, the Pardoner's performance is as much autobiographical as it is narrative. At the center of his tale lies an exemplum, or sermon, arguing the truth of his favorite text that cupidity is the root of all evil. Framing the gloss of that text is yet another virtuoso performance by a Canterbury pilgrim meant first to impress and then finally to bilk his fellow pilgrims, in which the Pardoner hypocritically proves himself to be the very embodiment of the greed against which he inveighs. But, like a number of others on the road to Canterbury, the Pardoner readily reveals himself to be too clever by half, and he is ultimately the cause of his own ignominious undoing. His sermon is a model of its kind replete with textbook examples of a variety of rhetorical and narrative flourishes, all perverted for the Pardoner's own selfish gain and ends.

Chaucer's tale recounts the adventures of three sociopaths in Flanders who set out to rob and eventually kill Death. Themselves models of vice like the Pardoner himself, the three young men devote their lives to a catalogue of deadly sins: drunkenness, gluttony, avarice, gambling, and lechery—all of which the Pardoner inveighs against. Directed by a mysterious old man, who is Death in disguise, the three uncover a hoard of treasure more fabulous than they can imagine. As the three discuss divvying up the spoils, the youngest of them is dispatched to a nearby town to buy food and drink. In his absence, the remaining two decide to kill him upon his return, so as to increase their share of the loot. Unbeknown to them, though, the youngest of the three laces the food and drink that he purchases with poison. When he returns, the two do indeed kill him, but they themselves soon die after they greedily devour the food and drink that he brings back to them.[9]

In the BBC version of the tale, the scene changes to present-day

Rochester. Almost a year to the day that Kitty Norman, a teenage girl who was eventually found raped and murdered, went missing, a second teenage girl has disappeared; she too will eventually turn up raped and murdered. The disappearance of this second girl mobilizes almost everyone in town to search for her, except for three young slackers: Arty, Baz, and Colin, who spend their days thinking up ways to scam people. Their contribution to the search for the missing girl is to collect money from passersby, which they promptly use to line their own pockets, under the pretext of helping to underwrite the costs of the search. Arty soon becomes fixated upon another girl, who appears out of nowhere and whom he imagines to be the girlfriend who will inspire him to do great things.

Egged on by the girl to engage in a bit of vigilantism, the three break into a house that the girl tells them is owned by the person who has murdered the two girls. Under the floorboards of the living room, they discover a cache of twenty-eight gold bars—eventually revealed to be worth £2.3 million. When Arty goes off to fence the gold—promising to return with Indian take-away—the dim-witted Baz and Colin plot to do him in, so that they can be richer for having divided the gold in two rather than in three. Arty returns, and Baz and Colin viciously bludgeon him to death with a cricket bat and fireplace poker. The two then sit down for a tasty curry dinner, unaware that Arty has laced the food with rat poison. Kitty turns out to be the teenager raped and killed a year ago—and the personification of Death.

The world of the BBC version of the Pardoner's tale is certainly grimmer than that of Chaucer's tale. While Baz and Colin may well be sociopaths, Arty is clearly a psychopath. He has repeated flashbacks to conflicts with his parents during what he now considers his overly religious childhood, and he is convinced on the basis of no evidence whatsoever that he is one of the extraordinary select few who are destined for greatness in his own time and in the pages of history. Increasingly, he cannot tell hallucination from reality. Possessed of a need to be the focus of attention from Baz and Colin as well as from complete strangers, Arty parades throughout Rochester's city center spouting poetry to never-quite materializing crowds of appreciative fans, his soliloquies—he is especially fond of John of Gaunt's encomium to Britain from Shakespeare's *Richard II*—falling on deaf ears as oblivious townsfolk and tourists alike quickly pass him by. His need for approval, especially from his parents, leads him to steal a tuxedo and Jaguar and show up at their front door. They fail to be impressed, or to understand what motivates his actions here or at any time in his life. The heinousness of Arty's attempt literally to cash in on the disappearance of the second teenager is only dwarfed by the fact that he has raped and murdered both missing girls. Even Baz and Colin are caught off guard when the full extent of his crimes is revealed.

The Man of Law's Tale

Chaucer's Man of Law's Tale is part saint's life and part fairy tale, ultimately derived from popular folk tales involving incest and a monstrous birth. In the Man of Law's version of the story, the central character is Constance, an unflappably constant Christian princess who suffers dreadfully at the hands of her less-than-noble, pagan relatives—including for good measure two evil mothers-in-law. Promised in marriage to the Sultan, she wins his conversion and that of most of his court to Christianity in exchange for her hand in marriage. Set adrift at the command of her mother-in-law who has had her own son and all his attendants hacked to death for renouncing Islam, Constance washes up years later on the shores of Northumbria, where she is cared for by vassals of the king, Alla. When she rejects the lustful overtures of another of Alla's knights, Constance is framed for a murder, only to be saved when her false accuser is struck down for his perjury and slander by a hand from above. Soon married to Alla, Constance now must deal with his mother, who accuses her of giving birth to a deformed creature. Constance is once again set adrift but eventually washes up on the shores of her father's kingdom. Thanks to coincidence, good fortune, and divine providence, she and Alla and their son are eventually reunited, and justice prevails.

In telling his tale, the Man of Law is in top form, declaiming it as if he were delivering a legal brief or making a court presentation on Constance's behalf. Rhetorical flourishes abound, although the Man of Law may be an overly eager advocate for his client. Repeated passages of pathos and the increasingly desperate situations that Constance finds herself in—not one evil mother-in-law but two, each rotten to the core—feature in the tale as Constance's nemeses. But the layering on of pathos eventually stretches the narrative's credibility, challenges the reader's credulity, and comes close to devolving into bathos. The Man of Law's eagerness to make his case in Constance's favor eventually begins to threaten the effectiveness of his presentation of that case.[10]

The BBC version of the tale is a decidedly different story. It is a commentary on racial bigotry and current British immigration policies that seem designed to support prejudice. Constance, a young Nigerian refugee, washes up in a small boat near the Chatham Estuary, from which she is rescued by Mark, who brings her home to his wife Nicky, both of whom agree to offer Constance sanctuary. The deeply religious Constance is unsure of a number of details about her past, including why she left

Nigeria and how she came to be set adrift in the small boat in which she was found. At church, Constance attracts the attention of Terry, while at Mark and Nicky's home she also attracts the attention of Alan, Mark's boss. Constance's rejection of Terry's increasingly crazed advances leads him to kill Nicky and frame Constance for the murder. Eventually cleared of the murder, Constance is nonetheless kept in detention because of her status in Britain as an illegal alien rather than a refugee.

To the horror of his mother, Leila, Alan proposes marriage to Constance, with whom he has fallen in love. Their marriage will eventually give Constance legal status as a landed-immigrant, but she must first return home to Nigeria to deal with bureaucratic red tape. When things go horribly wrong back in Abuja—thanks in large part to the interference of Alan's racist mother—the now pregnant Constance is ridiculed and beaten, eventually finding refuge in a church mission compound where she works as housekeeper to the pastor. Alan leaves for Nigeria, where, after a series of false leads, meetings with unhelpful officials and other difficulties, he is finally reunited with Constance and their son.

Chaucer's Man of Law's tale is generally not viewed as the most effective or successful of the *Canterbury Tales*, in part because the narrator, at times overly confident in his rhetorical skills (albeit in a more benign and good-natured way than the Pardoner), seems to lose control of the narrative thread of his tale. The BBC version of the tale features a much more tightly constructed plot. Indeed, it may be the best of the six televised tales. The pathos here for all involved is genuine. The Man of Law's almost hagiographic story of Constance exists in the abstract. The tale is set in an indefinite past, and it imagines a world in which almost instantaneous divine intervention to rescue the faithful and to punish the perfidious is commonplace.

The characters in the BBC version of the tale are not one-dimensional, almost allegorical types. They are real people coping with real situations. Here, the good do not always triumph—Nicky's kindness to Constance and her renewed embrace of Christianity are repaid by her savage murder by the irrationally jealous Terry. The already traumatized Constance, who has seen her Christian mother and Moslem father killed during repeated outbreaks of sectarian violence in Nigeria, is beaten and imprisoned by the same government officials whom she hopes will help her resolve her uncertain immigration status. Because of the actions of her mother-in-law, Constance thinks at first that she has been betrayed by Alan as well. Leila's racism is all the more contemptible since she is not some lower-class white person who misguidedly feels that her livelihood and economic well-being are threatened by an influx of third-world refugees into Britain from former member states of the Empire. She is a more-than-comfortably well-off woman whose racism seems almost innate. Leila simply hates people of color (she even had issues with Nicky and Mark's mixed marriage to her—not that it was any real business of hers), and she lamely tries to excuse her reprehensible views and actions by saying that she is only trying to protect her son.

* * *

Not surprisingly, critical reaction in the popular press to the BBC series in whole and in part was mixed.[11] Given that they present the efforts of six writers and four directors, there is also not surprisingly an unevenness to the telefilms. Chaucer's tales exist within several narrative contexts. They are predicated on a game of story telling, and many of the tales are framed in ways to add further narrative and dramatic levels to the work as a whole. The project announced in the *General Prologue* calls for each of the thirty pilgrims to tell two tales en route to and two tales coming back from Canterbury. But the work is not even one quarter finished. Nonetheless, the *Tales* has a recognizable beginning, middle, and end, and there is an overall narrative completeness to the work.

In contrast, the BBC tales are six stand-alone telefilms that, in the words of one critic, show "that the 14th century has something to say to the 21st about love, honor, friendship, betrayal and flatulence" (Lloyd E31). If anything, the opposite seems true. At the end of Chaucer's tales, the Parson steps forward to deliver a sermon on the seven deadly sins as the pilgrims find themselves not at the gates of Canterbury but at the gates of the New Jerusalem. The final concerns of the *Tales* become not narrative skill and enjoyment but spiritual solace and salvation.

No such formal narrative shift marks the BBC tales, whose only interconnection is the BBC's choice to broadcast them as a six-part series.[12] More importantly and perhaps somewhat surprisingly, the world of the BBC tales is far more bleak than that of Chaucer's fourteenth century. Characters in the BBC series, left to their own devices, more often than not give evidence of humanity's continuing inhumanity to humanity. Deceit, trickery, cunning all seem the rule. The series does end on a somewhat high note with the Man of Law's tale, but the cynicism of the first tale, that of the Miller, gives way to something much, much darker in the BBC Pardoner's tale, and Beth, the BBC's Wife of Bath, is a rank amateur and an almost innocent when compared to Meena, the shamelessly manipulative wife in the Sea Captain's tale. Ethical considerations in turn are in more than a bit of a muddle throughout the series. If the intent of the series is indeed to "hold a mirror up to [contemporary] society and produce ... [stories] with strong characters and an even stronger moral code" (Hamilton 20), the world of the BBC *Canterbury Tales* offers precious few examples of those who uphold that code.

Notes

1. For an overview of Chaucer's reception in modern popular culture, see Harty, "Chaucer in Performance," 560–75.

2. The reasons for Chaucer's failure to capture popular imagination are more complex than can be discussed here. But see Harty, "Chaucer in Performance," 573–74.

3. When the series aired on BBC1 in September and October 2003, six tales were shown in the following order: Miller, Wife of Bath, Knight, Sea Captain (Shipman in Chaucer), Pardoner, and Man of Law. In the United States, only the following four tales were shown in January 2005 on BBC America in this order: Wife of Bath, Knight, Sea Captain, and Miller.

4. For further details about Chaucer's version of the Miller's and the other five tales that are the basis of the BBC series, see the three standard college- and university-level textbooks used in Chaucer courses: Benson 7–8, 66–77, 841–48; Donaldson 105–29, 1066–70; and Fisher 8, 57–68.

5. For further discussion of the Wife's prologue and tale, see Benson 105–22, 864–74; Donaldson, 191–230, 1075–78; and Fisher 105–26.

6. For further discussion of the Knight's tale, see Benson 6–7, 34–104, 1061–66; Donaldson 191–230, 1075–78; and Fisher 7–8, 25–56.

7. For further discussion of the Shipman's tale and Chaucer's shift in narrators for the tale, see Benson 203–08, 910–13; Donaldson 405–27, 1091–94; and Fisher 214–15, 221–31.

8. Chaucer's original text reads: "Hardy and wise, and riche, and therto free, / And buxom unto hys wif and freesh abedde" (Benson 205, ll. VII 176–77).

9. For further discussion of the Pardoner's performance and tale, see Benson 193–202, 904–10; Donaldson 405–27, 1091–94; and Fisher 214–15, 221–31.

10. For further discussion of the Man of Law's tale, see Benson 87–104, 856–63; Donaldson 148–190, 1072–74; and Fisher 80–102.

11. For representative reviews, see *Daily Telegraph* (London), 30 August 2003, p. 8; 13 September 2003, p. 19; *Herald* (Glasgow), 12 September 2003, p. 37; *Independent* (London) 12 September 2003, pp. 29 and 20 September 2003, p. 20; *Independent on Sunday* (London), 14 September 2003, p. 29; *London Financial Times,* 12 September 2003, p. 20; *New York Times,* 7 January 2005, p. B3; *Observer* (London), 14 September 2003, p. 22; *Sunday Telegraph* (London), 14 September 2003, p. 9; *Sunday Times* (London), 14 September 2003, p. 76; *Times* (London), 11 September 2003, pp. 28, and 12 September 2003, p. 22.

12. Originally Kate Bartlett, the producer for the series, "had planned to link the stories as Chaucer does with six of the characters meeting up in a traffic jam on the M2 as they were making their way to Canterbury. Scripted by [Tony] Marchant, the linking device would have introduced each of the tales over six weeks, but the logistics of getting such a large cast together proved too much for even someone with Bartlett's organizational nous" (Hamilton 22).

Works Cited

BBC TV Programme Information Weekly, Week 37 (13–19 September 2003): 6–7.

Benson, Larry D., ed. *The Riverside Chaucer.* 3rd ed. Boston: Houghton Mifflin, 1987.

Donaldson, E. Talbot, ed. *Chaucer's Poetry: An Anthology for the Modern Reader.* 2nd ed. New York: John Wiley, 1975.

Fisher, John H. *The Complete Poetry and Prose of Geoffrey Chaucer.* 2nd ed. Fort Worth: Harcourt Brace Jovanovich, 1989.

Hamilton, James. "Chaucer on the Road Again." *Televisual,* June 2003: 20–22.

Harty, Kevin J. "Chaucer in Performance." In *Chaucer: An Oxford Guide*, ed. Steve Ellis. Oxford: Oxford University Press, 2005: 560–75.
Iannucci, Amilcare A., ed. *Dante, Cinema, and Television*. Toronto: University of Toronto Press, 2004.
Lloyd, Robert. "A Pilgrimage into the 21st Century." *Los Angeles Times*, 8 January 2005, E31.

Telefilmography

Episode One: *The Miller's Tale*. Original airdate: 11 September 2003, BB1 [cf. *Radio Times* 6–12 September 2003: 22–25, 102, 104]; writer: Peter Bowker; director: John McKay; producer: Kate Bartlett; cast: James Nesbitt (Nick Zakian), Billie Piper (Alison Crosby), Dennis Watetrman (John Crosby), Kenny Doughty (Danny Absolon), Ralph Riach (Malcolm Wickens), Eileen Essell (Jean Smallwood).

Episode Two: *The Wife of Bath's Tale*. Original airdate: 18 September 2003, BB1 [cf. *Radio Times* 13–19 September 2003: 98, 100]; writer: Sally Wainwright; director: Andy De Emmony; producer: Kate Bartlett; cast: Julie Walters (Beth Craddock), Peter Nicholls (Jerome), Pascale Burgess (Jessica), Bill Nighy (James).

Episode Three: *The Knight's Tale*. Original airdate: 25 September 2003, BB1 [cf. *Radio Times* 20–26 September 2003: 51, 92, 94]; writer: Tony Marchant; director: Marc Munden; producer: Kate Bartlett; cast: Chiwetel Ejifor (Paul), John Simm (Ace), Keeley Hawes (Emily), Bill Paterson (Theo).

Episode Four: *The Sea Captain's Tale*. Original airdate: 2 October 2003, BB1 [cf. *Radio Times* 27 September–3 October 2003: 116, 118]; writer: Avie Luthra; director: John McKay; producer: Kate Bartlett; cast: Om Puri (Jetender), Indira Varma (Meena), Nitin Gantara (Pushpinder).

Episode Five: *The Pardoner's Tale*. Original airdate: 9 October 2003, BB1 [cf. *Radio Times* 4–10 October 2003: 102, 104]; writer: Tony Grounds; director: Andy De Emmony; producer: Kate Bartlett; cast: Johnny Lee Miller (Arty), Samantha Whittaker (Kitty Norman), Ben Bennett (Baz), William Beck (Colin).

Episode Six: *The Miller's Tale*. Original airdate: 16 October 2003, BB1 [cf. *Radio Times* 11–17 October 2003: 110]; writer: Olivia Hetreed; director: Julian Jarrold; producer: Kate Bartlett; cast: Nikki Amuka-Bird (Constance Musa), Andrew Lincoln (Alan King), Adam Kotz (Mark Constable), Rakie Ayola (Nicky Constable), Kika Marhham (Leila), Leo Bill (Terry).

2 "If I Lay My Hands on the Grail"

Arthurianism and Progressive Rock

PAUL HARDWICK

In June 2000, the entertainment magazine *Uncut* began the build-up to the twenty-fifth anniversary of punk rock with the cover story: "The filth and the fury: The Sex Pistols and why PUNK had to happen." The line is repeated at the start of Gavin Martin's article beneath a photograph of a plumed knight raising aloft his sword as his horse prances proudly. Those unfamiliar with the image may need to give the picture a second glance to grasp its relevance. All is soon revealed, however, when, beneath the horse, the viewer notes the knight's protruding legs terminating in ice skates. For, of course, the photograph records what Martin terms "Rick Wakeman's ... grand folly," the performance of his third hugely successful solo concept work *The Myths and Legends of King Arthur*, which was staged over three nights in 1975 at the Empire Pool, Wembley—on ice (G. Martin, "Anarchy" 42–65). This event has perhaps more than any other come to be seen as a metonym for the extravagance and self-indulgence of progressive rock, that easy to spot but impossible to define genre which dominated the album charts of Britain and the United States during the first half of the 1970s. It is not my intention here to enter into debates concerning the definition of progressive rock.[1] What I shall explore in the present paper, however, is the place of Arthurian themes in progressive rock and why the image of the mounted Arthurian knight has become such an icon of the genre. In order to do this I will first briefly sketch the place of medievalism in progressive rock, before looking at the genre's use of Arthurian

28

themes in relation to their earlier occurrence in twentieth-century popular music.

Progressive rock is a uniquely European—and, more specifically, British—genre. Comparing the cultural climate in which it developed to the politically volatile psychedelic culture of the United States in the late 1960s, Gerry Lucky notes that British psychedelic music was

> more whimsical, almost ethereal giving rise to music that was less vehement. In many respects the genre was more musically driven and therefore open to other influences. There was no "political message" to dwell on, it was more a matter of artistic endeavour. This was combined with a much stronger "classical" influence coming from the whole European historical tradition. Once you add the elements of folk, jazz and even a little R&B you begin to understand why progressive rock is distinctly a British or European form of musical composition [19].

It is significant that this brief account foregrounds the influence of classical forms. In his pioneering study of progressive rock, the musicologist Edward Macan places the genre within an explicitly English musical tradition dating from the thirteenth century, most immediately mediated through Anglican church music (40, 149–51). Macan locates progressive rock as a specifically middle-class genre emanating from the most staunchly Anglican, as well as class-conscious, area of England, the southeast (147). While this common assumption regarding class is questionable, the Anglican influence is undeniable, with many leading musicians within the genre—including Keith Emerson, Robert Fripp and John Wetton—acknowledging this in interviews (Macan 149–50).

If we accept traditional perception of progressive rock musicians as public school educated products of privileged middle class backgrounds, the medievalism that permeates progressive rock may easily be accounted for. The ideology of the public schools became fully imbued with chivalric ideals throughout the latter half of the nineteenth century, and medievalised decorative features still abound.[2] However, as Durrell S. Bowman has noted, "[w]ith a few notable exceptions ... most progressive rock musicians came from the same small town and working-class British origins where hard rock and heavy metal originated" (185). Indeed, as Macan develops his thesis that

> the educational backgrounds of English progressive rock musicians as a group go a long way in explaining their familiarity with the European classical repertoire, without which progressive rock would not have developed [148],

there is a certain irony as he refers to Greg Lake of ELP for confirmation that "it was as natural for these musicians to draw on their European classical heritage as it was for popular American musicians to draw on their native blues, jazz and gospel heritage" (148). For Lake's childhood was spent on a working-class housing estate on the outskirts of Poole where, like Jon Anderson of Yes in Accrington, music offered a possible escape route.[3] During the period in which progressive rock musicians—and their initial audiences—were growing up, classical music was available to all through the wireless and through state schools, where Anglican hymns were commonplace in daily assemblies. A tradition of working-class access to high culture, dating back to the nineteenth century, had led to considerable democratisation of that which had previously been the preserve of the middle classes.[4] Concomitantly, social upheaval throughout the twentieth century had, as Mark Girouard notes, undermined ideologies of class-specific chivalry as promoted through the public schools system (292–3). It had also empowered a meritocratic reading of Arthurian matter that had long been a feature of American re-tellings.[5]

While bands such as Gryphon, Gentle Giant and Amazing Blondel went so far as to adopt pre-modern instrumentation and musical forms (and, in some cases, costume), a broader medievalism, ultimately derived from nineteenth century appropriations of the Middle Ages, informed the lyrical content and iconography of progressive rock. For example, the early albums of first-generation pioneers of the genre, King Crimson, are suffused with Pete Sinfield's medievalist lyrical imagery on tracks such as "In the Court of the Crimson King" and "The Battle of Glass Tears," from *In the Court of the Crimson King* (1969) and *Lizard* (1970) respectively. Indeed, the latter may be found on the *Lizard* album, which sports perhaps the most overtly "medieval" cover of the era, in which medieval and modern scenes vie for place in Gini Barris's elaborately illuminated lettering.[6]

That such a specifically English musical form, referencing as it does both the medieval and the medievalist, should embrace the "Matter of Britain" is perhaps inevitable. Arthurian themes had, of course, been present in popular music throughout the twentieth century. In view of the medievalism that permeated British culture throughout the nineteenth century, and the resulting proliferation of Arthuriana aimed at a broad social spectrum in a multitude of media, it would indeed be surprising if a strain of Arthurian popular music had not developed. Jerome V. Reel, Jr., has surveyed the growth of Arthurian musical productions from turn of the century burlesques such as *Lancelot the Lovely* and, aiming more up-market, the musical drama *King Arthur*, noting that throughout the twentieth century

> there have been many changes in the forms of delivery and also, although perhaps to a lesser extent, many changes in the thematics. In terms of audience, earlier twentieth-century Arthurian music was differentiated on the basis of social class; as the century progressed, age group rather than social status defined the target audiences [123].

As the century progressed, so the output increased, with the closing thirty years producing a "bountiful trove of Arthurian song" (Nastali 138).

Perhaps the most successful adaptation of Arthurian material in popular music—certainly in its time—was the Broadway musical *Camelot* by Alan Jay Lerner and Frederick Loewe, which premiered at the Majestic Theatre on 3rd December 1960, with a London run commencing on 19th August 1964 (Larkin 107–8; Everett 151–6). Touring performances, along with Joshua Logan's 1967 screen adaptation, ensured widespread familiarity with the songs, compounded by successful cast recordings of both the original stage show and the movie soundtrack. The show acquired a level of contemporary relevance through its association with the fleeting, tragically foreshortened Kennedy administration in the United States, with the closing scene's reference to "one brief shining moment" being taken up by commentators, and even a popular myth of the young president's survival casting him in an Arthurian role (Ashe 28). Such circumstances no doubt aided the growing popularity of the show itself which, in turn, allowed a number of songs such as "If Ever I Should Leave You" to gain independent status as modern love songs, divorced from the context of the film and stripped of any Arthurian resonance. As Reel notes, this was possible because of the film's "focus on what was the primary concern of the world in the middle of the twentieth century—love" (128).

Such is also the theme of one of the more enduring works in the rock/pop genre, David Crosby's "Guinnevere" from Crosby, Stills and Nash's eponymous debut album (1969). This folk rock composition eschews narrative and all but the most vague medievalism, merely using the Arthurian figure as a measure of beauty against which the singer's own "Lady" is measured. In British examples of Arthurianism in rock/pop, too, Guinevere is a key reference. Donovan's "Guinevere" appeared on *Sunshine Superman*, his 1966 album which saw him move from his folk and protest roots into the developing psychedelic idiom. While, like Crosby's song, this is essentially a portrait without narrative, its lyrics—later described by Donovan as speaking of "magical ways of seeing" (Donovan 194)—explicitly invoke a picturesque medievalism which recalls some of the more fanciful works of the Pre-Raphaelites who, while critically out of favor, were enjoying a popular revival in the emerging counterculture:

> Guinevere of the royal court of Arthur,
> Draped in white velvet, silk and lace;
> The rustle of her gown on the marble staircase,
> Sparkles on fingers slender and pale.
> The jester he sleeps but the raven he peeps
> Thru the dark foreboding skies of the royal domain.

> Maroon colored wine from the vineyards of Charlemagne
> Is sipped by the queen's lips and so gently,
> Indigo eyes in the flick'ring candlelight,
> Such is the silence o'er royal Camelot.[7]

While far from Pre-Raphaelite in its execution, Mick Taylor and Sheena McCall's cover painting for the British release refers to the medieval theme, mixing a wizard, a castle and a dragon with anthropomorphised animals, comic book heroes and characters from *Alice in Wonderland* in the illuminated "S," thereby lending the collection an air of medievalized fairy tale.

As Macan has discussed, it is from this British psychedelic scene that the initially very English genre of progressive rock emerged in the later years of the 1960s. Along with a dynamic juxtaposition of acoustic and electric passages derived from blending the essentially electric forms of psychedelia with a revived interest in folk music, Macan notes that

> a number of other characteristics which were to define English progressive rock style emerged between 1967 and 1970.... These include a persistent use of classically derived tone colors produced on the Mellotron, Hammond organ, and assorted acoustic instruments; rich vocal arrangements; lengthy pieces consisting of clearly articulated sections or movements; long instrumental passages; and a tendency to experiment with electronic effects and new recording techniques [22].

Bands such as the Moody Blues, Procol Harum, Pink Floyd and the Nice may, therefore, be considered psychedelic, "proto-progressive" bands (23), although each may have claims to being the first fully-fledged progressive act. What is certain, however, is that by 1969 the genre of progressive rock was firmly established and that the Moody Blues were at its forefront. "Are You Sitting Comfortably?," from their first British chart-topping album *On the Threshold of a Dream* (1969), superficially appears to be in the same vein as Donovan's "Guinevere," with its invocation of a picturesque, fantasy Middle Ages through reference to Camelot, Merlin and—once again—Guinevere. Yet within the context of the album the song fulfils another function. In the booklet accompanying the 1997 CD issue of the album, co-writer Justin Hayward commented on the album's theme:

> We wanted to collect religious and psychedelic influences onto an album and turn them into a pathway into enlightenment, if you like. I know it sounds terribly pretentious now but as young men, that's what we were searching for—we'd always seen ourselves as seekers. It really summed up *On the Threshold of a Dream*.

The "pathway," as described by the album, may be seen as progressing from a dystopian view of human isolation and individuality subsumed within "the Great Computer," through the mundane and emotional fulfilment, to a vision of spiritual fulfilment. "Are You Sitting Comfortably?" is the song which inaugurates this last phase; in looking back to the Arthurian past, therefore, the seeker finds succor and hope for the future.

Phil Travers's distinctive cover perfectly captures the clashing binary opposites of science fiction and medievalism which bookend *On the Threshold of a Dream*, a common juxtaposition which Macan characterises thus:

> Fantasy landscapes and medieval or Eastern imagery come to represent the idealized society—close to the earth, based on mutual dependence and a strong sense of community, linked with the past—to which the hippies aspired. On the other hand, bizarre sci-fi imagery is often used to represent the oppressive, soulless bureaucracy which the counterculture believed is crushing the life out of Western culture.... This same general dichotomy is evident in the lyrics as well [73].

As Bill Martin notes, one of the great paradoxes inherent in progressive rock is the performance of works which embrace "antitechnological romanticism," are firmly rooted in the "nonelectric" musical traditions of European classical and folk, and yet employ cutting edge musical technology, "to say nothing of megavolts of electricity" (B. Martin, *Listening* 133). Yet the simultaneous viewing of both past and future is, as he goes on to note, present in the New Left political thought of the sixties which impacted upon the counterculture which produced progressive rock (135). Indeed, one is curiously reminded of the Victorian artist and socialist William Morris, whose own paradoxically forward-looking medievalism grew out of the medievalist fancies of late-period Pre-Raphaelitism. The Moody Blues' invocation of the Arthurian past on *On the Threshold of a Dream* may be seen in parallel to the close of Morris's utopian vision of a medievalized future, *News from Nowhere*, as the narrator addresses the reader: "if others can see it as I have seen it, then it may be called a vision rather than a dream" (211).

With "Are You Sitting Comfortably?" then, the Moody Blues continue a movement in popular Arthurian song in the 1960s away from the concern with romantic love foregrounded in *Camelot*, through visions of a medievalized ideal past, to a spiritual quest.[8] In this, the Arthurian topos mirrors the developing lyrical themes in experimental popular music throughout the decade. Yet, as we saw at the start of this paper, no theme would come to represent progressive rock as well as the Arthurian. Perhaps the reason for this is best expressed in the track "Grail," from the little-known Leicester band Spring's sole, eponymous album (1974). The song's lyrics, characteristic of many works of their time within the genre of progressive rock, are less concerned with narrative than with impressionistically contributing to the mood and atmosphere of the musical whole.[9] While it would be presumptuous to attribute a specific meaning to the lyrics taken in isolation, it is safe to say that they convey an elegiac tone coupled with a quest for meaning, with the fool's finding and recognising Truth surely referencing the myth of the innocent fool who may heal the Grail king. The precise nature of this Truth, however, remains as enigmatic as the Grail itself; it is the quest, rather than its fulfilment, that provides the substance of the piece. As such, the Arthurian theme may be taken to represent aspiration in its broadest sense, including the aspiration of the music itself: as Bill Martin argues, "there is a fundamental connection between thoughtfulness and care in art and an engagement with the possibilities of human flourishing" (Martin, *Listening* 16). This finds perhaps its most explicit expression in the sleeve notes for Graham Bond's *Holy Magick* (1971), an album which, while firmly rooted in the blues tradition, was certainly progressive according to contemporary criteria by virtue of its extended form and esoteric leanings. Writing of the track "Return of Arthur," Bond invokes

> a Druidic and Celtic Legend of Arthur which states that the power of Arthur will return in this age of Aquarius to sustain this country in the vital part it has to play both in the sciences and in the arts.

Although the notion of rock music as art has, from the late 1970s, fallen into disrepute, this was not always the case. As John Covach notes,

> What was distinctive about the progressive-rock movement ... was an attitude of art-music "seriousness"—critics often called it pretentiousness—that many of these musicians brought to their music making. Among the most ardent fans of progressive rock at the time, there was the perception that these musicians were attempting to shape a new kind of classical music—a body of music that would not disappear after a few weeks or months on the pop charts, but would instead be listened to (and perhaps even studied), like the music of Mozart, Beethoven, and Brahms, for years to come. In their sometimes uncompromising adherence to what they took to be lofty art-music standards, progressive-rock musicians often seemed to be more interested in standing shoulder to shoulder with Richard Wagner or Igor Stravinsky than with Elvis Presley or Little Richard [4].

In both Spring's "Grail" and Bond's "Return of Arthur," we may see the Arthurian employed metaphorically for the quest of the progressive rock musician as he strives to create music that is at once popular and art, drawing both Richard Wagner and Little Richard to the same Round Table. This is most fully articulated on Rick Wakeman's 1975 album, *The Myths and Legends of King Arthur and the Knights of the Round Table*. Housed in a sumptuous, embossed gatefold cover and accompanied by a lavish twelve-page booklet of lyrics illustrated with medieval and pseudo-medieval woodcuts, the visual aspect of the *Myths and Legends* package is almost as important as the music in invoking the Arthurian milieu. At the time of its composition, Wakeman was recovering from a heart attack and, as Jerome Reel notes, the album "carries the long look back that a person who has faced such a crisis can bring to creativity" (132). The theme of love, so prevalent in earlier popular Arthurian song, is very much understated, as the concerns of the musician come to the fore. As Wakeman told *Melody Maker* journalist Chris Welch, in an interview reproduced in the program for the 1975 Wembley concerts,

> Although it's all about King Arthur and the legends and stories it's as much about me as Arthur pulling out the sword from the stone is like taking an opportunity of a career in music and not abusing it.... Everybody wants to be best in their field, and a lot of it is down to believing that you can do something [4].

Clearly aware of the tide of critical opinion beginning to turn against progressive rock, he goes on to compare Lancelot's quest with that of the musician, "because once you've written something, you've got to go out and prove it, take knocks and scrapes." The musician, then, may be seen as the helmed knight depicted inside the gatefold; victorious, triumphant, and almost—but not quite—within reach of the Grail, which surmounts the combatants and gives purpose to their endeavors. Indeed, the album itself, in Malorian terms, is a display of "prowess" in order to win "worship."

In spite of this autobiographical aspect, however, it is important to recognise that the musical quest is not concerned with self-glorification. Rather, the emphasis is upon what Macan terms "collective virtuosity," in which the individual performer is subservient to the group and, indeed, the music itself (67). Returning once more to the Wembley concert program, in reference to the musicians involved in the *Myths and Legends* concert, Wakeman commented, "I gave them parts for 'Arthur' that even I couldn't play" (5). This "collective virtuosity" is, as Macan notes, a defining quality of the genre which

> separates the progressive rock band from both the top-forty-oriented pop styles where a famous singer is accompanied by faceless instrumentalists, and from the hard rock/heavy metal styles in which the lead singer and lead guitarist are clearly predominant [67].

The quest itself thereby becomes communal, the musicians effectively forming a Round Table community. Such an analogy may, of course, be taken to imply the kind of elitism expressed by Mark Perry, editor of the seminal punk fanzine *Sniffin' Glue*:

> I'd always had this feeling that there was a gap between us, the fans, and them, the bands, that you couldn't cross. It was like a special club that had The Beatles and the Stones as founders and the only way to become a member was to sit for years alone in your bedroom learning how to play guitar [11].

The critical point here, however, is that this club *could* be joined, as it was essentially meritocratic and classless. Furthermore, the continued popularity of the multi-million selling *Myths and Legends* evinces an appeal beyond the "solidly middle-class" audience with which progressive rock is generally associated (Macan 152).[10]

In 1978, Simon Frith observed that "[t]he rock audience is not a passive mass, consuming records like cornflakes, but an active community, making music into a symbol of solidarity and an inspiration for action" (198). In our more cynical age, such a broad assessment may come into question. However, this is certainly the case regarding the post-hippie progressive rock audience. As Martin ruefully notes,

> [i]n a jaded society, it is difficult to get the idea of art-as-transcendence off the ground. Perhaps it is inevitable that progressive rock, as one of the last major art forms to take this idea to heart, comes in for special abuse in cynical and anti-utopian times [*Listening* 137].

Thus viewed, we may see progressive rock and its communal ideal—"based on mutual dependence and a strong sense of community, linked with the past" (Macan 73)—as "an expression of eighteenth-, nineteenth-, and twentieth-century attempts to substitute art for religion" (Martin, *Listening* 136). It is, then, strikingly appropriate that the defining visual symbol of all that progressive rock stood for should be one of Wakeman's Arthurian Knights, with all the connotations of community, quest and aspiration carried by the image.

However, as we saw above, this image is invariably used by recent critics as a by-word for folly, excess and pretension; an ironic counterpoint to the "authentic" upsurge of punk which swept it away in 1976–77. Punk poet John Cooper-Clarke recalls:

> the airwaves seemed to be clogged with overmanned combos of cheese-cloth shirted bozos with names like Supertramp, John Hiseman's Colosseum, Emerson Huntley and Palmer and Yes, to name but too many.... In an age where guys looked like Open University lecturers and even your uncle wore flares, The Ramones came in like a breath of fresh Carbona, inspiring Mark (Alternative TV) Perry from South London to launch *Sniffin' Glue*. First of the fanzines it featured the more realistic rock scene: The Damned, The Stranglers, Eater, Venus And The Razorblades, Hammersmith Gorillas, Slaughter And The Dogs, the lot [Perry 6].

The emphasis upon "realistic" rock as an opposition to progressive rock rehearses a common trope in discussion of music in late 1970s Britain. In a society fraught with high unemployment, high inflation, widespread industrial unrest and urban decay, progressive rock, it is frequently argued, had nothing to offer the disaffected teenager.[11] Yet contempt for the genre is frequently overstated; as Perry wryly confesses, "almost everyone involved in the [punk] scene was into other stuff but no one liked to admit it.... We were all trying desperately hard to be so hip" (31). Likewise, Perry's collaborator, Danny Baker, reflects on the affectations of punk and its legacy:

> Perhaps the most negative aspect of all punk rock that stuck, was the idea that all music beforehand was silly old hippy music.... When you remember, for instance, when people said, "What crap King Crimson turn out" but we knew every word of it and it was entirely what brought us there and gave you the desire to have a band to follow of your own when you're young [Perry 82].[12]

We may perhaps, then, to pursue our Arthurian metaphor, view punk rock as Mordred to progressive rock's Arthur; dependent upon its predecessor for life yet possessed of a single-minded Oedipal drive to destroy and usurp its progenitor. Yet, as Baker's comments reveal, it was not the music itself that was rejected; rather, it was allegiance to the ideology that it represented.

Peter Wicke neatly sums up the situation when he observes that

> [i]t is not surprising that the anarchy which the Sex Pistols demonstrated with the radical reversal of all rock music's conceptions of value offered the increasing number of unemployed school leavers in particular an opportunity for identification. Yet this in no way represented a politically articulated protest against their situation, but rather expressed an indifferent hopelessness [142].

While the broad demographic assumptions concerning the punk audience are as questionable as those rejected earlier when considering the progressive rock audience,[13] Wicke is surely correct to identify hopelessness as the crucial factor in rejecting the old aesthetic. As the crises in society mounted, "its political structures were paralysed in a right-wing conservatism which also became Government policy with the election of Margaret Thatcher as Prime Minister in 1979" (Wicke 141). Throughout the period leading up to Thatcher's election, the notion of community was becoming eroded, leading to the ascendancy of the cult of the self of the 1980s, one of the first popular cultural manifestations of which, it may be argued, was punk rock. No longer was it necessary to "sit for years alone in your bedroom learning how to play guitar"—the musical quest and its hard-won rewards gave way to instant gratification without effort, the collective project of producing lasting art to the nihilistic narcissism of temporary notoriety—or, at least, the affectation thereof. Whereas progressive rock had embraced the paradox of looking to the past while focusing on the future, punk returned to the roots of American rock and roll and remained there. Sid Smith draws attention to the Arthurian undertones of the cover imagery of King Crimson's valedictory live album *USA*, released in 1975, the same year as Wakeman's *Myths and Legends*. In Nicholas de Ville's striking design, there are intimations

of the Lady of the Lake holding aloft Excalibur (Smith 205). Retrospec-
tively, the design is ironically prescient, for even as Wakeman's Arthurian
epic was marking the peak of his career, King Crimson, whose medieval-
tinged progressive rock had helped to found and shape the genre, may
be seen as metaphorically returning the sword to the lake.[14] Within twelve
months, "Once and Future" would give way to "No Future."[15]

Although the reference is not made explicit, there can be no mistak-
ing the American social theorist Bill Martin's deliberate allusion at the
opening of his book, *Listening to the Future: The Time of Progressive
Rock*: "For a brief, shining moment, there was a time when the trend in
music known as 'progressive rock' captured the imaginations of millions
of listeners" (1). As we have seen, the phrase, borrowed from Lerner and
Loewe's *Camelot*, had been appropriated to describe what was seen as
an all-too-brief political golden age in the United States. Martin's allusion, then, implicitly casts the time of progressive rock as an Arthurian
idyll—appropriately so, as I hope I have shown. But as with Arthur and,
indeed, all myths which fashion themselves to the form of the Arthuriad,
the matter of progressive rock's demise remains unresolved. As Brian
Robison puts it, record companies' cashing in on ageing baby boomers
has meant that "[d]igital fossilization of classic progressive rock has preserved enough of the beast to imagine a reconstruction of its features, in
spite of the [critical] attempts to bury it" (233). However, it is not only
classic progressive rock that survives. While a progressive rock revival—
the most prominent act of which was Marillion, themselves no strangers
to medievalism in their early days—was a passing fashion in the early
1980s, it may be argued that the genre never really died in the first place.
As Baker notes, "*Sniffin' Glue* used to feature Camel!" (Perry 82). And
although there was no place for Arthurian themes within punk rock and
its descendants, they have, away from the novelty-obsessed attention of
mainstream popular media, remained a source of inspiration within progressive rock in works such as Halloween's *Merlin* (1994) and Ayreon's
The Final Experiment (1995).[16]

Interestingly, as the Arthurian song of *Camelot* came to represent
political idealism in the mid–1960s, so Arthurian material has been
shaped for political comment in the 1990s. On the surface, the song
"Mordred" from UK progressive rock band Legend's *Second Sight* album
(1993) may be read as Arthurian fantasy. However, in concert it
was pointedly introduced as a parallel to contemporary political corruption, with self-interest masquerading as right to the detriment of community:

> I'll right the wrongs and take my dues,
> My Kingdom my power, my glory,
> It is my birthright.[17]

The Arthurian myth, as it has been for centuries, is employed as a mirror for its own time. Whereas in the early 1970s it had been used as a metaphor for the collective project of progressive rock within the cultural zeitgeist of the age, we see it here re-fashioned for criticism of the self-serving individualism characteristic of subsequent decades. Yet, characteristically, this is not without optimism. For, as the collective, Round Table musical aesthetic of progressive rock has survived, so has the ideal which it represents, which, while apparently dead as far as popular culture is concerned, may yet reassert itself. The plea uttered in Graham Bond's "Return of Arthur" is envisaged as being answered elsewhere on *Second Sight* in "The Legend":

> Mist writhes upon the Lake, A single arm extends,
> Arise anew Excalibur, Let the Legend live again.[18]

> Now more of the deth of kynge Arthur coude I never fynde…. Yet som men say in many p[art]ys of Inglonde that kynge Arthure ys nat dede … and men say that he shall com agayne…. Yet I woll nat say that hit shall be so, but rather I wolde say: here in thys worlde he chaunged hys lyff. And many men say that there ys wrytten uppon the tumbe thys:
> HIC IACET ARTHURUS, REX QUONDAM REXQUE FUTURUS [Malory 717].

Notes

1. For a starting point I draw the reader's attention to Lucky 120–1. While devotees of the genre will no doubt disagree with many points, Lucky's attempt at a definition at least provides a framework which may be modified.

2. On the chivalric ideal and its material expression in public schools, see Girouard 163–76.

3. Early biographical details may be found in Forrester et al. 31–7 and Hedges 11–14. Jethro Tull's Ian Anderson—from a working-class Blackpool background—completes the triumvirate of possibly the most critically reviled progressive rock vocalists post–1977.

4. This is discussed by Rose. See especially pp. 196–206 for the ways in which classical music entered working-class communities.

5. See Lupack and Lupack for a wide-ranging discussion of American representations of Arthurian matter.

6. Further contenders may be the Canterbury band Caravan's almost inevitably titled compilation *Canterbury Tales* (1976) and their live CD and DVD, *A Night's Tale* (2002), both of which show a "merry company" of pilgrims (the former including the faces of band members) and Rick Wakeman's *The Myths and Legends of King Arthur and the Knights of the Round Table* (1975), which shows the sword in the stone, with the album's title displayed as a royal seal.

7. Donovan Phillips Leitch, "Guinevere." [Copyright (c) 1966 by Donovan (Music) Limited; Copyright (c) Renewed. International rights secured. All rights administered by Peermusic (UK) Ltd. Used by permission. All rights reserved.] While not returning to Arthurian matter again, Donovan's interest in Western myths and legends would lead to experiments with a distinctive feeling of British "Celtic Rock"—to quote a title from his 1970 *Open Road* album—a genre still flourishing today.

8. Picturesque, idealized Arthurianism would find its final flowering shortly after the release of *On the Threshold of a Dream*, in "The Glorious House of Arthur" on *From Home to Home* (1970), the debut release from Fairfield Parlour, a band re-modeled for the

pastoral, progressive audience after failing to find commercial success as the more overtly psychedelic Kaleidoscope.

9. Undoubtedly the fullest study of the role of lyrics within a progressive rock band's *œuvre* is Martin, *Music of Yes*, pp. xxv *et passim*.

10. On the continued popularity of *Myths and Legends*, see Nastali 146–7.

11. See, for example, Wicke 135–53.

12. In a 2003 interview, Rick Wakeman notes, "The Clash have just said that Yes were one of their biggest influences. Now that *was* a shock" (Ling 39).

13. This is most provocatively discussed by Home.

14. King Crimson would, of course, re-form—albeit in a markedly different configuration—in 1981. While Wakeman has continued his prolific career, both as a solo musician and a member of Yes, none of his subsequent releases has been as successful.

15. It should also be noted that, as Savage points out (123), progressive rock was, by its nature, "expensive to record, package and promote." Wakeman, for example, reflects on the Empire Pool performances of *Myths and Legends*: "We played three sell-out nights and the audiences loved it. The press hated it. The whole thing had cost an absolute fortune and ... I had to pay for everything myself. The culmination of all this was that in spite of having already sold nearly ten million records around the world, I was virtually broke" (132). In contrast, the stripped-down aesthetic of punk rock lent itself much more readily to the "instant return" business ethos of the late 1970s and beyond.

16. Arthurian themes also abound in New Age music, which, although beyond the scope of the present discussion, may be seen as an off-shoot of progressive rock. See Nastali 144–6.

17. Legend, "Mordred." (Pagan Media Ltd. Lyrics reproduced with permission.)

18. Legend, "The Legend." (Pagan Media Ltd. Lyrics reproduced with permission.)

Works Cited

Ashe, Geoffrey. *King Arthur: The Dream of a Golden Age*. London: Thames and Hudson, 1990.

Bowman, Durrell S. "'Let Them All Make Their Own Music': Individualism, Rush, and the Progressive/Hard Rock Alloy, 1976–77." In Progressive *Rock Reconsidered*, ed. Kevin Holm-Hudson, 183–218. New York and London: Routledge, 2002.

Covach, John. "Progressive Rock, 'Close to the Edge,' and the Boundaries of Style." In *Understanding Rock: Essays in Musical Analysis*, ed. John Covach and Graeme M. Boone, 3–31. Oxford: Oxford University Press, 1997.

Donovan. *The Hurdy Gurdy Man*. London: Century, 2005.

Everett, William A. "King Arthur in Popular Musical Theatre and Musical Film." In *King Arthur in Music*, ed. Richard Barber, pp. 145–60. Cambridge: D.S. Brewer, 2002.

Forrester, George, et al. *Emerson, Lake, and Palmer: The Show That Never Ends*. London: Helter Skelter, 2001.

Frith, Simon. *The Sociology of Rock*. London: Constable, 1978.

Girouard, Mark. *The Return to Camelot: Chivalry and the English Gentleman*. New Haven and London: Yale University Press, 1981.

Hedges, Dan. *Yes: The Authorised Biography*. London: Sidgwick and Jackson, 1981.

Home, Stewart. *Cranked Up Really High: Genre Theory and Punk Rock*. 2nd ed. Hove: CodeX, 1996.

Larkin, Colin. *The Encyclopedia of Stage and Film Musicals*. London: Virgin Books, 1999.

Ling, Dave. "Face Off: Rick Wakeman." *Classic Rock* 53 (May 2003): 38–42.

Lucky, Jerry. *The Progressive Rock Files*. Burlington, Ontario: Collector's Guide Publishing, 1998.

Lupack, Alan, and Barbara Tepa Lupack. *King Arthur in America*. Woodbridge: D.S. Brewer, 1999.

Macan, Edward. *Rocking the Classics: English Progressive Rock and the Counterculture*. Oxford: Oxford University Press, 1997.

Malory, Sir Thomas. *Works*. Ed. Eugène Vinaver. 2nd ed. London: Oxford University Press, 1971.
Martin, Bill. *Listening to the Future: The Time of Progressive Rock 1968–1978*. Chicago: Open Court, 1998.
_____. *Music of Yes: Structure and Vision in Progressive Rock*. Chicago: Open Court, 1996.
Martin, Gavin. "Anarchy in the UK." *Uncut* 37 (June 2000): 42–65.
Morris, William. *News from Nowhere*. In *The Collected Works of William Morris*, ed. May Morris. Vol. 16. Reprint New York: Russell and Russell, 1966.
Nastali, Dan. "Arthurian Pop: The Tradition in Twentieth-Century Popular Music." In *King Arthur in Popular Culture*, ed. Elizabeth Sklar and Donald L. Hoffman, 138–67. Jefferson, N.C.: McFarland, 2002.
Perry, Mark. *Sniffin' Glue: The Essential Punk Accessory*. London: Sanctuary Publishing, 2000.
Reel, Jerome V. "Sing a Song of Arthur." In *King Arthur in Popular Culture*, ed. Elizabeth Sklar and Donald L. Hoffman, 123–37. Jefferson, N.C.: McFarland, 2002.
Rick Wakeman: Official Programme Empire Pool Wembley. 1975.
Robison, Brian. "Somebody Is Digging My Bones: King Crimson's 'Dinosaur' as (Post) Progressive Historiography." In *Progressive Rock Reconsidered*, ed. Kevin Holm-Hudson, 221–42. New York and London: Routledge, 2002.
Rose, Jonathan. *The Intellectual Life of the British Working Classes*. New Haven and London: Yale University Press, 2001.
Savage, John. *England's Dreaming: Sex Pistols and Punk Rock*. 2nd ed. London: Faber and Faber, 2001.
Smith, Sid. *In the Court of the Crimson King*. London: Helter Skelter, 2001.
Wakeman, Rick. *Official Programme—Empire Pool Wembley*. Brueleum International, 1975.
Wakeman, Rick. *Say Yes!: An Autobiography*. London: Hodder and Stoughton, 1995.
Wicke, Peter. *Rock Music: Culture, Aesthetics and Sociology*. Trans. Rachel Fogg. Cambridge: Cambridge University Press, 1990.

Discography

Ayreon. *The Final Experiment*. Transmission Records TM 110, 1995.
Bond, Graham. *Holy Magick*. Vertigo 6360 021, 1971.
Caravan. *Canterbury Tales*. Decca DKLR 81/82, 1976.
_____. *A Night's Tale*. Classic Rock Productions CRP 1011, 2002.
Crosby, Stills and Nash. *Crosby, Stills and Nash*. Atlantic Records 588 189, 1969.
Donovan. *Open Road*. Dawn Records DNLS 3009, 1970.
_____. *Sunshine Superman*. Pye Records NPL 18181, 1967.
Fairfield Parlour. *From Home to Home*. Vertigo 6360 001, 1970.
Halloween. *Merlin*. Musea Records FGBG 4084 AR, 1994.
King Crimson. *In the Court of the Crimson King*. Island Records ILPS 9111, 1969.
_____. *Lizard*. Island Records ILPS 9141, 1970.
_____. *USA*. Island Records ILPS 9316, 1975.
Legend. *Second Sight*. Pagan Media PMR CD 6, 1993.
The Moody Blues. *On the Threshold of a Dream*. Deram SML 1035, 1969. CD reissue, Deram 844 769–2, 1997.
Spring. *Spring*. United Artists UAS 29363, 1974.
Wakeman, Rick. *The Myths and Legends of King Arthur and the Knights of the Round Table*. A&M Records AMLH 64515, 1975.

3 The Sound of Silents

Aurality and Medievalism in Benjamin Christensen's Häxan

ALISON TARA WALKER

"Medieval times: superstitions, potions and philters; the persecution of old crones," exclaims one review of the 1968 re-release of the silent film *Häxan*; "how a witch-hunt leads not only to the destruction of an entire family, but to general hysteria; how witches are made to confess by religious and physical 'persuasion'; what they confess to; demonic possession, the Black Sabbath; religion, flagellation and sexuality" (Milne 193). As this reviewer points out, *Häxan* illustrates the Middle Ages as a time when folk-magic ruled over science and superstition over fact. With gratuitous shots of devils, demonic possession, and torture, *Häxan* imagines the medieval period as a curio of antiquity, far-removed from the more enlightened and scientific twentieth century. With such salacious subject matter, it is surprising that *Häxan* remains forgotten by most film critics, especially those who focus on the "medieval film."

As more medievalists explore filmic representations of the medieval and film critics investigate many medieval films, where does a medieval film's score fit into the discussion? Musical scores and soundtracks can offer medievalists and film critics alike new ways of examining how films interpret the medieval period. Film scores and soundtracks can not only provide the critic of the medieval film with powerful aural cues in the forms of trumpet fanfare and traditional-sounding lutes and recorders; such music can serve as its own interpretive tool, providing more complex and multi-faceted readings of medieval films. Especially in silent films, which according to Mary Ann Doane "[are] certainly understood [...] as incomplete, as lacking speech," it becomes an important job for the film scholar to underscore that even though a silent film may not speak in the typical sense, its aural components are crucial parts to reach an understanding of silent cinema (162).

In this paper, I focus my discussion of film music and sound on the Danish silent film *Häxan* (*The Witch*); I inspect *Häxan*'s musical scoring and sound in combination with the film's images in both the 1922 and 1968 versions of the film. First I examine the original version of *Häxan* and the ways it attempts to create an uneasy distance between the contemporary time-period and the Middle Ages. I will then focus my analysis on a particular scene from *Häxan* and compare the 1922 and 1968 versions and how *Häxan*'s changing soundtrack dramatically alters the visual content of the scene. While the film does its best to distance the viewer from its imagined medieval mindset, *Häxan*'s musical score underlines aural links between the contemporary and medieval period.

The History of Häxan

Danish director Benjamin Christensen's *Häxan* premiered in Stockholm, Sweden, on September 18, 1922, and was first screened in Denmark on November 7, 1922, in Copenhagen at the Palads Teatret. During this era of silent cinema, it was common for a live orchestra to accompany screenings in large film halls, as was the case with the premieres of *Häxan*. Unfortunately, the musical program from the original premiere in Sweden has been lost. In the Criterion Collection DVD release of *Häxan* (2001), however, musician and music historian Gillian Anderson recreates *Häxan*'s musical program for its 50-piece orchestra from the Copenhagen premiere based on "a list of musical cues printed in the theater's weekly program notes" (*Häxan*, DVD). Anderson's musical team "assume[s] that the order of the music was that published in the program, and when [they] set the music to the picture, [they] found that this assumption could be made to work." While Anderson cautions that she cannot definitively say how much of each piece was used, when these pieces were used in the film, and which arrangements of each musical piece were used, Anderson's re-scoring of the film based on these musical cues allows film scholars to examine *Häxan* with new ears.

Häxan's history did not end after it was shown in silent film houses throughout the world. *Häxan* was re-released in 1941 with a prologue to the film by Christensen himself. As James Kendrick notes, Christensen's introduction "emphasise[s] again the film's pedagogical intents with a lengthy lecture on the history of witchcraft" (4). In 1968, British filmmaker Anthony Balch re-edited the film from its original 104 minutes down to 76 minutes. In addition to editing *Häxan* and marketing it under a new moniker, *Witchcraft Through the Ages*, Balch significantly changes the aural components of the film by adding an avant-garde jazz accompaniment and narration by Beat-author William S. Burroughs.[1]

History, Authority, and Red-Tinted Devils

Häxan can be divided up into three very different sections. The beginning segment of the film features an anthropological lecture on how various cultures perceive spirits, their universe, and witchcraft. The first intertitle claims that the film is "ett kulturhistoriskt föredrag i levande bilder i 7 avdelningar."[2] This portion traces the history of demons and witchcraft by presenting paintings, woodcuts, illustrations and photographs from anthropological books depicting evil spirits from various cultures. In addition, the beginning segment includes mock-ups of how various pre-modern cultures perceived their world. Throughout this section of the film, a disembodied pointer shows the audience where they should focus their gaze, adding to the film's pedagogical aims. After the more pedagogical section comes to an end, Christensen begins on the more overtly creative portion of the film; he presents his audiences with a dramatization that takes place in 1488 and features a witch named Karna. This section of the film includes witches flying on broomsticks to a Black Sabbath, scenes with various devils and demons, and witches confessing to church officials.[3]

After *Häxan*'s first intertitle, a close-up image of Benjamin Christensen's face appears as the film's first image. All the illustrations and scenes in the pedagogical portion of *Häxan* are shot with a red tint, and Christensen's face is no exception; it glows red against a black background, giving his head a disembodied aura. Christensen's eyes stare straight ahead, meeting the audience's gaze. After a few seconds, the image disappears and intertitles appear, telling audiences that Christensen wrote the script and directed the film. The next intertitle uses the first person "I" to give thanks to the art director and to point out additional information in the film's play bill. Christensen's looming face and the intertitles' authorial address to the film's viewers emphasize that Christensen created, researched, and conceptualized *Häxan*. In light of this section's overt pedagogical aim, Christensen's emphasis on his authorial possession over the upcoming images and text creates an uneven relationship between Christensen (the teacher) and the viewers (his students). In addition, Christensen's overt presence in this part of the film gives an over-tone of masculine, authorial knowledge that judges and condemns the "witches" and "hysterics" he seeks to historicize.

The academic disposition of *Häxan*'s initial section lends a factual air to the images and intertitles that Christensen presents to his audience.

After a brief description of early cultures' world-views, Christensen moves on to the medieval period and how early civilizations' beliefs in demons changed into the medieval belief of a powerful devil. The wood-cuts and illustrations are shown as a slide-show; the red tint on every illustration, coupled with the images of demons and devils, creates a menacing, threatening feeling. As Christensen introduces his audience to the medieval period, he screens a mechanically-animated, red-tinted image of hell, complete with dancing demons and fake smoke. The intertitle for this section reads: "Jag har funnit en egendomlig gammal mekanisk framställning av helvetet, som ger ett gott begrepp om medeltidens föreställningar."[4] The intertitle creates a pseudo-factual foundation about the medieval period's beliefs for the viewing audiences; the intertitle and the subsequent image substitute for any kind of nuanced historical discussion about the belief systems of medieval people, offering a single image as a stand-in for an entire culture.

After the intertitle, a dramatic, mechanically-animated image appears on screen; billowing red smoke partially covers the image, making it almost impossible to see the animated devils and their victims behind the haze. The image, reminiscent of Bosch's *Garden of Earthly Delights* due to its multiple foci and frenetic representations of fantastical creatures quickly waving their arms and legs, signals a link to the past to viewers. Another intertitle soon appears, sandwiching the image between textual interpretations: "Dessa djävlar, detta helvete var bittert allvar för medeltiden. Man tänkte på det med skrack, alltid, alltid."[5] This intertitle makes it clear to viewing audiences that the frantically moving devils on screen are considered real by people of the Middle Ages. Most of the subsequent wood-cuts and illustrations also have explanatory intertitles and are accompanied by a disembodied pointer, commanding the audience's attention to what Christensen considers important parts of the image. Christensen's attempts to illustrate the Middle Ages' belief system reveal his fear of the medieval period and its superstitious underpinnings. Christensen distances himself and his viewers from the Middle Ages by using overly-academic tools that attempt to separate pre-modern and thus less sophisticated beliefs from his own. As James Kendrick asserts, *Häxan* attempts "to explain the irrational past through the rational modernism of science and psychology" (5). Through the use of fantastic images and sardonic intertitles, Christensen makes a claim that the contemporary period is much more logical and rational than the medieval one.

With the addition of a musical score, the pedagogical section of *Häxan* takes on a more dramatic and distinctly less academic tone. During this segment, Franz Schubert's "Unfinished Symphony" plays in the background. The first movement starts out quietly, and provides a tranquil, musical background for the on-screen images. Soon, repeated upward scales by the brass instruments and the increasing crescendos drive the slide-show forward, creating momentum in the scene. Such crescendos followed by quiet interludes from flutes and strings occur at many points in the first part of *Häxan*, fashioning an emotional tug-of-war between the dramatic music and the screen's pedagogical images. The illustrations and intertitles attempt to historicize witchcraft and sterilize shocking images of devils by presenting them in an academic way. The musical background, however, undermines this effort and gives an emotive response to the wood-cuts of naked devils and demons tempting peasants. Musicologist Susan McClary points out that composers like Schumann "carefully established a dichotomy between the masculine example of Beethoven and the more sensitive, romantic Schubert" (18). Schubert's music was known by other composers as being romantic and dramatic, a style that seems even more feminine when compared with composers like Beethoven. The feminized, romantic music of Schubert contrasts with the more academic, masculine lecture that takes place on screen; the aural influences subtly undercut Christensen's lecture on the Middle Ages.

Film reviews following *Häxan*'s initial release remarked on the film's academic leanings as well as its preoccupation with attempting to understand the medieval period. One critic from *Variety* views *Häxan* as "in reality a pictorial history of black magic; of witches; of the Inquisition, and the thousand and one inhumanities of the superstition-ridden Middle Ages. Many of the scenes are unadulterated horror" ("Witchcraft" 30). As this reviewer notes, whatever *Häxan*'s genre, it is a film that attempts to portray its subject matter through factual means by presenting a "history." The reviewer also notices that *Häxan* means to distance the contemporary period from the medieval period it dramatizes by highlighting the Middle Ages' superstition and belief in demons and evil spirits. The last sentence of the quotation implies that Christensen's film not only distances the present time-period from the medieval period, but also that he does this through "unadulterated horror"—by making the Middle Ages frightening and appalling. Elsewhere in the review, the reviewer calls *Häxan* an example of "morbid realism," which highlights *Häxan*'s attempts to be historically accurate, but also underscores its preoccupation with emphasizing the more morbid aspects of the medieval period (30).

Anti-Semitism and Aurality: *Häxan* and Kol Nidrei

Although most reviews of *Häxan* focus on the film's uneasy ties to the medieval period and not the film's musical accompaniment, Gillian

Anderson has unearthed an interview in which Christensen praises *Häxan*'s music a month after the film premiered in Stockholm:

> I would [...] like to take the opportunity to offer my warmest praise for the musical arrangement done for the picture by the conductor Rudolf Sahlberg. It is simply ideal. At first, I myself wanted to have the film run without music, but Mr. Sahlberg has made the music follow the images in a masterly fashion. It is quite simply the best musical arrangement I have ever heard for a film! [qtd. in Anderson].

As Anderson notes, since Christensen liked Sahlberg's musical arrangements so much, it seems likely that he may have kept the same musical pieces for the Copenhagen premiere as well (Anderson). Like many silent films of the 1920s, the Copenhagen premiere used well-known orchestral pieces by a wealth of composers from Schubert and Mozart to Wagner and Bach. Most of the pieces chosen for *Häxan* come from the Romantic period with the exception of Bach, and most of the composers are German or Austrian with a few exceptions like Tchaikovsky. Max Bruch's *Kol Nidrei* stands out as the only piece that possesses a Hebraic name and melody.

Kol Nidrei (Kol Nidre), literally translated from Aramaic as "All Vows," is a Jewish prayer sung three consecutive times at the opening of the evening service of Yom Kippur. *Kol Nidrei* is a formal dissolution of unfulfilled vows made between congregants and God during that year. Even though *Kol Nidrei* has nothing to do with an annulment of vows between two men, historically it has been

> one of the means used by Jewish apostates and by enemies of the Jews to cast suspicion on the trustworthiness of an oath taken by a Jew. This charge was leveled so much that many non–Jewish legislators considered it necessary to have a special form of oath administered to Jews ("Jew's oath"), and many judges refused to allow them to take a supplementary oath, basing their objections chiefly on this prayer [*Jewish Encyclopedia*].

Kol Nidrei was so maligned that at a rabbinical conference held in 1844 there was a unanimous vote to abolish the *Kol Nidrei* from the Yom Kippur service, a practice that most Reform churches in Western Europe and America follow (*Jewish Encyclopedia*). Oftentimes these churches removed *Kol Nidrei*'s customary words and added new ones to the traditional melody. Even though *Kol Nidrei*'s place within the Yom Kippur service has been disputed, the *Jewish Encyclopedia* states: "the principal factor which preserved the great religious authority of the 'Kol Nidre' well into the nineteenth century, and which continually raises up new defenders for it, is doubtless its plaintive and appealing melody." Throughout its history, *Kol Nidrei*'s melody remains the most recognizable part of the prayer. In Max Bruch's arrangement of the song, *Kol Nidrei*'s familiar melody can be recognized by a solo cello and orchestra.

In a biography of Max Bruch, author Christopher Fifeld comments:

> The melody of Kol Nidrei is a haunting traditional one, and has long
> exerted a great emotional impact on Jews. It is traditionally sung on the eve
> of Yom Kippur, during the service of Atonement, and its elements of
> remorse, resolve, and triumph, corresponding to the three stages of repen-
> tance, are mirrored in the way Bruch breaks up the long-breathed Jewish
> melody into groups of three notes, interrupting each group with an emo-
> tional sigh by the insertion of a quaver rest [169–70].

Bruch's composition reflects *Kol Nidrei's* quiet power as both a musical
piece and one of the most sacred prayers of the Jewish calendar. In addition to phrasing his arrangement to mirror the three-fold repetition of
the prayer, his version's reverence reflects the prayer's journey, as it "gradually increase[es] in volume from pianissimo to fortissimo" each time it
is repeated (*Jewish Encyclopedia*). The softness of Bruch's arrangement
gives a sacramental air to *Häxan's* scenes that use *Kol Nidrei*.

In *Häxan*, Kol Nidrei occurs towards the middle of the film during
dramatizations of witches and witchcraft, directly after Schubert's bois-
terous *Rosamunde* Overture. As the scene opens, a single violin softly
plays a downward series of long notes as an introductory clause. The
images on screen are almost obscured by darkness: an open book and
candles reflect brightly in the dim scene. A devil stands before an altar,
holding a small human baby in his left hand; his mouth moves, incant-
ing, as he raises the baby up higher. A number of demons and women
standing around him raise their hands, as if blessing the sacrifice he holds.
As the music's downward scale progresses slowly, the image cuts to a
medium-close shot of another devil and a naked woman; she bows her
head in front of him as he pours liquid from a cup onto her waiting head.
The scene shifts back to the first demon, still holding the baby, who is
now shaking, as the onlookers raise their hands again. Then the scene
changes abruptly—two devils pointing at a cross at their feet, commanding a group of women to walk on the cross. As the musical stanza comes
to a close, an intertitle plays next: "Och där bespottade man mässan och
allt vad som heligt är."[6] When the scene returns, women jump and dance
on the cross with glee; the melody comes back with a crescendo of wood-
winds to a mezzo piano that mournfully establishes the primary melody
of *Kol Nidrei*.

After Bruch's quiet prelude to *Kol Nidrei*, its primary melody swells
as an intertitle appears: "Och maten kokades av Karna på paddor och
odöpta barn."[7] *Kol Nidrei's* melody moves forward in three note phrases,
evoking a feeling of sadness and of anticipation with a descending minor
second. During the quaver rest, an image of two women standing before
a cauldron replaces the intertitle. One of the women holds a baby in mid-
air, while the other holds an urn under the baby to catch blood that drips

from the infant. The camera focuses on a close-up of the infant's feet, as blood drips from its toes into the urn. All the while, *Kol Nidrei's* three-beat phrases continue to move emphatically forward.

Such grotesque images continue for the rest of the scene while the haunting melody of *Kol Nidrei* lends an air of misery and holiness to the film. When image and music are combined with *Kol Nidrei's* reputation, music and image begin to signify something altogether different than they do alone. *Kol Nidrei* is one of Max Bruch's most popular pieces, and as Alberto Cavalcanti notes, it has been used in other silent films besides *Häxan* (100). *Kol Nidrei* has become more than simply a Jewish prayer; by the time Bruch composes his version of *Kol Nidrei,* "the music world had come to consider [Kol Nidrei] the most characteristic tune of the synagogue" (Idelsohn 493). Indeed, *Kol Nidrei* becomes the most familiar musical marker of the Jewish faith. Rick Altman, in his book *Silent Film Sound,* notes that even in the silent period critics realized that playing music that was too familiar could influence an audience:

> In the early teens, critics sought to banish from the theatre any music that might compete with the film. In particular, they recognized that accompaniment by title or lyrics shunted the audience's attention from the film to the accompanist. Later critics witnessed the same process with overly familiar classical selections. When spectators recognize the music from an opera, these critics claimed, their knowledge of that opera interferes with their concentration on the film at hand [318].

Audiences' concentration shifts from image to music when films play familiar or notable songs. *Kol Nidrei's* importance within the Jewish calendar, its notability in the music world as a marker of Jewishness, and its popularity in silent cinema halls all create anti–Semitic underscoring when playing next to *Häxan's* images of Black Masses and baby killings. Music and image together connect to folk-tales about Jews desecrating Christian practices and killing Christian children.[8] These overtones change the scene from one of morbid spectacle to one of anti–Semitic exhibition.

Even though *Häxan* attempts to distance itself from the medieval period by presenting the Middle Ages as a time filled with superstitious and irrational beliefs, the film's soundtrack reveals that "medieval" suspicions still plague modernist practices through continued use of anti–Semitic folklore. During the medieval period, Christians claimed that Jews practiced "blood libel"; a practice where Jews "killed Christian children and drank or used their blood for ritual purposes" (Roth, "Blood Libel" 119). Coupled with accusations of blood libel are medieval folktales of ritual murder "involv[ing] the charge that Jews seized a Christian child [...] whom they then killed in some sort of secret ritual" (Roth, "Ritual Murder" 566).[9] Through salacious images of Black Sabbaths

involving the ritual blood-letting and killing of infants, *Häxan* reinvig-
orates medieval suspicions about the Jewish rituals.[10] Even though it
is primarily considered a medieval practice, Alan Dundes comments
that "the [blood libel] legend has been in constant circulation in oral
and written tradition from the twelfth to the twentieth centuries" (7).
He goes on to point out that "if folklorists considered the blood libel
legend credible, then it is no wonder that various folk groups did so
as well. It is, however, disheartening to realize that the legend has continued to exert its maleficent influence well into the twentieth century"
(15). Even though Christensen attempts to distance contemporary knowledge of the universe and religion from the medieval period's reliance on
false science and superstitious folk-tales, the film's soundtrack reempha-
sizes contemporary ties to the medieval period through continued
anti–Semitism.

Avant-garde Witches and William S. Burroughs: Witchcraft Through the Ages

As the previous section demonstrates, even a film that maintains a
nervous distance from the medieval period can have more in common
with its own interpretation of the Middle Ages than it may like to admit.
By examining *Häxan*'s musical score in conjunction with the images on
screen, abject associations materialize. Anthony Balch reedits *Häxan*
under the name *Witchcraft Through the Ages*, and Daniel Humair provides the newly-edited film with a contemporary soundtrack. By changing *Häxan*'s original music, the anti–Semitic linkages the original film
establishes break as Humair rewrites the film's score.[11] In 1968 *Witchcraft Through the Ages* begins its journey as "an ironic 'midnight movie,'
one relished by a new generation of cinema-goers who took sardonic
pleasure in the drug-inflected viewing of the flickering black-and-white
images of demonic mayhem set to funky jazz tunes" (Kendrick). *Häxan*'s
change in musical accompaniment alters the film's mood, the audience
reception, and any sound-specific referents within the film. With the addition of an avant-garde jazz score, the film's educational aims become
ironic and provincial. *Häxan*'s re-release as a "midnight movie" completely changes Christensen's original intentions; midnight movies are
meant to entertain, not to educate. The re-release highlight's Christensen's
achievements in early special effects, but also mocks its overly academic
posturing. Even so, the same distancing practices from the contemporary
period onto the Middle Ages are still in effect, as can be seen in reviews
of the film's re-release.

Reviews of *Witchcraft Through the Ages* comment both on the film's quaintness in terms of acting, but also on the gruesome way it depicts the medieval period (Gow 48). "What makes the film genuinely chilling," reviewer Tom Milne comments,

> is that these excesses are staged [...] amid an astonishingly *real* imaginative evocation of the medieval landscape in all its filth and squalor, its repressions, perversions, intolerances and cruelties: old crones tortured on the rack; young monks suffering the ecstasy of flagellation, old ones prancing the witches' Sabbath in obscenely naked corpulence; young girls burned to save their souls by a self-righteous, monstrous Inquisition [193].[12]

Milne's assertion that Christensen's depiction of the medieval period is imaginative and simultaneously *real,* corresponds to the contradiction voiced in *Variety's* 1923 review, which claims that *Häxan* presents its audience with "morbid realism" ("Witchcraft" 30). *Witchcraft Through the Ages* and *Häxan* present audiences with gruesome and sometimes fantastic images, but do so under the guise of a historical documentary. Even in 1968, when the film ironically stylizes and exaggerates silent-era cinema, reviewers still comment on how the film manages to portray history truthfully. Milne's review also makes the same type of comments as *Variety's* reviewer did: both categorize the medieval period as somehow alien to contemporary culture by highlighting its repressions, superstitions, and "inhumanities" ("Witchcraft" 5).

In the beginning of *Witchcraft Through the Ages*, Benjamin Christensen's face still appears, but this time as an authorial specter, since William S. Burroughs' gravelly voice begins to speak where Christensen's intertitles once played. "Lock them out and bar the door," Burroughs' musical voice intones against a black screen; "Lock them out for ever more. Nook and cranny, window, door, seal them out for ever more." This incantation, composed by Burroughs, sounds as though he is reading a medieval charm to ward off witches, and not experimenting with avant-garde poetry. Burroughs' narration takes the place of Christensen's authoritative intertitles, and Burroughs transforms from a Beat author into a lecturer as his narration keeps in time with the pointer that shows the audience where to rest their eyes. As one critic put it:

> Christensen would probably have been delighted by the spoken commentary which has been added to the present version of his film [...] and spoken by William Burroughs in the orotund and slightly absurd tones used in the days of Fitzpatrick travelogues, it maintains exactly the right distantiation [sic], never allowing the audience to become more involved in these mysteries and manifestations than Christensen is himself [Milne 193].

With the exception of the opening poetic gesture, throughout the rest of the film Burroughs takes his job as commentator and historian very seriously, presenting an aural soundtrack to Christensen's series of historical images. His voice becomes synonymous with Christensen's authority over the film's historical material. Indeed, Burroughs' tone lends itself to the dramatic, and it can be compared to Schubert's romantic violins that previously added emotion to the 1922 version of *Häxan*. Christensen and Burroughs in effect speak at the same time, creating a hyper-narration by giving the disembodied narrator a body that is not his own, but that of the director. Mary Ann Doane, speaking of the narrator's voice, comments: "In the history of the documentary, this voice has been for the most part that of the male, and its power resides in the possession of knowledge and in the privileged, unquestioned activity of interpretation" (168). Christensen's image and Burroughs' voice present the viewer of *Witchcraft Through the Ages* with a dual form of masculine authority, one so potent that even though Burroughs recites his own poetry at the beginning, it has the ring of the historic. Even though *Witchcraft Through the Ages* is meant as ironic entertainment, Burroughs' reinforces Christensen's educational aim by adding a vocal component to Christensen's silent lecture.

At many points throughout the film Burroughs' narration breaks off and lets Christensen's powerful images speak for themselves. Such is the case throughout the Black Mass scene in *Witchcraft Through the Ages*: the integrity of Christensen's silent film remains intact because there is no narration. Daniel Humair's musicians take over in the preceding portion of the film, his steady percussion guiding images of witches on broomsticks. The driving percussion of the previous scene fades away as the Black Sabbath takes place. A cello plays a series of three notes, then a single rest replaces frenetic percussion. Even though Humair probably didn't have *Kol Nidrei* in mind when he created the music for this scene, the three note phrasing, followed by a rest, strangely mirrors the musical phrases found in Bruch's piece. A violin hovers on a higher note above the cello, mimicking the sound of a baby crying, drawing attention to the sacrificial infant on screen. An organ plays downward progressing chords in the background, creating a more cluttered aural landscape, reminiscent of an organ practicing before a Christian church service. As women begin to jump and dance on the cross, a high-hat follows their stomping, drawing attention to the percussion in their movements. The high-hat stops abruptly when the image shifts to Karna blood-letting the baby; the percussion changes to almost-imperceptible pops on the high-hat, quietly marking the blood dripping into the urn.

Humair's attention to combining musical and visual details creates an unlikely conversation between image and soundtrack in *Witchcraft Through the Ages*. The shocking images of Christensen's Black Mass and the jazz soundtrack are strikingly different from each other, but together the music highlights the strangeness of the on-screen images, underscoring the eeriness of Christensen's portrayals of witches and demons. Even though it is obvious that Humair and Ponty take great care in reinterpreting the film through their music, it was not suited to everyone's taste: "someone ought to remove the strident, irritatingly mannered and highly unsuitable 'interpretative' jazz score which has been added" (Milne 193). Humair's score does not serve only to accompany the images on screen, but attempts to highlight certain aspects of the film through his scoring. The "interpretive" jazz score that Humair designs is only as shocking as the Christensen's images on screen. Together, music and image shock the viewers' senses.

Last Thoughts on *Häxan's* Medievalism and Musical Practices

Häxan provides its audiences with a novel example of an early filmmaker thinking about and filmicly portraying the medieval period. Christensen's opinions of the Middle Ages' belief-systems—especially their provincial beliefs in devils, demons, and hell—provide him a means for acclaiming his own culture's more scientific principles. His pedagogical intertitles laced with dramatic commentary on the Middle Ages sensationalize the Middle Ages but also serve to distance the more-enlightened 1920s from the time-period which Christensen so vividly portrays. Christensen seems frightened by eras that place their faith in churches and religions, but at the same time he remains fascinated by the grotesque, hedonistic, and fantastic medieval world that he creates in his film. Christensen's filmic world, full of flying witches and dancing demons, although presented to his audiences in a factual manner, serve to justify his own time-period rather than to portray another.

Christensen's film maintains uneasy connections to the medieval period through its scoring. Even though silent films have been categorized as missing the integral element of speech, *Häxan's* score speaks loudly—in some cases luridly promoting anti–Semitic ideals through combining on-screen images and Max Bruch's *Kol Nidrei*. While Christensen distances his own time from the medieval one which he represents, such aural cues within the film create invisible links to superstitious folktales of ritual murder and blood libel, akin to the provincial beliefs from which Christensen so keenly distances himself. In *Häxan*, the connection between film music and on-screen images highlights the role that sound plays as a force within a film that can make meaning and also change the interpretation of the images on screen.

Although the re-release of *Witchcraft Through the Ages* is meant as a sardonic look at a silent film, its narration complements Benjamin's pedagogical goals rather than poking fun at them. William S. Burroughs' narration for *Witchcraft Through the Ages* provides an additional authorial voice to Christensen's intertitles and pseudo-historic images. Even Burroughs's extemporaneous poetry serves as an apt introduction to *Witchcraft Through the Ages*. Burroughs's gravelly voice and Christensen's didactic direction give the film a hyper-authorial and thus factual focus, reinforcing Christensen's original aim for the film and adding another level of authority with the addition of Burroughs's voiceover.

The musical score of *Witchcraft Through the Ages* competes with these educational aspirations. Ponty pairs strings and drums frenetically playing mismatched musical phrases that highlight the film's fantastical elements. The film escapes its pronounced didacticism through the scores' ability to highlight the more emotional aspects of Christensen's vignettes and dramatizations. Ponty's arrangements focus on minute visual details in the film, like the movement of a baby's hand or dripping blood, and create a link between the visual and the musical that highlights these images for the viewer. In this way, the film score underlines emotional cues that serve to critique and undermine the overly-academic posturing that occurs in the first part of the film. In addition, the new scoring in *Witchcraft Through the Ages* erases *Häxan*'s ties to anti–Semitism and thus removes the overt connections to ritual murder and blood libel that, through Bruch's *Kol Nidrei,* become apparent in the original *Häxan.*

Häxan remains both a powerful example of medievalism in silent film and one of the few early films whose sound has been so thoroughly changed by contemporary filmmakers. More than simply featuring knights on horseback with lances raised, *Häxan* is a rare instance of a silent film dealing with a medieval subject in a documentary and academic manner. Studying *Häxan*'s soundtrack reveals that even though Christensen endeavors to detach his film from the superstitions of the Middle Ages, the anti–Semitism apparent when the film and score come together reveals links between Christensen's own time-period and the era from which he distances himself. The updated score and voiceover of *Witchcraft Through the Ages* highlight the ways that sound and score can alter a film's focus and substance. Both Haxan and *Witchcraft Through the Ages* provide film critics and medievalists alike with a multifaceted example of a silent film that speaks loudly through its aural components, giving scholars a compelling example of a silent film speaking about the medieval period.

Notes

1. Percussionist Daniel Humair leads the group responsible for the jazz score of *Witchcraft Through the Ages*. The music also includes Jean-Luc Ponty on violin.
2. "A presentation from a cultural and historical point of view in 7 chapters of moving pictures" (English subtitle).
3. *Häxan*'s final section presents its audiences with vignettes from contemporary life (the 1920s), linking the hysterical woman with devil-crazed nuns. While it is not in the scope of this paper to attend to these scenes, they deserve scholarly attention.
4. "I have found a strange old mechanical presentation of hell, which offers a good understanding of the beliefs of the Middle Ages" (English subtitle).
5. "During the Middle Ages, devils and hell were considered real and constantly feared" (English subtitle).
6. "And masses spat on all that was holy" (English subtitle).
7. "And a meal of toads and unchristened children was cooked by Karna" (English subtitle).
8. Gillian Anderson notes the "gratuitous anti–Semitism" in the choice of *Kol Nidrei,* although she asserts that the "chant works for dramatic reasons" as a fitting musical accompaniment, which may be missing the point. It seems impossible to wrestle *Kol Nidrei* away from its primary use as a prayer and simply view it as a fitting musical piece for this scene.
9. Alan Dundes points out that the terms "blood libel" and "ritual murder" are "used almost interchangeably but there are several scholars who have sought to distinguish between ritual murder and blood libel, arguing that ritual murder refers to a sacrificial murder in general while the blood libel entails specific use of the blood of the victim" (7). It is my assertion in this paper that *Häxan* participates in propagating both these myths.
10. Perhaps the most famous claim of ritual murder is the case of "Little" Saint Hugh of Lincoln, which Chaucer uses in "The Prioress' Tale."
11. In order to avoid confusion, I will call the 1922 film *Häxan* and the 1968 version *Witchcraft Through the Ages.*
12. Emphasis Milne's.

Works Cited

Altman, Rick. *Silent Film Sound.* New York: Columbia University Press, 2004.
Anderson, Gillian. "About the Music." The Criterion Collection. Available at http://www.criterionco.com/asp/release.asp?id=134&eid=155&section=essay.
Calvalcanti, Alberto. "Sound in Films." In *Film Sound: Theory and Practice,* ed. Elisabeth Weis and John Belton, 98–111. New York: Columbia University Press, 1985.
Doane, Mary Ann. "The Voice in the Cinema." In *Film Sound: Theory and Practice,* ed. Elisabeth Weis and John Belton, 162–76. New York: Columbia University Press, 1985.
Dundes, Alan. "The Ritual Murder or Blood Libel Legend: A Study of Anti-Semitic Victimization through Projective Inversion." *Temenos,* 1989, 7–32.
Fifeld, Christopher. *Max Bruch: His Life and Works.* New York: G. Braziller, 1988.
Gow, Gordon. "Witchcraft Through the Ages." *Films and Filming* 15.5 (1969): 48.
Häxan. Directed by Benjamin Christensen. With Maren Pedersen and Clara Pontoppidan. U.S.: The Criterion Collection, 1923.
Idelsohn, Abraham Z. "The Kol Nidre Tune." *Hebrew Union College Annual,* 1931–32, 493.
Jewish Encyclopedia. Jewish Encylopedia.com. Available at: http://www.jewishencyclopedia.com/index.jsp.
Kendrick, James. "A witches' brew of fact, fiction and spectacle Benjamin Christensen's *Häxan.*" *Kinoeye* 3.11 (2003). Available at http://www.kinoeye.org/03/11/kendrick11.php.
McClary, Susan. *Feminine Endings: Music, Gender, and Sexuality.* Minnesota: University of Minnesota Press, 1991.

Milne Tom. *"Häxan." Monthly Film Bulletin* 35.419 (1968): 193.

Roth, Norman. "Blood Libel" and "Ritual Murder." In *Medieval Jewish Civilization: An Encyclopedia*, ed. Norman Roth, 119–21, 566–70. New York: Routledge, 2003.

"Witchcraft." *Variety,* 30 August 1923, 30.

Witchcraft Through the Ages. Directed by Benjamin Christensen. With William S. Burroughs. U.S.: The Criterion Collection, 1968.

4 Antichrist Superstars

The Vikings in Hard Rock and Heavy Metal

SIMON TRAFFORD AND ALEKS PLUSKOWSKI

The near infatuation with all things Norse among a sizeable section of northern European intellectual elites in the nineteenth and early twentieth centuries is well-known, and its principal characteristics are easy to chart.[1] Founded upon romantic belief in the north as a home of barbarian liberty, it developed strong nationalist overtones wherever the population were able to stake some claim to descent from "Vikings": Scandinavia, the British Isles, Normandy and even the United States.[2] Attempts by the Nazis to hitch northern European Viking enthusiasms to their own beliefs in the twentieth century, however, certainly contributed to a termination of the love affair of European, and even Scandinavian, intellectuals with the Vikings in the post-war period, and their general disappearance from the realms of high culture (Lönnroth 247–9).

Popular interest in the Vikings, on the other hand, has been a different matter. Already well established in the early years of the twentieth century, it has gone from strength to strength in the last fifty years, with major museum exhibitions and such enterprises as the Jorvik Viking Centre both meeting and helping to foster demand.[3] The Vikings have entered the popular imagination: according to Raphael Samuel, they are among "our stock figures, our subliminal points of reference, our unspoken points of address" (27).

The Viking image has been adopted across a wide range of popular cultural forms, including films, cartoons, comic books, and advertisements, as well as works of fiction and popular history. Alexandra Service's 1998 doctoral thesis is the most comprehensive examination of popular usage of the Vikings and usefully highlights a number of its characteristic features. Vikings, firstly, are easily recognisable.[4] Their appearance is distinctive and well-defined. Generally it is males who are portrayed: indeed the Viking is hyper-masculine. They are big and strong with blond or red hair, and equipped with swords or axes and winged or horned helmets (64–113). Typically they are also accompanied by an equally archetypal piece of Viking material culture: the longship, bedecked with dragon figureheads, stripy red-and-white sails, and shields. Of course, little of this supposed Viking appearance is supported by historical or archaeological evidence—a fact regularly bemoaned by academic specialists—but that is rather beside the point. Even if the audience recognises—as it perhaps increasingly does—the dubious historical accuracy of elements of this Viking kit, that does not mean it ceases to use, for instance, horned helmets as the central diagnostic symbols that "mean" Vikings: their effectiveness as a superlative brand identifier is perhaps enhanced by the pleasing sense of one's own cleverness to be derived in seeing through them.

Service identifies a number of characteristic qualities, behaviors and attributes associated with Vikings. Most obviously the Vikings are violent: in both art and literature, their primary activity is the raid, complete with longships drawn up on the shore, burning villages, and panicked inhabitants (131 ff.). However, almost as important is the image of the Vikings as great sailors and explorers (211 ff.). Closely allied is their association with freedom: they are seen as restless and individualistic spirits following their own stars and not submitting easily to any acknowledged authority (196 ff.). Finally, Service notes that the Vikings of popular culture tend to extremes: they are the greatest sailors, the hardiest warriors, the biggest eaters and drinkers, the tallest and toughest men and so on. There is simply something about them that attracts superlatives (64).

This diverse and potent combination elicits reactions that are frequently both emphatic and complex. While the dominant image of the Vikings is of bloodthirsty and rapacious attackers, barbarian disrupters of civilized life, and definitely not to modern tastes, there is enormous admiration for their energy, dynamism, military strength and sense of adventure; they are romantic anti-heroes, bad boys of a past far more exciting than, but also safely remote from, our own times.

In this paper we shall explore how various elements of the Viking image have been used by an important popular cultural form not addressed by Service: rock music, and, specifically, hard rock and heavy metal.

"*Everything Louder than Everyone Else*": The Semiotics of Heavy Metal

Before going on, it is important to say a little about heavy metal (also "metal" or "HM"), if only to offer a partial explanation of why it is in this musical form, and in the subculture associated with it, that the Viking image has had most resonance.[5]

Excess is the stuff of metal. Bands aim to be the loudest, the fastest, and the dirtiest. Subtlety is not especially prized: everything about HM— the music, the lyrics, the appearance of band and audience members, and the artwork of album covers, promotional material and stage sets are designed to convey their messages simply, directly and emphatically (Weinstein 21–43). The subjects to which HM addresses itself in its imagery are many and varied, but there are recurrent themes which are particularly distinctive and characteristic, and these bear out the predilection for the lurid, the grotesque and the extreme. Deena Weinstein, in her authoritative study of the genre, divides these into two broad categories: those concentrating on Dionysiac pleasure (sex and drugs and rock 'n' roll) and those invoking images of chaos, which in this context she defines as "the absence or destruction of relationships, which can run from confusion, through various forms of anomaly, conflict, and violence, to death" (38). It is squarely within this latter category that the employment of the Vikings in heavy metal falls.

A particularly rich source of inspiration for ideas of chaos is popular entertainment in all its manifold forms: literature, television and, above all, film have all been thoroughly worked over by bands seeking material (Weinstein 40). In selecting from such sources bands invariably concentrate on garish and powerful imagery, and on anything which will appeal to the teenage males who constitute the principal (though by no means the only) consumers of metal. Fantasy, science fiction, horror and death are particularly favoured, as is anything to do with Satan or hell. If the subject matter happens to be the sort of thing that makes parents, teachers or other guardians of moral wellbeing cross, then so much the better, a habit which has led to a long-running campaign against HM by the conservative Christian right in the US.[6] Metal, though, has reveled in its outlaw, bad boy image, and, indeed, has emphasized it, lionising macho masculine maverick heroes and anti-heroes such as bikers, cowboys, or, indeed, Vikings.

Heavy metal emerged as a distinctive and self-aware sub-genre within the broader category of rock music in the late 1960s and early 1970s: it was in this period that the characteristic visual, cultural, musical and lyrical signifiers that would ever after define heavy metal—the "code"—were assembled and crystallised into a distinctive medium (Weinstein 8). This was also, though, the period of a boom in fantasy literature, kicked off by the enormous popularity of J.R.R. Tolkien in the United States in the later 1960s (James 180–81). The two emergent genres grew alongside each other, attracting audiences with similar demographic profiles and interests, and it is only natural that heavy metal should have drawn extensively on fantasy in its subject matter. This interleaving of sub-cultures was only reinforced by the success of a number of fantasy films, and by the popularity of both fantasy role-playing games, such as Dungeons and Dragons, and fantasy adventure computer games, all of which appealed to the same audience. These converging cultures of music, gaming, books and film served and serve extremely effectively as recruiting grounds for each other: those who are members of any one are almost inevitably exposed to the others, thus considerably multiplying the audience for all. Members of the metal audience tend to be highly conversant in the norms and topoi of swords 'n' sorcery fantasy, which is of particular importance to the current study given the close links between stereotypical fantasy barbarians and the Vikings of popular discourse (Service 80).

Blood and Irony: Popular Vikings and Metal

Evocation of Viking imagery has been a feature of hard rock from the very beginning of its development as a distinct musical genre. Indeed, it is in the oeuvre of Led Zeppelin, arguably the band that did most to define and popularise the style, that the earliest and best-known exploitation of Norse themes can be found. The lyrics of "Immigrant Song" (1970) and "No Quarter" (1973) conjure an air of romance and adventure—albeit tinged with menace—through striking allusions to the characteristic and familiar Viking behaviours: seaborne voyaging, violence and exploration. Interestingly, neither song ever actually mentions the word "Viking," nor details their subject in any direct way: on the contrary, there is complete confidence that a general audience will understand the references and surmise on the strength of their behavior and context alone the Viking identity of the song's subjects.

Where Led Zeppelin led, many other mainstream hard rock and heavy metal bands from the 1970s to the present day have followed, with songs that draw upon the general received popular Viking iconography, but normally laying most stress upon the violence, chaos and danger which are their most lurid and attention-catching features.[7] In every case, interest in the Vikings is ephemeral; they will form the subject matter for one song, but then bands will turn once more to war or Hammer Horror–style Satanism or motorbikes or any of the other standard lyrical fare of HM. Equally, no attempt is made in the music to capture a "Viking" sound, whatever that might be: the lyrics apart, none of these songs could be differentiated from the rest of their performers' output. The Vikings are just one more item on an à la carte menu of popular culture, to be picked up and used as a strong and easily-recognized image with well-defined meanings, and perhaps also the ability to impart an air of romance and mystery, but then to be put down again in favor of other subjects. Authentic historical representation or context is not really an aim: what matters is what they stand for in popular cultural terms, as that has been communicated by books and films, and as it is understood by performers and audience.

It is perhaps worth noting that allusions in metal—or any other form of pop music—to any early medieval culture or people other than the Vikings are very few indeed.[8] It is precisely, we may conclude, because the Vikings have escaped from the ghetto of historical knowledge into a wider cultural milieu alongside characters from fiction or film that we see them in use thus in popular music. In this way, if in no other, the peers of the Vikings are not dowdy old Anglo-Saxons or Franks or Allemannii, but the colorful, larger-than-life, superstars of every other reach of popular culture: flesh-eating zombies or cowboys or serial killers.

Ad hoc appropriation of Viking imagery in this way continues to the present in rock music. The image of the Viking received from films, literature and the rest of its vast panoply of platforms is one of a multitude of iconic ideas used freely and in the certain knowledge it will communicate messages about the sorts of qualities attributed to the Vikings: freedom, masculinity, adventure and chaos. Rock music thus becomes another medium transmitting and reinforcing that Viking "package."

However, there has sprung up a second usage of the Vikings by heavy rock bands, which lays far more stress on their historical context. Although developing out of the occasional and unsystematic allusions dealt with so far—which established the Vikings as a staple subject of heavy metal—this new usage transformed them, so that the Vikings became, in some cases, the sole focus of bands' lyrics, identity and image.

Barbarians and the Viking Life

The trail was blazed by a number of bands who started to adopt a Viking or Viking-based persona as a permanent part of their identity. Prime amongst these, and notable in apparently taking it seriously, were Manowar. Champions of the furry loincloth, they were widely ridiculed even within heavy metal, but won a sizeable—and fanatical—following.

Making regular references to the Vikings and Norse mythology in their lyrics, they relished the Viking image, although stopping short of completely embracing it: although a significant minority of their songs are indeed on Viking themes, the bulk of them stick to more routine heavy metal fare, with songs about the majesty of rock, the awe-inspiring manliness of Manowar and typical themes of chaos, war and death. In any case, the Manowar version of the Vikings owes as much to Conan the Barbarian as to history, saga or Edda: what matters to Manowar is untamed masculinity, and the Vikings are for them merely the archetypal barbarian males.[9] Unlike the Viking bands discussed below, Manowar were not bothered about the historical actuality lying behind the popular Viking image, and never attempted to claim religious or racial identity with the Vikings in any serious way: that would have been practically impossible for a band whose leading member has the less than wholly Scandinavian name of Joey di Maio.

It was in Scandinavia itself, and particularly in the more extreme Death and Black Metal scenes from the late 1980s onwards that some bands, following Manowar's lead, began to identify far more totally with the Vikings. Pioneers in this field were Bathory, from Stockholm, who, after three albums of routine Satanism-by-numbers, changed direction and released 1988's "Blood, Fire, Death," including two songs on Norse themes and completed with the striking cover image of *The Wild Hunt of Odin* by the nineteenth century Norwegian artist Peter Nicolai Arbo. This, though, was a mere prelude to 1990's "Hammerheart," again with nineteenth century sleeve art, which was a complete concept album entirely devoted to the Vikings. This, in turn, was followed up with further Viking-themed concept albums: 1991's "Twilight of the Gods," "Blood on Ice" (recorded in 1988–9 though not released until 1996), and, most recently "Nordland" vols. 1 (2002) and 2 (2003).

Bathory's songwriter and dominant figure, known only as Quorthon, commented on the band's new interest in the north:

Since I am an avid fan of history, the natural step would be to find something in history that could replace a thing like the dark (not necessarily always the evil) side of life (and death). And what could be more simple and natural than to pick up on the Viking era. Great era, and great material for metal lyrics. Being Swedish and all, having a personal relation to, and linked by blood to, that era at the same time as it was an internationally infamous moment in history, I sensed that here I just might have something. Especially well suited was it since it was an era that reached its peak just before the Christian circus came around northern Europe and Sweden in the tenth century, establishing itself as the dictatorial way of life and death. And so that satan and hell type of soup was changed for proud and strong nordsmen, shiny blades of broadswords, dragon ships and a party-'til-you-puke type of living up there in the great halls [*Blood on Ice* sleeve-notes].

What was new in Bathory's approach was, firstly, the all-embracing character of their enthusiasm for the Vikings—the likes of Manowar may have alluded to them a few times, but they certainly did not produce album after album entirely dedicated to them—but more important was the personal link forged between the band as Swedes and the Vikings. Previously, heavy metal bands' interest in the Vikings had been based almost purely upon their emblematic status as hyper-masculine anti-authoritarian role models, propagators of Weinstein's "chaos." An element of racial or national identification between bands and/or audience and the Vikings, although not, perhaps, ever absent, was never as important as enthusiasm for the Vikings' supposed behavior. What Bathory did, however, was emphasize a romantic nationalist link between themselves (and their predominantly northern European audience) and the Vikings, portraying themselves as inheritors of their blood, and thus linked to them in a special and exclusive way. Once this was established, the way was open for the transformation of what had been a mere interest into a philosophical, religious and even political program.

Viking Metal

Extreme and obsessive loathing of Christianity had long been a norm— a cliché, even—of death and black metallers,[10] but Bathory and, in the 1990s, many other bands and fans began to turn away from Satan and place their faith in the Vikings, and more specifically in Oðin, as the foremost champions of opposition to Christianity. Many claim affiliation to Ásatrú, a religion founded in Texas in the late '60s and attempting to revive Norse heathenism.[11] Whereas many proponents of Ásatrú are hippyish and peaceable New Agers, the slant put on the religion by most of the black metallers who claim devotion to the Aesir is militant and normally fiercely patriotic or racist: Christianity is regularly dismissed as a "foreign, slave religion," whereas northern Europeans should actually be true to their old gods. The conversion of Scandinavia to Christianity is normally portrayed as entirely forcible and as a wrong that needs to be righted.[12] Some members of the scene have proved themselves willing to back up their words with actions: indeed, it first gained attention—and notoriety—as a result of a spate of church-burnings in the early and mid 1990s by its members, including that of the 12th century Fantoft Stave Church outside Bergen by Varg Vikernes, the leader of the Norwegian band Burzum.

Thanks to the church-burnings and his murder of a rival black metaller, Vikernes has become an infamous figure in Norway, and his views and beliefs have been widely reported. Besides a penchant for self-mythologizing, they reveal the confused character of ideas about the Vikings in the black metal scene. Vikernes at first claimed to be a Satanist, the well-worn pose of extreme metallers wishing to portray themselves as evil. His tastes seem originally to have been not so much for the unmediated medieval itself as for J.R.R. Tolkien: he adopted the name of "Count Grishnackh," based upon an orc in *The Lord of the Rings*, and named his band Burzum after a Tolkienian word for "darkness." Only in retrospect, and taking advantage of the considerable opportunities for reflection offered by a life jail sentence, did Vikernes cloak his actions in an Oðinic garb and claim the motivation of an attempt to restore Norse paganism for his church burning (Moynihan and Søderlind 151–2). From prison he has issued his own racist and anti–Semitic interpretation of Norse mythology entitled *Vargsmål*, obviously a deliberate echoing of *Håvamål*, although also obviously with an eye on *Mein Kampf* (Moynihan and Søderlind 151). Vikernes has also released albums on Norse themes—in a musical style which increasingly draws upon Norwegian folk music rather than heavy metal—and has become a hero of the Norwegian far right. Proving both that it is not just the early medieval past to which he looks for inspiration, and that he will use any historical weapon at his disposal to offend liberal Norwegian opinion, it is notable that he has recently added the name Quisling to his own, and is even attempting to claim some sort of kinship to the wartime collaborator (Moynihan and Søderlind 165, 170).

Very few bands or individuals have gone quite as far as that, but an undercurrent of racism, nationalism and anti–Semitism continues to permeate many parts of the black metal scene. On the other hand there are a number of bands who are merely extremely interested in the Vikings, and Norse mythology in particular. There has grown up a broad church of so-called Viking Metal bands—such as Enslaved or Einherjer—who entirely eschew tired old Satanism and write songs almost exclusively on Norse themes (Moynihan and Søderlind 183, 191–2). There are perhaps as many definitions of what constitutes Viking Metal as there are fans, but something of the ethos can be captured from the description provided by one American enthusiast:

> Viking Metal is about Norse Mythology, Ásatrú, Nature, the Nordic landscape, pride and strength, characteristics of the Vikings, historic events relating to the Vikings, and so forth. VM also deals with the Heathen/Pagan "soul" (if you will), and the eternal battle with judeo-x-ianity, as well as all foreign slave religions.... One can even say that VM is enshroud in social Darwinism [sic] ... and the survival of the fittest—the survival of the finest—of Nature's creation (e.g. the Vikings, the Norse, Heathens, etc.). Moreover, VM is a medium for viewing and celebrating life and the world through our eyes—eyes of European folk, kin, and our ancestors—without foreign influence, perversions, and lies. VM is not just music, it's not meant for bleeding hearts or those laden with European ancestral guilt, and it's not about a bunch of rowdy pirates wearing horns, getting drunk from mead, and swinging axes around [http://members.aol.com/Einherjer/VM.html].

Viking metallers tend to take their subject seriously, evincing contempt for the popular and Hollywood version of the Vikings: no self-respecting Viking metaller would be caught dead in a horned helmet. Frequently they have read extensively, if uncritically, and songs are filled with allusions to Norse mythology: indeed it is not uncommon for bands to provide glossaries or encyclopedias on record sleeves or Web sites to help their fans understand all of their references. These sleeves, similarly, are often decorated with archaeological finds of the Viking Age: Thor's hammers are favored, but other items, such as the Oseberg posts, or even the Sutton Hoo helmet have also appeared. Yet these iconic emblems of the Viking Age, found in innumerable text books and museum catalogues, are contextualised within the violent and misanthropic world-view projected by Scandinavian Black Metal bands.

A Love of the North: The Iconology of Viking Metal

Music, belief and outlook are closely related in Black Metal (Moynihan and Søderlind 33). The dark and violent outlook of Scandinavian Viking Metal as expressed in lyrics and associated literature (and in extreme cases in the actions of individuals) is underlined, even spearheaded, by visual media ranging from album art and band photographs through to merchandise and Web site design. From Bathory the Viking Metal bands have inherited an iconographic blueprint for "thoughtful explorations of ancient Viking heathenism" (Moynihan and Søderlind 22). The imagery used in Viking Metal is largely formulaic, but it is not exclusively based on the material culture of the Viking Age. It encompasses the broad semiotic system favored by many Black and Death Metal bands, not least of all the exultation of violence and hyper-masculinity expressed through weapons and battlefields. In Viking Metal, this is combined with a consistent interest in ancestral roots, specifically pre–Christian heritage, expressed visually through Viking mythology and the aesthetics of northern landscapes. This is evident in the iconography of the most influential Viking Metal bands: Einherjer, Enslaved, Moonsorrow, Thyrfing and Windir.

The album covers of Einherjer give the Norwegian band perhaps the most "Viking" feel of all, rivalled only by Enslaved, as they include actual artefacts: a Thor's hammer pendant (*Leve Vikingånden*, 1995 and *Far Far North*, 1997), a carved post from the Oseberg ship burial (*Dragons of the North*, 1996) and part of a harness bow of a type in the "Jelling style" found in Denmark (Blot, 2003). A more unusual combination is found on the cover of *Odin Owns Ye All* (1998) which includes a representation of the one-eyed god and his two ravens, flanked by ornamentation reminiscent of the spiralling tendrils and animals found on Urnes stave church. The entire composition is represented as a wooden carving, fire-lit from below. In this respect, the band's artwork spans the full chronology of the Viking Age: from the eighth/ninth century Oseberg to the eleventh/twelfth century Urnes art styles. You could be forgiven for assuming these were album covers from a Scandinavian folk band, but images of the band members themselves—sullen and aggressive, wearing black leather and chain mail—leave no doubt and exemplify the dual character of Viking Metal: the diabolical and masculine heritage of earlier Metal combined with a conscious link to a glorious pre–Christian

Enslaved's cover for *Eld* (1997) shows both the Thor's hammer (pendant) and typical examples of medieval Scandinavian animal carving. (Copyright ©1997 Osmose Records. All rights reserved. Used by permission.)

ancestral past. Indeed, few Viking Metal bands would be mistaken for the re-enactors that can be regularly encountered in Scandinavia or Britain during Viking-themed festivals or "living history" displays; an exception that instantly springs to mind is the cover design of Norwegian band Enslaved's album *Eld* (1997) (fig. 1) which pictures vocalist Grutle Kjellson as a Viking chieftain, sitting on a throne decorated in the manner of dragon-headed posts recovered from the Gokstad ship burial, wearing chainmail, a large Thor's hammer pendant and carrying a sword in one hand and a drinking horn in the other. The other band members just out of shot, but represented elsewhere in the album, are dressed similarly as Viking warriors (although one appears to be holding a Scottish claymore). The quintessential Viking-ness of Enslaved is underlined by the band's logo, which includes the name constructed from knotwork, reminiscent of Viking Age zoomorphic art and incorporates the shape of Thor's hammer at its center. Interestingly, the prolific use of the Thor's hammer pendant today overshadows its function in conversion period Scandinavia, when it probably only played a minor role (Staecker 89–104), but as a recognisable Viking and pagan symbol, it conveys a very clear message. On the other hand, there is widespread evidence for martial culture in Viking Age (and earlier) Scandinavia, and this has become central to the image projected by Viking Metal bands.

Martial imagery clearly plays an important role in the iconography of many Metal bands, with eras of inspiration ranging from prehistory through to the Gulf War. The Viking Age is certainly not short of suitable material, and weapons and warriors are readily incorporated into the iconography of Viking Metal bands, ranging from logos, such as that used by Norwegian "folkloric black metal" band Windir, which substitutes two Viking-Age swords for the "i"s,[13] through to band member personas.

Promotional photographs of band members of Moonsorrow standing in chainmail, wearing Thor's hammer pendants and carrying swords (photo shoot Verisäkeet, 2005) typify the visual presentation of Viking Metal bands and underline their interests: dressing in black, often leather, represents a virtual uniform that identifies them with Metal (rather than folk music); wielding weapons identifies them with the violent and masculine concepts associated with Black Metal; and sometimes carrying authentic Viking arms represents a deliberate link to the glorious age of their ancestors. The backdrop is often a forest but includes any typically northern, and particularly Scandinavian, landscape such as fjords and mountains. With the exception of the odd promotional photograph of band members wielding firearms or carrying bullet-belts, there is a distinct lack of references to modern, Western civilization and this links back to a key motivation of north European Black Metal as an extreme reaction against mainstream European culture, as well as emphasising a natural connection with the ancestral lands. Indeed, Thyrfing's most recent promotional photographs have the individual band members literally rising out of a forest bog.[14] The use of Viking motifs to emphasize an ancestral connection extends beyond Scandinavia; when Austrian Black Metal band Amestigon released a promotional album in 2000 titled *Remembering Ancient Origins*, they chose for its cover a widely published carving from the stave church in Hylestad, Norway, depicting the hero Sigurd slaying the dragon Fafnir. Although written down within a Christian milieu, many elements of the story are frequently linked to pre–Christian oral tradition.

Einherjer stand out visually because of their use of iconic examples of Viking material culture, and other bands dip into this bountiful resource: the instantly recognisable symbol of the square-sailed Viking ship is readily used. The album art of Falkenbach includes a number of images of longships and seascapes, as well as a familiar burning dragon-headed prow from a re-enactment of a ship burning (*Magni Blandinn Ok Megintiri*, 1998), represented in full on the cover of Swedish group Månegarm's album *Dödsfärd* (2003) (fig. 2). Similar fjord landscapes are found in the album art of Windir, while longships and seascapes are also used by Thyrfing. Enslaved, seen by many as a foundational Viking Metal band, went as far as representing themselves as Viking warriors standing on a rocky shoreline with their boat moored in the background (on the cover of *Blodhemn*, 1998). Moonsorrow make use of equally familiar late Viking Age runestones (on *Kivenkantaja*, 2003) but draw on even earlier prehistoric material such as rock carvings and megaliths for their ancestral connection.

The cover of Månegarm's 2003 album *Dödsfärd*, which translates as "Death Journey," features the stereotypical Viking funeral.

Many Viking Metal bands focus on their local roots first, and perhaps a north European identity second; in the case of Moonsorrow this is Finland, and with Einherjer it is Norway. All however see Christianity as the common enemy, whether in the past, or, as in the case of groups such as Burzum, into the present. Moonsorrow's exultation of their pagan heritage and the struggle against Christianity is explicitly stated on their Web site:

> Picture vast battlefields with ravens soaring above them. Now picture the forest nearby. Therein skulk the oppressed heathens of the barren North. The brazen sons of the earth fighting against the scourge from the West.... During their journey of nearly ten years Moonsorrow have gained prestige as advocates of the pagan ways. Telling credible tales of the struggle of the tribes of the northern heathens, and combining this with their recognizable brand of epic folk metal.[15]

While scenes of Christian oppression are uncommon in Viking Metal iconography, a notable exception is found on Burzum's *Daudi Baldrs* (1997), which depicts pagans being offered a choice between baptism and death. Yet scenes where Christianity is directly targeted are equally rare. They are perhaps most vividly associated with Månegarm's recent albums, such as *Vredens tid* (2005), which pictures a troll emerging from the woods and pounding away at a stave church (fig. 3), perhaps interpreted as "the land" fighting back against the intruding belief system, while *Havets vargar* (2000) depicts two squabbling monks about to be cut down by a Viking warrior stepping off his ship.[16] The opposition to

The cover of Månegarm's 2005 album *Vredens tid*, which translates as "The Time of Wrath," depicts what seems to be one of the Jotun, or giants, who appear in Scandinavian mythology, smashing a medieval stave church. (All rights reserved. Copyright Displeased Records.)

Christianity is not always aggressive in band iconography. Many Viking Metal bands choose to focus on themes from pagan Scandinavian mythology, as found on the cover of Bathory's *Blood on Ice* (1996), which represented characters from the apocalyptic battle of Ragnarök set against a background of forests and mountains, and in the art of Dutch band Fenris, whose album *Offerings to the Hunger* (2001) appropriately represents the great wolf himself on the cover, whilst Thyrfing's *Valdr Galga* (1999) depicts a scene in Valhalla. Explicit anti–Christian iconography is relatively uncommon and tends to be found more frequently where clear Satanic rather than pagan interests are expressed. Of course, within Black Metal ideology the line between the two is blurred (Moynihan and Søderlind 191 ff.), but many Viking Metal bands choose to focus on ancestral, martial imagery, sometimes having initially begun their careers with Satanic motifs drawn from the stock pictorial vocabulary of Black Metal.

Their use of Viking imagery ranges from the pristine, such as directly incorporated artefacts, through to more elaborate interpretations of the Vikings within a suitable context, whether violent or contemplative. Although there is much diversity in how individual Viking Metal bands present themselves, they all share, or at least project, a common world view— a world of snow, frost, mountains and woods, a world of endless conflict with undertones of a universal struggle for survival from some of the more extreme groups, in particular the struggle against Christianity. In general, the predominance of pagan themes, particularly apocalyptic ones, may reflect the general tendency towards using martial Viking imagery rather than a direct statement against Christianity. In other cases, this opposition is more explicit. Actual representations of misanthropy are comparatively rare in Viking Metal iconography and so the overall impression is that the ancestral culture of the north is at the heart of the band's image, whether expressed through Viking material culture, landscapes, or creative vignettes drawn from Scandinavian mythology and history. Alternatively, the recurring metaphor of life as a battle, as a struggle, and the band members as heathen warriors is reinforced with more widely employed imagery, particularly martial imagery that can verge on the animalistic and the barbaric.

Practically all of the bands in the scene believe that they are descendants of Vikings: predictably, the Viking Metal scene is strongest in Scandinavia, but it is also active in other areas of Europe that saw Scandinavian settlement in the Viking Age: England, Russia, and even Normandy. Indeed, the Vikings have currency across northern Europe, particularly for those who find common ground within a shared Germanic culture; in Austria, for example, the Vikings, complete with horned helmets, are central to the ideology and iconography of "Teutonic War Metal" band Valhalla.[17] There are also a number of Viking Metal bands in the United States and Canada, who generally claim Viking blood either directly from Scandinavian forebears or through English descent. Some members of the scene indeed state explicitly that it is impossible to be a Viking if one is not oneself of northern European descent.[18] By way of contrast, it is interesting to note that there has recently sprung up a new genre of so-called Celtic Metal in Ireland and France (and, more surprisingly, in Germany), which sounds essentially like Viking metal, albeit with the addition of a few harps, but celebrates Celtic gods and myths.

Conclusions

Over the last four decades, popular music has become active alongside film, literature and history in the production and dissemination of the Vikings. It is in heavy rock and metal that enthusiasm for the Vikings has been most evident, largely because the characteristics typically attributed to the Vikings—machismo, chaos, freedom, irreverence for authority and so on—correspond closely to those most lauded by heavy metal culture. Also there are close links between the popular image of the Vikings and the barbarians of fantasy literature and film, which is another area which has provided rich lyrical pickings for heavy metal.

However, although most bands remained playful and casual in their allusions to the Vikings, since the late 1980s or early 1990s an extremist fringe have come to identify themselves with them in a far more determined manner. Viking Metal is, by its nature, evangelical and attempts to engage the listener in an integrated, if not especially profound, religious, philosophical and sometimes political outlook. In doing so it resembles far more the nationalist, racist and romantic appropriation of the Vikings generally associated with the nineteenth and early twentieth centuries than the popular post-war usages of the image.

In concluding, it is reasonable to allow a measure of conjecture about how this development has come about, and why it has happened where it has in the last ten or so years. It is tempting to treat this as yet another manifestation of the pan–European anxiety about identity in the wake of global realignment and mass migration since 1989, which has also produced a wave of nationalist demagogues. Alternatively, and paradoxically, it may perhaps also be correct to seek causes in the very stability and liberalism of contemporary Scandinavia. Escape into a stirring past, like rock 'n' roll decadence, may be an understandably attractive alternative to the horrors of respectable middle-class life in an affluent, enlightened European democracy.[19]

Notes

1. See Wilson and Roesdahl 39–63; Wilson, "The Viking Age in British literature and history" 58–71; Wilson, *Vikings and Gods in European Art*; Lönnroth, "The Vikings in history and legend" 225–49; the papers collected in Wawn (ed.), *Northern Antiquity*; Wawn, *The Vikings and the Victorians*; and Shippey 215–236.

2. Wilson and Roesdahl 48–58; Wilson, "Viking Age," *passim*; Lönnroth, "Vikings in history" 235–44, Wawn, *Vikings and Victorian*, *passim*. On French and Norman reactions to the Vikings see Boyer 69–81.

3. See Wilson and Roesdahl 59 and Addyman 257–64.

4. In popular usage the word "Viking" is applied in a broad and ill-defined manner to refer to all the inhabitants of Scandinavia in the Viking Age. The academic hesitations regarding usage of the word "Viking" have made no impact upon its currency and meaning in the wider world, which remains broad and un-nuanced (c.f. Service, 7–10). Throughout this paper I have used "Viking" in this sense.

5. Heavy metal is an under-researched topic, but a small literature does exist. Deena Weinstein's *Heavy Metal* is an important but dated sociological study. See also Robert Walser's *Running with the Devil*.

6. See Weinstein 245–75.

7. Examples are many, and have been produced by leading luminaries of the HM scene such as Black Sabbath and Iron Maiden.

8. Although see below, p. 71.

9. Space forbids proper discussion of the complex and reflexive interface between popular ideas of Vikings and the barbarians of sword 'n' sorcery fantasy as they appear in literature, film, rock music or role-playing games. See Service 74.

10. This probably originated in a milder form as part of the rejection of what were perceived as the mores and cultural values of adult society, but was given greater impetus by attacks on heavy metal by right-wing evangelical Christians in the United States. See Weinstein 245–70 and Baddeley 113 ff.

11. See Moynihan and Søderlind, 180–1. For the core beliefs of Ásatrú, see Gundarsson, *Teutonic Magic* and *Teutonic Religion*. There are numerous Ásatrú and Oðinist-related Web sites.

12. See, amongst others, Bathory, "One Rode to Asa Bay" from *Hammerheart* (1990).

13. http://www.windir.no/default.aspx?p=biography&lang=engelsk.

14. See image gallery at http://www.thyrfing.com/.

15. http://www.moonsorrow.com/2005/mainpage.html.

16. http://www.manegarm.com/?meny=albums.

17. http://www.truemetal.org/legion-of-eternity/.

18. "Another criterion I firmly adhere to is that only bands of ancestral European decent [sic]—which can include American, Australian, Canadian, and Russian bands (but excludes those from the vile Mediterranean lands ... thus wannabe Italian Vikings can give up the disgusting, ridiculous act)—can be VM" (http://members.aol.com/Einherjer/VM.html, accessed 18 July 2003).

19. See Service 44; Roesdahl and Wilson, "What the Vikings Meant," 39.

Works Cited

Addyman, P. "Reconstruction as interpretation: the example of the Jorvik Viking Centre, York." In *The Politics of the Past,* ed. P. Gathercole and D. Lowenthal, 257–64. London: Unwin Hyman, 1990.

Baddeley, G. *Lucifer Rising: Sin, Devil Worship & Rock 'n' Roll.* London: Plexus, 1999.

Boyer, R. "Vikings, sagas and wasa bread." In *Northern Antiquity: The Post-Medieval Reception of Edda and Saga,* ed. A. Wawn, 69–81. Enfield Lock: Hisarlik Press, 1994.

Gundarsson, K. *Teutonic Magic.* St. Paul, Minn.: Llewellyn, 1990.

_____. *Teutonic Religion.* St. Paul, Minn.: Llewellyn, 1993.

James, E.F. *Science Fiction in the 20th Century.* Oxford: Oxford University Press, 1994.
Lönnroth, L. "The Vikings in history and legend." In *The Oxford Illustrated History of the Vikings,* ed. P.H. Sawyer, 225–249. Oxford: Oxford University Press, 1997.
Moynihan, Michael, and Didrik Søderlind. *Lords of Chaos: The Bloody Rise of the Satanic Metal Underground.* Venice, Calif,: Feral House, 1998.
Samuel, Raphael. *Theatres of Memory: Volume One, Past and Present in Contemporary Culture.* London: Verso, 1994.
Service, Alexandra. "Popular Vikings: Constructions of Viking Identity in Twentieth-Century Britain." Unpublished DPhil thesis, University of York, 1998.
Shippey, T.S. "The undeveloped image: Anglo-Saxon in popular consciousness from Turner to Tolkien." In *Literary Appropriation of the Anglo-Saxons from the Thirteenth to the Twentieth Century,* ed. D. Scragg and C. Weinberg. Cambridge: Cambridge University Press, 2000.
Staecker, J. "Thor's Hammer—Symbol of Christianization and Political Delusion." *Lund Archaeological Review* 5 (1999): 89–104.
Vikernes, V. *Vargsmål.* N.p.: 1997.
Walser, R. *Running with the Devil: Power, Gender and Madness in Heavy Metal Music.* Lebanon, New Hampshire: University Press of New England, 1993.
Wawn, A. (ed.). *Northern Antiquity: the Post-Medieval Reception of Edda and Saga.* Enfield Lock: Hisarlik Press, 1994.
_____. *The Vikings and the Victorians: Inventing the Old North in 19th-century Britain.* Cambridge: D.S. Brewer, 2000.
Weinstein, Deena. *Heavy Metal: The Music and Its Culture.* Revised edition. Cambridge, Mass.: Da Capo Press, 2000.
Wilson, David M. "The Viking Age in British literature and history in the eighteenth and nineteenth centuries." In *The Waking of Angantyr: The Scandinavian Past in European Culture,* ed. E. Roesdahl and P.M. Sørensen, 58–71. Aarhus: Aarhus University Press, 1996.
_____. *Vikings and Gods in European Art.* Højbjerg: Moesgård Museum, 1997.
Wilson, David M., and Else Roesdahl. "What the Vikings meant to Europe." In *The Source of Liberty: The Nordic Contribution to Europe,* ed. Svenolof Karlsson, 38–63. Stockholm: The Nordic Council, 1992.

Discography

Amestigon. *Remembering Ancient Origins.* 2000.
Bathory. *Blood, Fire, Death.* 1988.
_____. *Blood on Ice.* 1996.
_____. *Hammerheart.* 1990.
_____. *Twilight of the Gods.* 1991.
Burzum. *Daudi Baldrs.* 1997.
Einherjer. *Blot.* 2003.
_____. *Dragons of the North.* 1996.
_____. *Far Far North.* 1997.
_____. *Leve Vikingånden.* 1995.
_____. *Odin Owns Ye All.* 1998.
Enslaved. *Blodhemn.* 1998.
_____. *Eld.* 1997.
Falkenbach. *Magni Blandinn Ok Megintiri.* 1998.
Fenris. *Offerings to the Hunger.* 2001.
Iron Maiden. *The Number of the Beast.* 1982.
Led Zeppelin. *Led Zeppelin III.* 1970.
Månegarm. *Dödsfärd.* 2003.
_____. *Havets vargar.* 2000.
_____. *Vredens tid.* 2005.
Moonsorrow. *Kivenkantaja.* 2003.
Thyrfing. *Valdr Galga.* 1999.

5 The Future *Is* What It Used to Be

Medieval Prophecy and Popular Culture

STEPHEN YANDELL

P rophecy flourishes in popular culture today. We may like to believe that rationality trumps superstition in the twenty-first century, but the success of twenty-four-hour psychic hotlines, the popularity of daily horoscopes, and television programs like NBC's *Medium* and the syndicated *Crossing Over with John Edward* reveal something different. Society clearly values having access to the future. Does this fascination with prophecy really suggest a challenge to rationality, though? One might point to countless other prophetic activities embedded in popular culture—from Groundhog Day to bridal bouquet-throwing—that show how little credibility is actually given to prophecy. Prophecy here is innocuous. At best it ameliorates anxiety about the future; at worst it offers unfounded advice to the naive. The fact that prophecy is pervasive, therefore, does not indicate that it actually impacts any of society's discourses of power.

This position, however, ignores the real breadth of prophecy and the weighty consequences it can carry. In checkout lines, tabloid headlines proclaiming ever-imminent ends of the world bombard buyers. Apocalyptic prophecy moves from the personal to the global; from the mere banal to the gruesome. And with this shift comes a meaningful impact on mainstream society's worldviews. Granted, some apocalyptic prophecy is transient. A missed apocalyptic deadline from a tabloid is forgotten as quickly as the next week's issue comes to the shelf. The *Sun* boldly announced "End Times Begin 9/11/05" on September 12, 2005, for example. However, Tim LaHaye's *Left Behind* series, perhaps the largest apocalyptic industry ever created, represents a much longer-lasting text, reaching far larger audiences. The first twelve novels alone, which blend dispensational theology with current events and fiction, have sold more than sixty-two million copies (Gates 46).

Knowing the actual number of believers in any of these forms of prophecy is impossible, but the significance of such huge numbers cannot be overlooked. To say all prophecy in popular culture is mere entertainment or simply fringe radicalism risks seriously underestimating its impact. A crucial first step in making sense of prophecy in popular culture is to understand its roots. Almost all prophecy created and circulated today borrows its major features from medieval prophetic discourse: its forms, its methods of authorization, and its uses. Only by looking here can we understand why modern prophecy functions in the ways it does and see how effectively it has been impacting modern political discourse, just as it did in the Middle Ages.

Prophetic Forms and Functions

According to Michael Shermer, part of prophecy's success can be attributed to the ease with which it is digested and can offer immediate gratification: "As a culture we seem to have trouble distinguishing science from pseudoscience, history from pseudohistory, and sense from nonsense. [...] People believe weird things [...] because they want to. It feels good" (275). Any number of supernatural pursuits, he argues, provide people with a counter to science, which most view as a comfortless "cold and brutal logic." In seeking order and happiness, therefore, people are "willing to grasp at unrealistic promises of a better life or to believe that a better life can only be attained by clinging to intolerance and ignorance" (277–8). For Shermer, negative effects can easily result from supporting certain prophecies.

In most cultures prophecy is tied intimately to power. Those who predict the future are a prized commodity, whether they generate their own prophetic texts or interpret others', and identifying oneself among the chosen can bring huge payoffs. This is true today and was true in the Middle Ages. Lesley Coote argues that power was always the central concern of medieval political prophecy: "[It] is not a game, nor is it a code or a form of intellectual exercise, and it is most certainly not unimportant" (238). Today, telephone psychics represent a growing, multi-billion-dollar industry (Glass 70). Six books in the *Left Behind* series have reached number one on *The New York Times* bestseller list (LaHaye and Jenkins, *Handbook* 3). Sylvia Browne's Web site (sylvia.org) assures readers of her "genetic predisposition to psychic excellence," in order to justify her rate of $750 or more for a personal reading. With this kind of money and power at stake, it is not surprising to find in every generation at least a handful of individuals who have recognized the power of prophecy and learned to manipulate others with it. This was true for the Greek oracles interpreting cryptic Sibylline verses, Hebrew prophets warning of God's displeasure, and medieval visionaries describing God's plan for people's lives.

Although prophecy has been prevalent in many cultures, prophecy's relationship to the Middle Ages, the thousand-year period between, roughly, 500 and 1500, is particularly important. The Middle Ages inherited the greatest diversity of prophetic traditions. Classical, Biblical, and Celtic traditions were all adopted, circulated, and transformed, and entirely new forms sprang up. "Galfridean" prophecy, for example, named after the twelfth century historian Geoffrey of Monmouth, who popularized the form, depicted political figures as animals in prophetic verse (Taylor, *Political Prophecy* 4). This diversity of forms allowed medieval prophecy to accommodate multiple functions, shaping a discourse that ultimately proved something more than a simple, unified whole, and more than a mere amalgamation of disparate parts.

Another reason turning to medieval prophecy is so important for understanding its uses today is that in the Middle Ages a popular audience became increasingly integral to the reception of the discourse. By the fourteenth century in Britain interest in prophecy permeated all levels of society (Coote 7). In the Middle Ages we see prophecy used as a crucial tool for placing leaders in and out of power. Umberto Eco, in making a case for the importance of the Middle Ages in modern society, first concedes a large number of ideas that had their origins in ancient Greece and Rome. Crucial to Eco's argument, however, is what happened to these ideas in the Middle Ages: it is "from the Middle Ages [that] we learned how to use them" (65). This is true of prophecy as well, whose classical forms were inherited and transformed by medieval authors.

The diverse forms of prophecy we see today reflect a diversity spawned in the Middle Ages. Thomas Aquinas notes a troubling proliferation of vaticinal arts in the second section of part two of his *Summa Theologiæ*, question 95:

Astrologers cast horoscopes by consulting the position and motions of the stars, augurers observe the flight and calls of birds and the sneezes and involuntary spasms of men, omens make meanings out of words said unintentionally, palmistry inspects the lines of the hand. But sometimes men base their divinations on the outcomes of actions specially engaged in for the purpose: drawing lots, pouring molten lead into water and examining the shapes, picking out different-length sticks, throwing dice, opening a book at random [411].

Although he attempts to capture the entirety of Christian theology in his text, Aquinas seems to find prophecy straining the seams of his completeness and posing problematic questions. How can the same discourse that entrusts a true servant of God with divine messages about the future also be appropriated by vain individuals wanting to gain inappropriate knowledge? He comes to no easy conclusion.

Modern guides to prophecy claim that hundreds of forms of divination are used today, many of which gained popularity in the Middle Ages. The 1997 *Illustrated Encyclopedia of Divination*, for example, cites a diversity of signs that can be read prophetically, including the natural (stars, weather, bird-flight patterns), the textual (tarot cards, runes, randomly opened books), the bodily (bones, palms, dreams, overhead conversations), and the obscure (tea leaves, jewelry, broken coconuts). Isolating prophetic signs as a distinct kind of text has been difficult in many cultures, including medieval and modern. In *Prophecy and the Biblical Prophets* John Sawyer explains that prophecy has a longstanding tradition of merging multiple forms:

> "Prophecy" means both prediction (foretelling) and proclamation (forthtelling), so that "prophets" include not only people with supernatural powers, able like Cassandra, for example, to foresee events in the future, but preachers like St. Francis of Assisi, John Wesley, Martin Luther King and other "proclaimers" as well [1].

Despite the inherent difficulties of prophesying accurately, to gather an audience around oneself for the purpose of prophesying is not particularly difficult, and the same techniques used in the Middle Ages are employed today: use vague language in making prophetic claims, offer a large number of them, allow an indefinite amount of time for their fulfillment, and ignore any misses. Using this time-proven advice has allowed countless creators of prophecy to gather loyal followings, and these spokespersons of prophecy are often interested in promoting their specific worldviews.

Prophecy was also crucial in developing Christian theology in the Middle Ages. Jeffrey Russell's *A History of Medieval Christianity: Prophecy and Order*, for example, is one of the first studies to defend the essential role prophecy played in the development of church doctrine. He claims that the

> search for order and the urge to prophesy [...], the constitutional structure of the Church and the mystics and ascetics who cried down or ignored the structure, the orthodox, and the heretics—all these opposites are necessary [... for Christianity] to preserve its doctrinal and institutional identity while at the same time producing (or at least permitting) a wealth and variety of religious experience [6].

Just as in the Middle Ages, prophecy today is concerned more with present-day beliefs than with future events. Consequently, those able to authorize themselves as prophetic spokespersons gain control of prophetic interpretation and in turn wield great control over beliefs within a popular audience.

Authorized Voices

The form of a prophecy often had little to do with its credibility among a medieval audience or with its ongoing usefulness as a prophecy. Instead, effective authorization of a text typically came through established genres (such as apocalyptic verse), established prophet figures (like Merlin), or established prophetic works (like the Bible) (Kerby-Fulton 319; Coote 7; Watt 13–14). The prophet played the most important role in prophetic authorization, though, by positioning himself to mediate messages between divinity and humanity. Creating a flexible vantage point for himself, the prophet aligned himself neither with the supernatural source nor the secular audience completely, and this allowed him to control meaning of a text more easily. The prophet remained in a crucial middle space, not belonging fully to either the supernatural or human world. This allowed him to not only maintain a rhetorical flexibility, but also shift alliances as it proved advantageous.

In the Middle Ages only a handful of figures were granted the position of otherworldly mediator. These included figures such as the Biblical prophet Daniel, Merlin, Thomas (Rhymer) of Erceldoune, Thomas Becket, and John of Bridlington. Although many medieval prophecies remained anonymous, those attached to an author were typically attached to one of these. For creators of new prophecies, writing under one of these key names was crucial in giving their words credibility. Geoffrey of Monmouth is believed to have composed all the Merlin-related prophetic verses in his works, but by claiming he had copied them from an ancient Celtic book that had previously recorded Merlin's words, his verses held instant authority.

Prophets in modern popular culture use similar authorizing strategies. Some have taken the more difficult task of posing themselves as modern-day visionaries. Figures such as Edgar Cayce (1877–1945), Jeane Dixon (1904–1997), Sylvia Browne, James Van Praagh, and John Edward have each produced books and made media appearances with their predictive skills. Jeane Dixon was perhaps the most famous American psychic of the late twentieth century, and until her death in 1997, she gave advice to various public figures, including Nancy Reagan. More recently, figures like Sylvia Browne, John Edward, and James Van Praagh have perfected the art of "cold reading" techniques as a way of authorizing themselves. They are able to offer information about individuals that seems very specific, but is in fact based on simple observation of people and human nature, as well as statistically sound conclusions: "I see a male figure with the letter J—perhaps James or John." Once authorized, they have won over an audience eager to hear any prophetic messages.

Aside from these self-authoring figures, a large number of prophecies being written in books and magazines today make use of already established prophetic sources, as was done in the Middle Ages. Merlin continues to be a recognized prophet figure whose manuscripts some believe continue to turn up with new words about our present-day condition. He has been joined in the list of top prophetic authorities by Michel Nostradamus, the sixteenth century French author of 942 ambiguously worded quatrains. The *Sun*, in particular, invokes newly discovered verses from Nostradamus on a regular basis, and his name becomes one of the easiest mouthpieces for the newspaper's own, typically conservative beliefs (Wilson xii).

The neo-prophets of conservative Christianity in the present day are part of a relatively recent theological movement, born in America from the teachings of John Nelson Darby. This former priest in the Anglican Church of Ireland developed Dispensationalism in the 1870s, based on the premise that God has been dealing with humanity through a series of covenants or dispensations. These large periods divide human history and are associated with key Biblical figures such as Adam, Noah, Moses, Abraham, and Jesus Christ (Allis 13). Darby's rubric sees the Book of Revelation as a guide to the final dispensations. The Church Age will end when Christ raptures the church just before the seven-year period of tribulation begins, a fulfillment of Daniel's prophecy in the Hebrew scriptures of a "seventieth week" of suffering. The thousand-year period of God's kingdom on earth will then begin, the Millennium, after which the Earth will be destroyed and replaced by the New Heavens and New Earth (Weber 21). Darby's theology of a historical time scheme was not new. Augustine in the *City of God*, book twenty, is very traditional, for example, in arguing for a figurative reading of Revelation, and one of the controversies behind Joachim de Fiore's apocalyptic visions was his challenging of Augustine's long-accepted reading and suggestion that Revelation offered a literal timeline one might follow (McGinn 127–30). But in Darby's time, a fairly literal reading of the book of Revelation had never reached mainstream acceptance before.

Hal Lindsey became dispensationalist theology's popular spokesperson in the 1970s, and his best-selling books *The Late Great Planet Earth* (1970), *Satan Is Alive and Well on Planet Earth* (1974), and *The 1980s: Countdown to Armageddon* (1982) outlined what he said was God's clear plan in the Book of Revelation for the imminent return of Jesus for the church. Tim LaHaye wrote about Revelation in a similar vein at this time, in books such as *Revelation Illustrated and Made Plain* (1973). Along with Pat Robertson, these men have become the most visible spokespersons of Dispensationalist theology today.

One distinctive feature of Lindsey and LaHaye's books, including LaHaye's more recent *The Rapture*, and *Charting the End Times*, is the inclusion of visual depictions of God's timeline for Earth. None of the diagrams includes specific dates about when the rapture of the church will occur—wisely, since a lesson had been learned from many other visionary spokespersons of the nineteenth and twentieth centuries after rapture dates they insisted upon came and went uneventfully. These colorful charts do, however, make the Book of Revelation look digestible and worthy of a literalist reading, which partly accounts for why the public has embraced the books so easily. The transition from twentieth to twenty-first century also seemed like the ideal point at which to begin a thousand-year reign of peace; real-life events have proven otherwise, though. While the theology of these men is fairly modern, it is worth noting that their desire for an all-encompassing world view fueled by a taxonomic impulse seems to grow from a very medieval scholarly position.

Like the medieval Thomas Rhymer, whose visit to the Otherworld gave him the gift of speaking cryptic prophecies, these modern speakers pose themselves not as generators of prophecy themselves, but as mouthpieces of God. Self-appointed spokespersons for God authorize themselves in part by maintaining the same rhetorical, mediating position as their medieval predecessors. They merely interpret divine texts that have already been determined prophetically significant by others. That authority, however, gives some of their interpretations—on war in the Middle East and the inevitable destruction of the Earth, for example—monumental implications for world politics.

The power of prophecy and the authority granted to figures such as Merlin, Nostradamus, or Pat Robertson becomes clear when considered in Michel Foucault's discussions of discourse. Foucault's conception of discourse and discursive formation suggests a useful foundation for explaining how prophecy functions within the socio-political sphere (Foucault 37, 107). As with all discourses, the production of prophecy is both controlled and organized. What holds prophetic discourse together is not only that it generates contested interpretive space, or that it is always mediated by key individuals we identify as prophets, but that prophetic statements affect how people think. Admittance into prophetic discourse, therefore, has serious social ramifications. Once a text had been made available, it can be linked to countless future events to support myriad causes.

Ambiguity Glossed

Ambiguity served as a crucial underpinning of prophetic discourse throughout the Middle Ages because it increased a prophecy's chances of remaining in circulation. Prophetic authors quickly learned the importance of surrounding their prophetic texts in increasingly layered ambiguity (Ashe 15; Karcher 22). Modern examples demonstrate what happens when authors predict with too much specificity. A key technique of controlling prophetic interpretation, then, is to attach to a highly ambiguous text heavy glosses that lead a reader to intended meanings. This makes the reader dependant on the glossator and allows the text to maintain its unblemished state even if none of the predicted interpretations comes true. One can continue to hold up the source text as accurate and point to the interpretation as wrong or the fulfillment delayed. We see several examples today of prophecies using vague symbols with attached interpretations. When the *Sun* offered "100 New Nostradamus Prophecies" on May 23, 2005, for example, their expert reminded readers that Nostradamus's quatrains are known for their ambiguities, and that modern interpretive experts, like himself, were necessary for proper understanding. For the verse, "Blow winds, lash rains, unleash thy fury; / Mankind's wickedness shall reap thy wrath. / Punished sinners will pray God's mercy / Before the deluge shall run its path," readers are told that "hurricanes will ravage the East Coast of the United States" (27). Here the vagueness of both the text and the gloss allows the text to be labeled "true" as long as hurricanes occur in the east at any point in the twenty-first century—a fairly reasonable claim.

The glossing of medieval prophecy worked in similar ways. Geoffrey of Monmouth first authorized the prophetic passages in his *Historia Regum Britanniae* by back-dating them, claiming they had been copied from a source centuries older. Geoffrey then transcribed a lengthy section of prophecies that he attributed to Merlin. This portion is typical of the earlier, historical sections:

> The Lion's cubs shall be transformed into salt-water fishes and the Eagle of Mount Aravia shall nest upon its summit [174].

By the fourteenth century, many copies of Geoffrey's text were in circulation, and several of them included extensive glossing. Because Geoffrey's early verses represent past events couched in symbolic language (as a way of moving readers easily into the later verses where a discussion of contemporary events could take place), the glossator can be very explicit in describing clear matches between prophetic symbols and historical events. For example, many contemporary readers would already have recognized the "Lion's cubs" as a reference to Henry I's two sons:

William, Henry's heir, and Richard, an illegitimate son. The narrative's details make the link explicit for an audience: William and Richard had drowned in the infamous 1120 wreck of the White Ship, thus "transforming" them into fish. Henry's eldest child, his daughter Matilda, is represented in the verse as an eagle, for she had gained notoriety by moving (in eagle-like fashion) to a mountain-top home with her new husband, the Count of Anjou (Eckhardt 44, 80–81).

The centrality of ambiguous prophetic signs is something the fourth century scholar Macrobius notes in one of the most well known medieval texts on dreams, his commentary on the "Dream of Scipio," the closing portion of Cicero's *De re publica*. Macrobius warns that no symbol in a dream should be taken at face value:

> All portents and dreams conform to the rule that their announcements, threats, or warnings of imminent adversity are always ambiguous. [...] Even commonplace examples teach us that when a prediction about the future is made, it is always clothed in doubt, but in such a way that the diligent inquirer—"unless divinely opposed," as we say—may find clues to the information he is seeking concealed in the prophecy [118].

Macrobius's description hints at a crucial role played by ambiguity in prophecy: an inevitable doubleness. At the same time prophecy promotes its revelatory nature, it obscures meaning.

When authors move from vagueness to specificity, they risk shutting down the usefulness of their text. However, in the case of religious beliefs, this is not always insurmountable. As Pascal Boyer notes in *Religion Explained*, as long as prophetic sources have first authorized themselves for an audience, counter evidence will not necessarily send followers away. Researchers found that if a specific date of the end of the world passed, it "seemed to deepen commitment rather than shake it" (302).

Reading the Past

Literary scholars have identified retroactivity as a key interpretive practice for narratives (Todorov 64; Kermode 67; Parker 186, 211). This is also useful for understanding the uses of prophecy: Reading prophecy requires constructing meaning both backward and forward. In analyzing the strategies of Lancastrian legitimation, for example, Paul Strohm highlights prophecy's appropriation of the past as a key tool for trying to "control the field of imaginative possibility" (2). Along with chronicle accounts, gossip, imagination, and other prophecies, Strohm looks at prophetic inclusions in the *Chronicle* of Adam of Usk as one set of evidence for a battle waged on "a field of symbolic action within which adversarial claims might be discredited and even extirpated at their point of origin" (1). The king's exile of Henry Bolingbroke played a crucial part in the conflict between Richard and Henry, and Strohm points to the following prophecy within Usk as evidence for Usk's Lancastrian agenda:

> The return from exile of the aforesaid duke of Hereford—also now, through the death of his father, duke of Lancaster, and thus a duke twice over—fulfilled the prophecy of Bridlington, where the verse reads,
>
>> The double duke will come with scarce three hundred men,
>> Let perjured Philip flee, regardless of the slain.
>
> According to the prophecy of Merlin, this duke Henry is the eaglet, for he was the son of John; following Bridlington, however, he should rather be the dog, because of his livery of linked collars of greyhounds, and because he came in the dog-days, and because he drove utterly from the kingdom countless numbers of harts—the hart being the livery of King Richard [Given-Wilson 51–3].

The propagandistic value of this prophetic allusion, as Strohm reveals, is its suggestion that, "far from being an adventurous usurper, Henry is actually engaged in fulfilling a venerable prophetic mandate" (12).

The verse also aligns Richard with the unflattering image of "perjured Philip," a murderous ruler who was destined to be—indeed was known to have already been—overthrown. The final allusion in the prophecy to a retreat attempts tidy closure to the conflict, assuring readers metaphorically that Richard and his supporters had been driven "utterly from the kingdom." This was not the case, of course, and reveals a key motivation of prophecy as stabilizer: not only to use history to show that what has happened was supposed to happen, but also to posit a historical reality that can write over any instability.

A culture's moments of emergency tend to produce increased prophecies, according to Rupert Taylor. For example, political prophecies "become more numerous at times of crisis or when patriotic emotion was deeply moved" (87). Consequently, natural disasters such as tsunamis and hurricanes, technological crises such as the Y2K computer bug scare, and terrorist attacks such as on September 11, 2001, serve as a nexus for prophesying. In the case of the Y2K bug, people published prophetic warnings leading up to the year 2000 predicting how modern society, without commodities like electricity, would be plunged back into power monopolies that we last saw in "the medieval feudal system" (Mills 68).

Another effect of prophetic ambiguity is that it allows more easily for events in the past to be interpreted retroactively as prophetic signs. After tragic events, people look desperately to the past in order to locate signs that might help confirm order in the world—signs by which society should have seen the tragedies coming. The retroactive process of prophetic justification is one we see throughout popular culture. Traumatic events such as the attack on New York's World Trade Center were followed by the popular press immediately scrutinizing the past for identifying signs that could be interpreted as prescient warnings. Creative writers constructed new Nostradamus prophecies and sent them out into the Internet, for example:

> Earthshaking fire from the world's centre
> Will cause tremors around the New City [Wilson xi].

These lines circulated much more quickly than the average e-mail user could confirm their authenticity. Tom Clancy's novel *Debt of Honor*, which includes a scene of a plane flown into the capital, was retroactively labeled prophetic by the press because it appears to predict the 9/11 attacks. The book's 2000 back cover even announces "a shocker climax so plausible you'll wonder why it hasn't yet happened!" ("Clancy Novel" 2). The label "prophetic" attempts to cover over the randomness of traumatic events, and also allows the press a novel way of re-packaging already over-exposed news stories. As with medieval prophecy, the predictive texts tend to be too vague to be meaningful until after a fulfillment presents itself.

Part of what is at stake in believing the retroactive readings of prophecy is the blame that gets generated. In her article "The Blame Game," Emily Heil argues that after major national and world disasters, spokespersons of the Christian right have been quick to leverage the tragedies for political causes, pointing to the hedonism of gays and lesbians (among others) as leading inevitably to God's wrath. For example, in reference to Hurricane Katrina's devastation of New Orleans, Michael Marcavage, director of Repent America and a former White House intern, proposed that "the day Bourbon Street and the French Quarter was flooded was the day that 125,000 homosexuals were going to be celebrating sin in the streets. We're calling it an act of God" (42). The fact that the Gay Pride parade was to take place in an unaffected portion of the city was inconsequential. Similarly, after the September 11th attacks in 2001, Jerry Falwell blamed terrorist victories on a wide range of sinful behaviors he believed were going on in America. Heil also points to Pat Robertson's 1998 wide-sweeping claim that tolerance of a gay celebration in Orlando, Florida, "will bring about terrorist bombs, it'll bring earthquakes, tornadoes, and possibly a meteor" (42). In all of these cases, we find vocal leaders following the medieval habit of pointing retroactively to signs in the past as causes for things that have already happened.

Apocalyptic Politics

Prophetic discourse has real influence in people's lives today. Its texts hold power not merely in affecting the decisions individuals may make according to a newspaper horoscope, but in terms of where wars are fought, how huge amounts of national money are spent, and how political power is wielded. One of the forms of prophecy that has gained considerable interest during the shift between the twentieth and twenty-first centuries is apocalypticism. This resurgence of what has been a long-standing popularity of apocalyptic prophecies is due to a number of reasons, one of which is the effectiveness of the discourse as it evolved during the Middle Ages.

Apocalyptic prophecy in the Middle Ages was perfected as a way of allowing authors to talk about what they disliked in society at the moment. One medieval example, "The Last Six Kings to Follow John" (c. 1312–1470), is attributed to Merlin and comes to us in eight extant versions (Smallwood 572):

> Than in that ilk time the castels all
> That standes on Tems bank doun sall thai fall.
> And the water sall seme als it war dry,
> So many ded bodise sal tharin ly.
> The foure chefe waters that er in Ingland
> Sall rin all of rede blude, als I vnderstand [Hall 104].

The picture described here is bleak, revealing the apocalyptic direction in which the author sees England heading. The author employs an authorizing strategy similar to Geoffrey of Monmouth's presentation of his Merlin prophecies in that earlier sections of the prophecy depict well known historical events under a thin allegorical veil so an audience will recognize them easily. Later sections describe where the world is going and become increasingly ambiguous. What the poet claims his audience will see in the future is fantastic, but is described with increasingly literal language. Audiences are presented with real castles falling into the Thames and rivers running with blood of the dead. These are not presented as metaphorical images, but literal pictures of the future.

One reason apocalyptic prophecy has proven to be so productive in the twenty-first century is because that shocking kind of imagery appeals to a popular audience. In the Dispensational movement from the 1970s to the present, several writers have gained huge followings by arguing that the end of the world is imminent. Apocalyptic prophecies are also extremely flexible. The Book of Revelation allows both literal and figurative interpretation extremely easily. In his 1969 book *Why I Preach That the Bible Is Literally True*, W.A. Criswell explains how a fundamentalist ought to make sense of figurative language in the Bible:

> A simple rule to follow in determining what is literal and what is figurative is this: If the literal meaning of any word or expression makes good sense in its connections, it is literal. But if the literal meaning does not make good sense, it is figurative. [...] Any term ought to be regarded as literal until

there is good reason for a different understanding. [...] When we do not use the plain, normal literal method of interpretation, all objectivity is lost [142].

A Biblical book like Revelation, however, falls precisely between the cracks Criswell tries to ignore. More than any other text it the Bible, Revelation can be cast as literal or figurative as one's exegetical needs require.

Barbara Rossing, author of *The Rapture Exposed*, challenges those who claim Dispensationalism is an inevitable theological choice for Biblical literalists:

> The dispensationalist story creates a comprehensive, overarching narrative. [...] But the dispensationalist system's supposed clear-cut answers rely on a highly selective biblical literalism, as well as insertion of nonexistent two-thousand-year gaps and dubious re-definitions of key terms. The system is not true to a literal reading of the Bible, as they claim [173–74].

One of Rossing's greatest concerns is that the theology underlying the *Left Behind* series is dangerous:

> The genius of the *Left Behind* novels is their use of fiction to advance a political and theological agenda. *Left Behind* [...] gets inside people's heads to try to convince us that the violent, absolutist script is how God's victory will happen and is happening in the world. The script is most dangerous for the people of the Middle East, but it has dangerous ramifications for everyone's political and democratic future. From denial of global warming to support for militarism and expansionism in the Middle East, Rapture theology can lead in directions that are dangerous for our world [xi].

Kevin Phillips is equally worried that the right-wing theology which manipulates prophecy for power has been embraced by the Bush administration in the twenty-first century. In his book *American Theocracy* Phillips quotes Tim Weber, a professor of church history, in his conclusions regarding belief in Rapture-based prophecies: "If Jesus may come at any minute, then long-term social reform or renewal are beside the point. It has a bad effect there" (250). For a society that accepts prophecy of this kind, the world is going to be destroyed and Christians will be removed, so environmentalism is pointless, social change is impossible, and the Arabs are irrevocably God's primary enemy. Rossing believes apocalyptic Christianity has taken over America in the wake of George W. Bush's administration, and "since the election I am more convinced than ever that the political agenda driving the *Left Behind* storyline is the most dangerous aspect of the *Left Behind* phenomenon. [...] [It details] a full-blown program of theocracy for the United States" (viii–ix).

There are real social dangers, then, when popular culture gives credence to Dispensationalist presentations of the rapture; but there are also theological dangers for traditional Christianity. In the second section of part two of his *Summa*, question 95, Aquinas attempts to distinguish between divine prophecy, a kind of communication to which all humans should aspire in their closeness to God, and sinful human divination, an inappropriate desire humans should shun:

> By divining the future we mean predicting it. [...] Men [can predict events according to their effects] by seeing them happen in the present; to know events in themselves before they happen is God's prerogative, since he alone in his eternity sees future things as though they were present. If anyone else claims to foreknow or foretell the future without God having revealed it, then clearly he is arrogating to himself what belongs to God. So by divining the future we don't just mean predicting what will happen necessarily or normally, for that can be reasoned out; nor knowing non-determined future events by divine revelation, for that is not so much divining them as receiving them from the divine. Divining means arrogating to oneself without justification the prediction of future events, and this is clearly a form of wrongdoing [411].

The prophecy being harnessed in Western politics today takes as its premise the belief that politicians are part of a divine plan that will inevitably culminate in the apocalyptic destruction of the earth. This enacts in many ways the kind of hubris against which Aquinas warns his readers.

But do people actually believe rapture theology? Phillips points to statistics from Paul Boyer, a University of Wisconsin historian, to argue that up to forty percent of Americans "believe that Bible prophecies detail a specific sequence of end-times events" (253). Phillips attributes this high rate of belief in part to the kind of creativity prophecy has always allowed: "The Bible includes no specific sequence of end-times events, as most theologians point out, so belief that it does is largely a product of a century of amplified Darbyism, which is consummated in the *Left Behind* series" (253). There is, then, a great deal at stake in understanding prophecy's roots in the Middle Ages. This powerful discourse became intimately tied to popular culture in the Middle Ages, and in the Middles Ages we find individuals modeling techniques for influencing people's action in the here and now. For those using the same techniques today it remains an equally powerful tool.

Works Cited

Aquinas, Thomas. *Summa Theologiæ: A Concise Translation.* Ed. Timothy McDermott. Westminister, Md.: Christian Classics, 1989.

Allis, Oswald T. *Prophecy and the Church.* Philadelphia: The Presbyterian and Reformed Publishing Company, 1945.

Ashe, Geoffrey. *The Book of Prophecy: From Ancient Greece to the Millennium.* London: Blandford, 1999.

Beaton, Graham. "Armageddon 2006." *Sun,* 6 Feb. 2006, 18–19.

Becker, John E. "The Law, the Prophets, and Wisdom: On the Functions of Literature." *College English* 37 (1975): 254–64.

Boyer, Pascal. *Religion Explained: The Evolutionary Origins of Religious Thought.* New York: Basic Books, 2001.

Burgroft, Alan. "100 New Nostradamus Prophecies." *Sun*, 23 May 2005, 26–29.

_____. "The New Nostradamus Predicts World War 3!" *Sun*, 22 Aug. 2005, 18–19.

"Clancy Novel Predicted Attack." *Bloomington Herald Times*, 13 Oct. 2001, 2.

Coote, Lesley. *Prophecy and Public Affairs in Later Medieval England.* Woodbridge, Suffolk: York Medieval Press, 2000.

Criswell, W.A. *Why I Preach That the Bible Is Literally True.* Nashville: Broadman Press, 1969.

Eco, Umberto. *Travels in Hyperreality: Essays.* Trans. William Weaver. New York: Harcourt Brace, 1986.

Eckhardt, Caroline D., ed. *The Prophetia Merlini of Geoffrey of Monmouth: A Fifteenth-Century English Commentary.* Cambridge: The Medieval Academy of America, 1982.

Fairfield, Gail. *Choice Centered Tarot.* Smithville, Ind,: Ramp Creek, 1990.

Foucault, Michel. *The Archaeology of Knowledge and the Discourse on Language.* Trans. A.M. Sheridan Smith. New York: Pantheon Books, 1972.

Gates, David. "The Pop Prophets." *Newsweek*, 24 May 2004, 44–50.

Geoffrey of Monmouth. *The History of the Kings of Britain.* Trans. Lewis Thorpe. New York: Penguin, 1984.

Given-Wilson, C., ed. and trans. *The Chronicle of Adam Usk, 1377–1421.* Oxford: Clarendon, 1997.

Glass, Stephen. "Prophets and Losses." *Harper's Magazine*, Feb. 1998, 69–79.

Hall, Joseph, ed. *The Poems of Laurence Minot.* 3rd ed. Oxford: Clarendon, 1914.

Heil, Emily. "The Blame Game." *The Advocate*, 17 Jan. 2006, 42–3.

Karcher, Stephen. *The Illustrated Encyclopedia of Divination.* Rockport, Mass.: Element, 1997.

Kermode, Frank. *The Sense of an Ending: Studies in the Theory of Fiction.* Oxford: Oxford University Press, 1977.

Kerby-Fulton, Kathryn. "Prophecy and Suspicion: Closet Radicalism, Reformist Politics, and the Vogue for Hildegardiana in Ricardian England." *Speculum* 75 (2000): 318–41.

Kugel, James L, ed. *Poetry and Prophecy: The Beginnings of a Literary Tradition.* Ithaca: Cornell University Press, 1990.

LaHaye, Tim. *The Rapture: Who Will Face the Tribulation?* Eugene, Ore.: Harvest House, 2002.

_____. *Revelation Illustrated and Made Plain.* Grand Rapids: Zondervan, 1975.

LaHaye, Tim, and Thomas Ice. *Charting the End Times: A Visual Guide to Understanding Bible Prophecy.* Eugene, Ore,: Harvest House, 2001.

LaHaye, Tim, and Jerry B. Jenkins. *The Authorized Left Behind Handbook.* Wheaton, Ill.: Tyndale House, 2005.

_____. *Left Behind: A Novel of the Earth's Last Days.* Wheaton, Ill.: Tyndale House, 1995.

Lindsey, Hal. *The Late Great Planet Earth.* Grand Rapids: Zondervan, 1979.

_____. *The 1980's: Countdown to Armageddon.* New York: Bantam, 1982.

_____. *Satan is Alive and Well on Planet Earth.* Grand Rapids: Zondervan, 1974.

Macrobius, Ambrosius Aurelius Theodosius. *Commentary on the Dream of Scipio.* Trans. William Harris Stahl. New York: Columbia University Press, 1990.

McGinn, Bernard. *Visions of the End: Apocalyptic Traditions in the Middle Ages.* New York: Columbia University Press, 1998.

Mills, Dick. "Power Grid Breakdown! Chilling, Dark, and Possible!" In *How to Survive the Y2K Crisis: Harris' Farmer's Almanac Presents No. 14*, ed. Gerald C. Bethge, 68–70, 79. New York: Harris Publications, 1999.

Parker, Patricia. "Preposterous Events." *Shakespeare Quarterly* 43 (summer 1992): 186–213.

Phillips, Kevin. *American Theocracy: The Peril and Politics of Radical Religion, Oil, and Borrowed Money in the 21st Century.* New York: Penguin, 2006.

Rossing, Barbara R. *The Rapture Exposed: The Message of Hope in the Book of Revelation.* New York: Basic Books, 2005.

Russell, Jeffrey B. *A History of Medieval Christianity: Prophecy and Order.* New York: Thomas Crowell, 1968.

Sawyer, John F.A. *Prophecy and the Biblical Prophets*. Ed. P.R Ackroyd and G.N. Stanton. Rev. ed. *Oxford Bible Series*. Oxford: Oxford University Press, 1993.

Shermer, Michael. *Why People Believe Weird Things: Pseudoscience, Superstition, and Other Confusions of Our Time*. New York: W.H. Freeman, 1997.

Smallwood, T.M. "The Prophecy of the Six Kings." *Speculum* 60 (1985): 571–92.

Strohm, Paul. *England's Empty Throne: Usurpation and the Language of Legitimation 1399–1422*. New Haven: Yale University Press, 1998.

Taylor, Robert. "Martyr's Visions of the End of the World." *Sun*, 22 Aug. 2005, 27–28.

Taylor, Rupert. *The Political Prophecy in England*. New York: Columbia University Press, 1911.

"Things That Make You Go Hmmm ..." *Entertainment Weekly*, 18 Sept. 1998, 12.

Todorov, Tzvetan. *The Poetics of Prose*. Trans. Richard Howard. Ithaca: Cornell University Press, 1987.

Watt, Diane. *Secretaries of God*. Cambridge: D.S. Brewer, 1997.

Weber, Timothy P. *On the Road to Armageddon: How Evangelicals Became Israel's Best Friend*. Grand Rapids: Baker Academic, 2004.

Wilson, Ian. *Nostradamus: The Evidence*. London: Orion, 2002.

6 Idealized Images of Wales in the Fiction of Edith Pargeter/ Ellis Peters

LESLEY JACOBS

Edith Pargeter (1913–1995) was one of the twentieth century's major authors of medieval historical fiction. Her novels combine historical figures with characters of her own creation and display careful research and a deep familiarity with the history and historical writing of the period. Under her own name, Pargeter published *The Brothers of Gwynedd Quartet*, comprising *Sunrise in the West, The Dragon at Noonday, The Hounds of Sunset*, and *Afterglow and Nightfall*. This monumental epic tells the story of Llewelyn ap Griffith, the last prince of unified Wales, and of his struggle to unite his country against the pressures of the English kings Henry III and Edward I. She had previously published *The Heaven Tree Trilogy*, comprising *The Heaven Tree, The Green Branch*, and *The Scarlet Seed*. Set on the Welsh border in the twelfth century, they focus on the nature of a particular artist and architect and feature Llewelyn ap Iorworth (the Great), grandfather of the later Llewelyn. Also set in the medieval period, although later, is a novel of the boyhood of Henry V entitled *The Bloody Field* (reissued as *A Bloody Field by Shrewsbury*), which treats another Welsh hero, the fifteenth century Owen Glendower.[1] These novels foster an idealized version of medieval Wales that is often set up in contrast to its more powerful neighbor, and focus on compelling historical personalities in the Wales and England of the twelfth and thirteenth centuries.

Pargeter is perhaps better known as Ellis Peters, the author of the medieval mystery series featuring the fictional Brother Cadfael. Cadfael, a Welsh monk at the abbey of Shrewsbury, stands out from his fellows in many ways: his crusading background and his herbalist wisdom make him unique among the cloistered brothers, but most important is his ethnicity. Cadfael's Welshness in the disputed border region of Shropshire gives him the ability to comment on English values and offer alternatives to them. As an observer not implicated in English society, he repeatedly notes for the reader the many ways in which medieval Welsh values are not only better than the English alternatives but also similar to our modern ways of thinking. In the Cadfael novels as in her other historical fiction, Peters presents idealized images of England's most intimate neighbor to construct the Middle Ages, and specifically medieval Wales, as both intimate and alien to the modern reader.[2]

Jeffrey Jerome Cohen discusses this kind of intimate alterity in his article on the twelfth-century cleric Gerald of Wales, whose works serve as useful companion pieces to Peters' fiction. The descendant of a princess of South Wales and an Anglo-Norman marcher lord, Gerald wrote several pieces describing Wales and the Welsh marches, the borderlands where he spent much of his childhood and around which his adult ambitions centered. *The Journey to Wales* and *The Description of Wales*, Gerald's major works, alternately praise and denigrate Welsh institutions, taking up what Cohen describes as a "hybrid" attitude—one marked by, among other things, competing allegiances—toward Gerald's own situation of being of mixed descent in the border region (Cohen 85–6). Ultimately, although Gerald waxes eloquent on some celebrated vices of Welshmen—including their habits of marrying their first cousins and killing off their brothers in fratricidal warfare—he presents some of their institutions as instructive contrasts to those of Norman England. Peters follows this lead, depending in her characterizations of the region on the qualities Gerald defines as being particularly Welsh. However, Peters goes beyond Gerald and sets up Welsh values as the ones with which we as modern readers should identify. Thus we feel our intimacy with the Middle Ages through identification with the "better" qualities of medieval Wales while still remembering our distance from the medieval through the contrast that Wales offers to medieval England.

Peters' Work on the Borders

In *History on the Edge*, Michelle Warren argues that the drawing of boundaries between countries seeks to establish "an absolute difference at the place of most intimate contact between two spaces" (2). Warren's analysis focuses on the Arthurian "histories" that sprang up around the borders between England and Wales and in the British possessions on the Continent during the centuries following Arthur's supposed reign. We can also apply her analysis of border writings to literature from long after that period: Pargeter's novels can be defined most succinctly as border fiction. Taking shape in the space between England and Wales, they explore the conflicts between English and Welsh identity that occur in the regions dividing the two countries. Pargeter's novels examine the interweaving of life between medieval England and Wales in Shropshire, her own home region, and in the center of its divided loyalties, the town of Shrewsbury. The Cadfael novels are set in Shrewsbury but extend their reach into both England and Wales, acknowledging the town's ties to both sides in the medieval struggle for power. Other novels move further into Wales, but still center on the ties of loyalty extending both sides of the disputed border between Wales and England.

In *The Brothers of Gwynedd*, Pargeter's narrator describes Shrewsbury as "a noble town, formidably walled all around and everywhere moated by the Severn, but for a narrow neck of land open to the north, for the whole town lies within a great coil of that river" (Pargeter 1989, 23). The choice of Shrewsbury was a shrewd one for Pargeter as a setting; besides being her own home and an area she knew well, its location in the border county of Shropshire situated it excellently for providing an objective point of view on politics both sides of the border. During the period in which Pargeter's novels are set, Shrewsbury functioned basically as a frontier town keeping watch over the independent, and then semi-independent, regions of Powys and Gwynedd in Wales.[3] It was thus a place where Englishness was felt deeply in the times of conflict against Wales, but also a town with many connections to markets and families west of the border.

In border regions, language remains an important marker of difference between the peoples living in proximity to one another (Warren 11–12). Cadfael, of course, is bilingual in the border region and can thus shift his identity as needed between English and Welsh. As a Welshman in an English order and an English town, Cadfael remains a kind of outsider within the monastic system. As a herbalist and physician to the people of the town, he can go where he wishes and do more or less as he wants, occasionally making excuses to journey into the town for his own purposes. Cadfael's mobility is further enhanced when he becomes godfather to a friend's son, necessitating the paying of sponsoral visits in *The Potter's Field* and other novels. Cadfael's Welsh language skills are also often called upon by the various abbots and bishops he serves. At various times during the Chronicles, Cadfael goes into Wales to act as a translator and a messenger to bishops and kings. Even in Shrewsbury itself, he is sometimes called upon to use his mother tongue for the better workings of English order, translating for Welsh merchants at the abbey fair. In *Saint Peter's Fair*, one of these merchants uses the Welsh language to manipulate his fellows, pretending to be in need of Cadfael's translating services since "tongues wag more quickly in front of the deaf man" (Peters 189). Ultimately, the merchant's information-gathering serves the purposes of Owain, prince of Gwynedd, who naturally has his "intelligencers" at such a great gathering of tradesmen and customers from across the region (Peters 188). Here, as elsewhere in Peters's fiction, language enters into the niceties of plot as well as of identity.

The topography of the border region and of Wales also plays a part in Peters's novels, especially the location of Shrewsbury on the river Severn. Warren argues that rivers "embed instability in the permanent features of the landscape," drawing settlement and rivalries toward their shifting banks (5). Peters defines Cadfael's Shrewsbury by its relationship with the river that forms its shape, and makes it a place of mingling not only between England and Wales, but between Englishness and Welshness. Many of her novels point out the impossibility of dividing the two kingdoms, for, as she points out in describing the residents of Shrewsbury, "hardly a native-born family in the borough was without kin on the western side of Severn" (Pargeter 690). In *The Heaven Tree* trilogy, Shrewsbury actually changes hands as a historical conquest by Llewelyn Fawr is made personal to the novel's characters: he occupies the town in order to regain his foster-son, held prisoner there (Pargeter 374–7). In *The Brothers of Gwynedd*, Welsh and English meet to discuss affairs of state in Shrewsbury, and in *The Bloody Field* it is the English hub of communications with the Welsh under Glendower. Shrewsbury thus, in the Cadfael novels and in Pargeter's other fiction, directly represents the space of divided loyalties between England and Wales.

Not only spaces but also characters exist on the emotional borders of Pargeter's novels. David ap Griffith, Prince Llewelyn's youngest sibling in *The Brothers of Gwynedd*, serves as a device to focus the action and sympathies of the novel, torn between Wales and England but ultimately siding with Wales. He crosses the border multiple times during his life, from the age of six with his fleeing mother to the later betrayals of his brother that send him fleeing into England. Pargeter uses David in *The Brothers of Gwynedd* as a study of the psychology of loyalty and betrayal, his constant conflict between his Welsh blood and his English upbringing demonstrating for the reader the real conflict of values between the two systems. Three times David betrays his brother, and three times Llewelyn forgives him: David epitomizes all the Welsh nobles who change sides for gain or jealousy but are inevitably drawn back by their love of their homeland. As he says to Llewelyn after their final reconciliation, "I *am* Welsh, birth and blood urge me, the very air I breathe wrings my vitals, and tells me *I am Welsh*!" (Pargeter 696, original emphasis). After Llewelyn's death, David has the responsibility of leading Wales even in defeat, for with Llewelyn's death defeat becomes inevitable (797). However, he remains loyal to his brother's memory and continues to fight. After their final victory, the English brutally execute David in Shrewsbury (811–12), the proper setting for the physical dismemberment of a body who had been all his life emotionally torn between the two regions. David is the glass through which we see his brother and through which we judge Llewelyn as ultimately greater than the Edward who conquered him. In all of David's painful conflicts in the novel, he never ceases to see Wales as the principality tied more truly to justice than England and the one more dedicated to its people's well-being. This construction, epitomizing Pargeter's idealized version of Wales, echoes throughout the tragedy of *The Brothers of Gwynedd* and forms the basis for her comparison of Wales with England in the Cadfael novels.

The Virtues of Wales

Peters portrays medieval Wales as providing alternatives to some less-than-ideal social practices of its more powerful neighbor, and perhaps of her contemporary society as well. In this, she follows in the footsteps of Gerald of Wales, who intended for his descriptions of Wales to point up certain deficiencies in the English society of the time. For Peters as well as contemporary observers, the most important Welsh virtue is that of hospitality. Gerald devotes an entire chapter of his *Description of Wales* to "Their hospitality and eating habits," opening the chapter with the categorical statement: "In Wales no one begs. Everyone's home is open to all, for the Welsh generosity and hospitality are the greatest of all virtues" (236). He notes that "when you travel there is no question of your asking for accommodation or of their offering it: you just march into a house and hand over your weapons to the person in charge" (236). We experience this Welsh virtue of hospitality in the first Cadfael novel, *A Morbid Taste for Bones*. When Cadfael and his prior and fellows journey into Wales to bring back the relics of Saint Winifred, they are met and greeted with openhandedness by the local people. Although the parish priest may be alarmed at the sight of so many strangers, wondering how his small property can house and feed them, he cannot hesitate, for "guests were sacrosanct, and must not be questioned on the proposed length of their stay, however ruinous" (Peters 35). Peters's insistence on Welsh generosity and hospitality continues during the later books in the series. When Cadfael and Brother Mark make their way to Owain Gwynedd's court in *The Summer of the Danes*, they are immediately approached by welcoming hosts and the offer of food and drink (Peters 23–7), following Gerald's description of how the Welsh welcome visitors to their homes (236). Peters' idealization of Welsh hospitality sets it off not only as a way to show the shortcomings of England, during this period of the early 1140s torn by civil war, but also as a quality to which we as contemporary readers should aspire.

We have seen how Peters offers medieval Wales as an example for the modern reader's emulation. Her idealized version of medieval Wales is one with which the modern reader can often identify. Most of these identifications take place in the realm of social practices, where medieval Wales is set off as different from the less enlightened regions of medieval England—an inversion of the usual (English) medieval discourse that presented Wales as barbaric.[4] One Welsh quality that Peters aligns with modern sensibilities is the Welsh differentiation between degrees of killing. In early medieval Wales, manslaughter was not the same as murder and could be compounded for a blood-price. Peters opposes this practice to the English one of executing all killers, even accidental ones. The plot of *Dead Man's Ransom* revolves around precisely this difference between murder and manslaughter. Cadfael argues fervently against an English sheriff for a young man in the novel who has killed and instantly regretted it, for as the daughter of the murdered man comments, "it seems a sad waste that all a man's good should not be able to outweigh one evil, however great" (Peters 210). In the back-story to the novel's main plot, we learn of a Welsh trader who was hanged for stabbing a town porter during a drunken brawl. His half-brother resents the trader's punishment, for as Cadfael points out, "in Wales the young man would not have hanged. A blood-price would have paid it" (144). However, instead of starting a blood-feud with the man responsible, the half-brother follows another Welsh custom and accepts a price for his brother's death. Peters presents this compromise as one that saves lives otherwise ended because of drunken or instantly regretted mistakes. This attitude, aligned with modern progressive judicial practices rather than with those of medieval England, sets off medieval Wales as a place where some modern readers, in their progressive idealism, would feel at home.[5]

Peters also uses Wales as a counterpoint to play up medieval England's shortcomings in her depiction of Welsh deviance from certain Christian customs, offering the Welsh attitude toward children born out of wedlock as a critique of medieval England's strict imposition of Christian rulings. Although Peters's outlook in the Cadfael novels, for the most part, remains steadfastly Christian—focused on traditional values such as forgiveness and generosity to the poor—her espousal of what she presents as natural law sets her and the Welsh apart from medieval religious customs today's society would condemn as unjust. The view that prevailed over most of medieval Europe was that children born outside of Christian marriage deserved neither their father's name nor any part of his inheritance. The Welsh, although orthodox in most of their religious practices, held that any child acknowledged by the father belonged to the father's kinship and should share in the eventual division of his property. In the Cadfael novels at least, Peters continually stresses the superiority of the Welsh system over that of England. In *Monk's Hood*, we see the illegitimate half–Welsh son of an English father murder that father for the inheritance that can only be his by Welsh law, not English. Since the young man was popularly known to be his father's son, he can claim inheritance by the Welsh law that does not bar bastards from succession (Peters 185–8), until, of course, Cadfael unmasks him as a murderer. Peters places the blame here to a great extent on the father, whose refusal to acknowledge his son legally and give him title to his land tempts the young man to gamble for his inheritance with patricide. This tragedy, like others, is brought about by the narrowness of English law, as it works with the strictures of orthodox Christianity to limit the transition of property to those blessed by the Church.

A tragedy of greater proportions, as it involves a greater property, we see played out on the larger stage of the civil wars during which the Cadfael novels are set. When Henry I of England died with no son left to succeed him, the daughter he had designated as heir, Maud (or Matilda), was not in a position to take immediate possession of the throne. At this juncture, Stephen of Blois, the king's nephew, took the crown and held it against the armed resistance of Maud and her supporters. This conflict was resolved only near the end of Stephen's reign, outside the scope of the Cadfael novels, and only by the agreement that Maud's son would succeed to Stephen's throne. However, Peters hints at a solution that could have been reached by Welsh law, although never considered in England. Robert of Gloucester, the oldest of King Henry's sons—but not by his legal wife—supported his sister throughout her crusade for the crown. Cadfael sees him only a few times, but judges him "the best of [Henry's bastard children], who ... could have outrivalled both these royal rivals had his pedigree accorded with Norman law and custom. In Wales he would have had his rights, the eldest son of his father, and the most royal" (Peters, *Brother Cadfael's Penance*, 57). Had Peters' version of Welsh customs—to Cadfael as, perhaps, to her readers the more just—prevailed in England, the waste of civil war could have been prevented.

For the Welsh, pride in their own identity leads to a lack of servility to others. In *The Description of Wales*, Gerald notices that "Nature has endowed [the Welsh] with great boldness in speaking and great confidence in answering, no matter what the circumstances may be, and even in the presence of their princes and chieftains. This is true of all of them, from the highest to the lowest" (245). A lack of servility marks many of the Welshmen who appear in Peters' novels and contrasts with the eagerness to please of the lower orders of England before their social betters. In *The Pilgrim of Hate*, a rider must ask directions from a herd-boy, who is described as "half–Welsh and immune from servility" (Peters 153). Despite the rider's clear social advantages—his horse and its gear, not to mention his own—the child is unafraid to approach and guide him. Similarly, in *Monk's Hood* Cadfael knows he is in Wales by the attitude of a servant he is questioning; the servant answers back to him and asks him why he is asking questions, and Cadfael thinks, "An English servant, if he ventured to challenge your proceedings at all, would do it roundabout and obsequiously, for fear of getting his ears clipped, but your Welsh lad speaks his mind to princes" (Peters 169). This presentation of the Welsh as confident and egalitarian remains constant throughout Peters's works. Cadfael himself finds obedience the most difficult part of his vows (Peters, *Potter's Field*, 29), and often comes into disfavor with his prior for his manner of speaking freely to his social betters. Identifying with Cadfael and his free speaking, the modern reader takes this pride to himself as a quality shared over time with the medieval Welsh.

Peters frequently stresses the Welsh devotion to freedom and independence and to the assertion of their rights and their equality with other races. Gerald describes the Welsh as "passionately devoted to their freedom and to the defence of their country" (233), and Cadfael's own clinging to his Welsh identity in the midst of an English monastery shows one instance of this devotion to freedom. The many fighters for Welsh autonomy in Peters's novels echo Cadfael's dedication to his homeland. Throughout the Cadfael Chronicles, Owain Gwynedd serves as a prime example of single-minded devotion to his country. Similarly, the second Llewelyn's fierce devotion to the cause of Wales forms the center of *The Brothers of Gwynedd*. Following in his grandfather's and namesake's footsteps, Llewelyn tries to carve out a free Welsh principality against what Pargeter presents as the corruption and trickery of the English kings. Again and again, Henry III and Edward I move against Llewelyn either in arms or in the lawcourts, trying to bend Wales and its leaders to their control. They do not scruple to use Llewelyn's own liegemen against him, including his own rebellious brothers (Pargeter 510). In contrast to English maneuverings for power and gain, Llewelyn, like his grandfather in *The Heaven Tree Trilogy*, appears as a man motivated by unselfish patriotism. Pargeter's fierce idealization of the men who fight for the cause of Wales reflects back on the civil wars in the Cadfael Chronicles as well as on the supposed abuses of power of the English kings. In the political sphere as in so many others, she constructs the medieval Welsh as decidedly superior to their English neighbors.

Peters uses the popular impression of Celtic Christianity as comparatively pure and free from corruption to criticize the worldliness of the English Church as well as to emphasize the ideal character of Welsh religion.[6] Throughout the Cadfael novels, as well as in her other historical works, she inserts reminders of the difference between the practices of the Welsh and English churches and peoples. Here she follows Gerald's example once again: he states that "nowhere can you see hermits and anchorites more abstinent and more spiritually committed than in Wales" (254). Peters notes that "Welshmen preferred their own ancient Celtic Christianity, the solitary hermitage of the self-exiled saint and the homely little college of Celtic monks rather than the shrewd and vigorous foundations that looked to Rome" (*Monk's Hood* 162). In his *Description of Wales*, Gerald titles one of his chapters "How they [the Welsh] received the true religion long ago, their piety and their devotion to the Christian faith" (253). He describes the Welsh as still faithful to early practices taught them centuries before and asserts that they have great respect for relics, men of the cloth, their churches, and the Cross itself (253). Peters's version of Welsh spirituality is filled with unselfish priests and local hermits wholly dedicated to their communities and their calling. The construction of a superior form of Christianity mirrors her construction of idealized political and social customs in Wales, which forms the background even for her acknowledgment of problems inherent in the Welsh character and social system.

The Problems of Wales

A common English view of the Welsh during the Middle Ages was that they were particularly prone to conflict and bloodshed. In *The Journey through Wales*, Gerald asserts in the context of narrating the Welsh resistance to Henry II that "the Welsh are more prone to anger and revenge in this life than other nations, and similarly their Saints in the next world seem much more vindictive" (189). This emphasis on the Welsh as easily moved to anger and martial resistance echoes throughout Pargeter's fiction. Her Welshmen tend to follow Gerald's outline physically and emotionally, typically "light and agile. They are fierce ... and totally dedicated to the practice of arms" (233). In *The Brothers of Gwynedd*, Llewelyn's quest to unify Wales is beset by local chieftains who closely resemble other characterizations of Gerald. For one thing, they have great pride in their descent, which often leads them into violence. Gerald says in *The Description of Wales* that "[the Welsh] avenge with great ferocity any wrong or insult done to their relations. They are vindictive by nature, bloodthirsty and violent. Not only are they ready to avenge new and recent injuries, but old ones, too, as if they had only just received them" (251). These statements follow only a few chapters after Gerald's descriptions of Welshmen's "natural acumen and shrewdness"; he describes them as "very sharp and intelligent" and "quicker-witted and more shrewd than any other Western people" (238–9). Cohen describes Gerald's writing as motivated by "competing allegiances conjoined with tortured abjections" (87), as it deploys almost simultaneously his respect for the Welsh and their customs and the prejudices of his Norman upbringing and associates. These competing allegiances also characterize Pargeter's work, as she constructs a romanticized version of the medieval Welsh that turns even their acknowledged defects to good.

Pargeter's conflicted attitude toward the Welsh character is reflected most clearly in *The Brothers of Gwynedd*, where she presents Wales as "beset with brothers ... the cords of the rack that broke her joint from joint" (819). Not only do the second Llewelyn and his brother war constantly, but so do their father and his half-brother. Even before even the death of their father, the two are in conflict. The elder Llewelyn's legitimate son's imprisonment of his half-brother provokes much anger from Welshmen who hold to the old ways and the division of property equally among sons (9–11).[7] The second Llewelyn calls feuding between brothers "the whole story of Wales, this blessing and curse of brotherhood, the spring of loyalty, of jealousy, of murder, of all the heroisms and the villainies of our history" (563). We also see Wales as a land disturbed by warring brothers in the Cadfael novels. The conflict between Owain Gwynedd and his brother Cadwaladr forms the backdrop for *The Summer of the Danes*. Cadwaladr's followers, at his orders, had ambushed a close ally of Owain's, and Owain's retribution and his brother's attempt to regain his property bear out Cadfael's statement that "brothers have been the ruin of Welsh princedoms through all ages" (Peters 10). Peters presents conflict between brothers as never-ending, fed by the hostility inherent in the tradition of dividing land equally, but always marked by a love that draws blood-kin back to reconciliation.

The Summer of the Danes also focuses on the relationship of foster-brothers, a frequently discussed relationship in medieval Irish and Welsh society. Gerald describes the institution of fosterage as a damaging one for the country's peace in *The Description of Wales*, since each foster-father of a prince's son will tend to fight for his own protégé if there is war (261, 273). Peters, however, chooses to highlight the more positive aspects of fosterage in her Cadfael novels. *Dead Man's Ransom* centers around the ties of two foster-brothers, close enough that each offers to die in the other's place when they fall into English hands. Another stark example of foster-brothers' loyalty is the case of the fictional Cuhelyn in *The Summer of the Danes*, who lost an arm in the defence of his prince and foster-brother and determines throughout the book to avenge him (37). We see that although Peters idealizes the foster-brother relationship, she posits it as another relationship so strong that it can lead to violence, further splintering Welsh unity and ability to resist infiltration by its more powerful neighbor.

Pargeter's novels of the last Welsh prince of Wales follow Gerald's lead in identifying Welsh resistance to unification as that which will eventually destroy Wales. Gerald outlines resistance to unification as one of the three things "causing the ruin of the Welsh people and preventing them, generation after generation, from ever enjoying prosperity," saying that "through their natural pride and obstinacy, they will not order themselves as other nations do so successfully, but refuse to accept the rule and dominion of one single king" (271). *The Brothers of Gwynedd* chronicles the constant to-and-fro of loyalties as Welsh marcher lords switch their fealty between their Welsh prince and the king of England. Here Pargeter causes her English kings to follow Gerald's advice on "how the Welsh can be conquered": he advises that "[they] must sow dissention in their ranks and do all [they] can by promises and bribes to stir them up against each other" (267). Henry and Edward do this very thing, "pick[ing] off one by one" the loyalties and fealties of unstable Welsh allies (120). Still, perhaps because of the constant betrayals Llewelyn suffers, Pargeter manages to construct his story as a resounding tragedy instead of a tale of fickle followers. She takes the problems outlined by Gerald and transforms them into the flaws that bring Llewelyn's independent principality down.

In her novels of Welsh history as well as in the Cadfael series, Pargeter manages to reconcile these acknowledged problems in the medieval Welsh system with the idealized version of Wales she has constructed. She deploys what she construes as the particular virtues of Welsh society—its hospitality, its espousal of natural law over imposed Christian hierarchies, its lack of concern with artificially constructed social systems—not only to critique English society of the period, but also to present Welsh society as being more in line with our contemporary democratic values. Pargeter constructs Cadfael's world and the world of *The Brothers of Gwynedd*, *The Heaven Tree Trilogy*, and her other historical novels as one which is not unrecognizable in spite of its great historical distance from our own period. The values she offers as specifically Welsh provide a bridge to our own understanding and identification, and those she identifies with England are set off as other and alien. They belong on the other side of the great divide between us and the Middle Ages, a divide which Cadfael and the great leaders such as Owen Glendower and the two Llewelyns have no difficulty in overcoming.

Notes

1. Pargeter's medieval works also include a romance set in early Plantagenet England called *The Marriage of Meggotta*. I will not consider this novel in this essay, as it deals more with events in England than with comparisons between England and Wales.

2. In citing, I will use the name under which the book was published (thus Peters for the Cadfael novels and Pargeter for the other fiction).

3. From being more or less independent principalities in the eleventh century, Powys and much of South Wales gradually came under royal control during the twelfth and thirteenth centuries.

4. See Cohen on representations of indigenous peoples as barbaric. For centuries, the Welsh had been configured by English chroniclers as primitive and subhuman "in order to render the taking of their lands unproblematic" (Cohen 87).

5. I see Peters' vision here as a left-wing point of view, one that favors political solutions stereotyped in the United States as "liberal." It is thus the politically left-leaning reader who would feel most at home in the world that Peters constructs.

6. For sources that reflect the changing views of Celtic spirituality since Peters was writing, see Marion Bowman, "Contemporary Celtic Spirituality," in *New Directions in Celtic Studies*, ed. Amy Hale and Philip Payton (Exeter: University of Exeter Press, 2000), 69–91.

7. See Gerald 261 on the division of property.

Works Cited

Cohen, Jeffrey Jerome. "Hybrids, Monsters, Borderlands." In *The Postcolonial Middle Ages*, ed. Jeffrey Jerome Cohen, 85–104. New York: Palgrave, 2000.

Gerald of Wales. *The Journey through Wales and The Description of Wales*. Trans. Lewis Thorpe. London: Penguin, 1978.

Pargeter, Edith. *The Bloody Field*. London: Macmillan, 1972. Reprinted by Headline Book Publishing in 1989 as *A Bloody Field by Shrewsbury*.

_____. *The Brothers of Gwynedd Quartet*. London: Headline Book Publishing, 1989.

_____. *The Heaven Tree Trilogy*. New York: Warner Books, 1993.

Peters, Ellis. *Brother Cadfael's Penance*. New York: Mysterious Press of Time Warner, 1994.

_____. *The Confession of Brother Haluin*. New York: Mysterious Press of Time Warner, 1988.

_____. *Dead Man's Ransom*. New York: Ballantine of Random House, 1986.

_____. *The Devil's Novice*. London: Morrow, 1984.

_____. *The Hermit of Eyton Forest*. New York: Mysterious Press of Time Warner, 1988.

_____. *Monk's Hood*. New York: Fawcett Crest of Ballantine, 1986.

_____. *A Morbid Taste for Bones*. New York: Fawcett Crest of Ballantine, 1977.

_____. *One Corpse Too Many*. New York: Fawcett Crest of Ballantine, 1985.

_____. *The Pilgrim of Hate*. New York: Morrow, 1984.

_____. *The Potter's Field*. New York: Mysterious Press of Time Warner, 1990.

_____. *A Rare Benedictine*. New York: Mysterious Press of Time Warner, 1991.

_____. *Saint Peter's Fair*. New York: Mysterious Press of Time Warner, 1992.

_____. *The Sanctuary Sparrow*. New York: Mysterious Press of Time Warner, 1995.

_____. *The Summer of the Danes*. New York: Mysterious Press of Time Warner, 1991.

Warren, Michelle. *History on the Edge: Excalibur and the Borders of Britain, 1100–1300*. Medieval Cultures, volume 22. Minneapolis: University of Minnesota Press, 2000.

7 Places Don't Have to Be True to Be True

The Appropriation of King Arthur and the Cultural Value of Tourist Sites

BENJAMIN EARL

When looking for an Arthurian cultural site in Britain to analyse for this chapter, I was not exactly restricted in my choice. In addition to the well-known sites such as Tintagel, Glastonbury, and Cadbury, recent books by the likes of N.J. Higham have seen fit to present evidence for culturally authentic artefacts. These have included the Pillar of Eliseg (110). Higham's argument is not necessarily to prove the historicity of Arthur, but rather to prove the historicity of "the *idea* of King Arthur" (3) and consequently show a lineage of national identity and how that has been constructed over the centuries (4). Meanwhile, Steve Blake and Scott Lloyd's book *Pendragon: The Origins of Arthur* has resulted in the Llangollen tourist board jumping on the bandwagon and marketing their site as "Arthurian Llangollen." However, one site in particular intrigued me, that of King Arthur's Labyrinth at Machynlleth, near Aberystwyth in mid–Wales. Unlike sites such as Tintagel, where the sedimented authority of texts linking the castle to King Arthur's birthplace grant it some authenticity,[1] such claims to authority do not exist for King Arthur's Labyrinth. Indeed, originally the site was a series of slate mines, only closing in 1970 and opening in 1994 as the labyrinth.

In this chapter, I attempt to offer a theory as to why the Machynlleth site should be successfully marketed as an Arthurian site, whereas Caerleon in South Wales ignores its Arthurian heritage entirely, in favour of highlighting Roman Caerleon. This despite Caerleon's far greater claims to authority, being featured as Arthur's court from texts as diverse as Malory and Tennyson, to Rosalind Miles' recent "bonk-busters."[2]

Secondly, I consider it important to discuss in what form the site appropriates the myth. Finally, it was necessary to think about what the site's motivation was for appropriating the myth in that form and what effects this produces.

A Mythic Discourse

In order to answer these questions, it might be wise for me first to consider what I mean by myth. There is clearly not room within this chapter for me to go into great detail[3] and indeed, the amount of literature produced on the subject is vast, meaning it is impossible to arrive at a simple definition. It would be wise to remember, as Coupe says, that anybody's "own chosen emphasis (on myth) is only one of many" (6).

For this chapter, I wish to look at myth in the sense of an adaptation of Roland Barthes's definition. Barthes's famous statement concludes that myth "transforms history into nature" (*Mythologies* 129). Myth in Barthes's case makes society's structures and ordering appear to have been consistent throughout time. So, Barthes concludes that by the use of myth, the constructs of society and society's power relations appear not man-made, but natural. So the systems of dominance and submission created and maintained by society utilizes a myth such as Arthur in order that these power relations are maintained. As Warner's critique of Barthes makes plain, myths aren't set in stone, but the story can change drastically in what it means.

> Myths convey *values* and expectations which are always evolving, in the process of being formed, but—and this is fortunate—never set so hard they cannot be changed again, and newly told stories can be more helpful than repeating old ones [13–14, my emphasis].

It is perhaps inappropriate to think, as Barthes does, of the average person unquestioningly accepting myth's naturalised ideologies, but it is nevertheless important to see how people appropriate meaning. Bourdieu would argue that this meaning is appropriated in order for particular social groups to assert their distinction, to maintain their cultural capital. Joanna Overing provides a good analysis of this process: "Myth ... provides a necessary sticking plaster for the social structure. It serves as a symbolic statement about the social order, and as such it reinforces social cohesion and functional unity by presenting and justifying the traditional order" (7). Mythic discourse reminds a community of its own identity through the public process of specifying and defining for that community its distinctive social norms.

Caerleon

In respect of the Arthurian myth both reminding a community of its identity, and enabling it to shape its own identity, Machynlleth has the advantage over Caerleon. The very elements that are able to be appropriated by other sites prove to be a hindrance for Caerleon's Arthurian claims.

When texts such as Malory's *Morte Darthur* feature Caerleon as an Arthurian site, this proves to be a problem for the Welsh tourist board. Although Malory may very well hold the status of "the most influential of all Arthurian texts" (Field 225), and "has exerted a unique shaping influence on other literary works and on the popular consciousness" (Parins 1), Malory's own presentation of Arthur is that of a particularly Anglicised king. Stephen Knight offers a persuasive argument that Malory's text "defined in credible terms the tensions and shocks" (107) of English aristocratic disputes and struggles for power in the fifteenth century and during the Wars of the Roses.

For a *Welsh* tourist site, looking to bring to the fore ideas of *Welsh* heritage, this automatically proves to be a problem.[4] A clash arises between the aims of the site and the dominant myth coupled with it. Consequently, Caerleon works in tension with the dominant sedimented myth associated with it, and as such is unable to use this interpretation of the site. While travelling the site, the visitor will note that mention of Arthur is restricted to a brief reference to Geoffrey of Monmouth in the Roman Baths; the rest of the site and promotional material focuses on the Roman remains.

And yet the question begs to be asked why Roman remains should escape this censure, given that these too have exactly the same problem associated with them as an Anglicised Arthur, belonging as they do to a culture associated with colonising the island and of repression of the aboriginal people.

This tension is partly negotiated by presenting the Roman remains as a site of heroic resistance for the Welsh, while also mentioning how Roman occupation was limited within Wales as a whole. The guidebook says that "the Silures, whose territories included much of south-east Wales, had resisted a series of Roman governors for nearly thirty years, and had inflicted several major defeats on the legions" (J. Knight 8). However, it soon becomes clear that when faced with the "real" history of the Roman settlement made visible, the mythical history of Arthur becomes subservient.

The money was raised for the excavation of the Roman amphitheatre in 1926–1927 by the *Daily Mail*'s drawing on the site's legendary status of being King Arthur's Round Table. By looking at captions of postcards and prints from the eras before, during and after the excavation of the amphitheatre, it is possible to see how the status of the amphitheatre changed depending on how much of the Roman remains were visible. Before excavations began, in 1861,[5] the caption was purely "King Arthur's Round Table." Meanwhile, as segments were revealed, a postcard taken between the 1909 and 1926 excavations (so only some of the amphitheatre was revealed) had the phrasing changed to an intermediary stage of calling it the amphitheatre remains in round table field.[6] Finally, in the present day, by which time all excavations have been completed, Cadw's signs and captions within the field mention the Roman remains here and the Roman way of life, but all mention of its being Arthur's Round Table is now expunged.

The reassuring solidity of a history that can be seen, rather than the ever-shifting fluidity of myth, therefore appears to have an effect on how the site has been perceived and presented, and consequently this appears to have impacted on visitors' opinions on what they expect from the site. Indeed, when I visited in the summer of 2004 in order to interview people on their perceptions of Arthur, very few were interested in discussing the myth. Moreover, one woman went so far as refusing to give me an interview, and instead spent the time she could have spent answering my questions bringing into dispute the validity of my research. I was told I was wasting time on this "New Age rubbish" when there was so much "proper" history around me that was far more worthwhile of my time and energy. She finished her tirade with the pithy comment that "they let people waste their time studying anything now." This brought home the low cultural value that the Arthurian myth held to many visitors to the site when compared to the "authentic" and tangible Roman history. Although most people's views were a little less opinionated, the trend still existed, that people were not interested in myths when there was a "real" history staring them in the face, with real bricks and mortar. Many when questioned by me mentioned that an important facet of their visit was being able to touch the ruins, and feel a connection to the past. Geraldine went into particular detail on her experience:

> It's almost like you're touching the past when you come. Even though I wasn't actually able to tou—when I *can* touch, I put my hand on it cause it just feels like—I mean to know that somebody thousands—two thousand years ago, were the same as we basically weren't they, except there was a future, they weren't trying to blow each other up. Then it was much easier with just a sword, and you just stab somebody, whereas here we're trying to wipe out half a world. Different and the same.

This aided people in making the site more "real" and as such adds to its heritage, and authenticates the validity of its production. The ruins work as a "metaphor of memory" which "connect[s] the intangible with the material, either [to] convey notions of fixity and stability or ... highlight process and transformation" (Hallam and Hockey 27). In this process, the tangible, physical remains of the Roman ruins are more useful than the intangible myth of Arthur.

King Arthur's Labyrinth in contrast does not suffer from these tensions, as there is no ancient history there fighting for position, in contrast to Caerleon, which has its own ancient history there to rival that of Arthur, now visible after excavations. If the "authentic" site of Caerleon cannot be used by virtue of the tensions arising from the place, then the use of the slate mines as an Arthurian site suddenly seems to become a lot more appropriate. They are not tarnished by any sedimented cultural associations that have built up over time, and effectively the space of the slate mines is an open canvas. As "space is [only] claimed for man by naming it" (Relph 16), this means that without any association with the dominant chivalric interpretation, King Arthur's Labyrinth has the freedom to impose its own reading. This is especially important if we consider that "heritage sites, do not preserve the past, they represent it. ... authenticity and originality are, above all, matters of technique. The staging, design and the context of the preserved object become crucial in establishing its 'reality' for us" (Rojek 16).

Presentation of Arthur at the Labyrinth

Indeed, this "staging" becomes a self aware strategy in itself, as an appeal to authority is not made in the historical accuracy of the stories presented at King Arthur's Labyrinth (we are informed that "stories don't have to be stories to be true") but rather in their age. Although such luminaries as Roland Barthes have famously proclaimed "the death of the author," in a cultural context the authority attached to the writer is still prevalent and still used as a potent marketing tool.[7] As Seán Burke sums up neatly, "Nietzsche never read Kierkegaard, and it would doubtless be possible to read him as though he had, but immeasurably stronger intertextual currents open up between Schopenhauer and Nietzsche, Nietzsche and Heidegger, precisely because there is influence, succession, recession and revision, withal, an act of strong reading between their work" (173). Nonetheless, each individual text can still have its own individual identity. Although wishing for the Death of the Author, perhaps it is better to see Barthes's work as providing scope for the author to be decentred, thus providing the opportunity for other forms of authority to be presented. This therefore allows the site to move away from an interpretation tied to the "great works" of Malory and Tennyson.

Barthes's rhetoric in *The Death of the Author* is particularly antagonistic as he speaks of how "we know now that a text is not a line of words releasing a single 'theological' meaning (the 'message' of the Author-God) but a multi-dimensional space in which a variety of writings, none of them original, blend and clash. The text is a tissue of quotations drawn from the innumerable centres of culture" (*Image* 146). That is, the text is language; it is a system of signs and the author is merely the agent in putting these signs on to the paper. It is the responsibility of the reader to interpret these signs, to "disentangle" them. This thus opens up a multiplicity of readings, and allows for a polysemic text. The death of the author can in many ways equate to the reassertion of traditional values, as myths enable a multiplicity of visions, meanings and experiences, in contrast to the limiting forces acting upon the word on the page, as literate cultures by fixing the word in time and space exclude many elements of culture (cf McLuhan 266).

When the text appropriated for cultural authority is a collection of folk tales, such as the *Mabinogion*, then it is clear that the text's recourse to a means of authority must not only position itself against the dominant interpretation, but also find some authority that is not tied up in the author-god. In something as fluid as myth, where myth "always refers to events alleged to have taken place a long time ago," recourse to its status and the value that comes with its age is a valuable tool to activate cultural authority. "But what gives the myth an operational value is the specific pattern described as timeless; it explains the present and the past as well as the future" (Smith 51). As such, are we able to refer merely to authors of the myth? For the Arthurian myth rises from a time when its "anonymity caused no difficulties since their ancientness, whether real or imagined, was regarded as a sufficient guarantee of their status" (Foucault 109).

When talking of the "author-function" as society's need to close meaning, Foucault might have equally have written of the "ancient-function" or the "Arthur-function." These work to both close and open meanings, according to need and according to their dominance at different stages of the myth, at different moments. These three functions are always in tension. The functions live in a constant state of flux, with each becoming ascendant depending on which meanings are activated within each site in turn. Each holds equal value until brought out by various intertextual devices utilized by the site.

And if a text is indeed a tissue of quotations, this does not mean we have to automatically sideline any appeals to authority. Each text, each site will have its own individual set of cultural flows acting upon it. That they act on the text is beyond dispute; the importance lies in the inter-textual devices used by the text in an effort to close down the particular meanings, and in analyzing this we find that the combination of flows is unique to each text. Analytical focus should be given to how these inter-textual elements are activated in order to close down meanings within the text, and guide the participant towards the site's preferred meaning. In order to see how this preferred meaning is arrived at, it is necessary to analyse the unique combination of cultural flows particular to this site. In this particular case, the site makes a specific effort to channel its flows through the ancientness of the source text. So despite not having the sed-imented authority that other sites possess, the slate mines seek to estab-lish their own authority by consciously positioning themselves against the Anglicised versions. Machynlleth makes a certain claim to authen-ticity as it markets itself as a place where you can "learn about the *orig-inal* legends of King Arthur, the wizard Merlin, Avalon and much more" (my emphasis).

The style of Arthur that the site wishes to present becomes evident as soon as you enter the gift shop. According to the site's own publicity, "the Labyrinth shop sells books and gifts on the Celtic Arthurian theme." We get the grittier popular versions, such as Steven Lawhead's, and all that is available with regards to the Anglicised chivalric versions is a copy of Malory tucked carefully out of sight in the corner. The T-shirts sold also focus on Celtic crosses and other motifs, rather than an Anglo-chivalric Arthur. The presentation of the site displays some elements of theme parks in that, as Bennett discusses, "it is an assimilated otherness that is on offer, an already recuperated and tamed fantastic" (Bennett 243), yet this is not as obvious as in many theme parks, who present themselves openly as such without the appeal to authority. Instead of sig-nage simply warning you not to jump the queue, the signs are written in a way that disguises their message within the context of a story. As such, we are told that "the boatman holds the key to the Labyrinth. Wait for him here. Dire peril awaits those who venture further on their own." In this way, the myth helps to naturalize the fact that your path through the caves is heavily controlled and consists of carefully planned chore-ography, and enables the experience of Arthur's Labyrinth to become heavily regulated around a dominant ideology of a version of the myth that they wish to present.

Entry to the labyrinth, as the quote above suggests, is by boat, which achieves the effect of establishing a distance between "reality" and "fan-tasy," possibly by recalling Arthur's boat journey to the Isle of Avalon. The effect of this is that the boat journey "creates the emotional illusion of authenticity" (Mestrovic 83) for the site. The distance between the everyday world and the world we are about to enter is hammered home by the tagline that boasts of an otherworldly experience: "Behind that waterfall is the past. Do you want to go there?" (Symonds back cover). However, this entrance to the labyrinth is itself an artificial creation, as "the boat takes visitors in on the old level 6 tramway that was opened around 1850 and flooded in 1994 to create river access to the Labyrinth" (Symonds). Descending into the labyrinth, Celtic themed music is played to further emphasize which version of the myth is being presented.

The attraction consists of a series of set pieces, evocatively lit, which consist of waxwork displays of figures over which a story is told. The order this is arranged in means that the first "exhibit" we come across is that of the sword in the stone. However, rather than tell us the story as given by Malory, Tennyson and others, a challenge is made to the dominant English tradition. We are told that "you all know that story, that's English!" The authority of this story is then challenged. Here, we are told how in actual fact there are older stories than those we know, that the "story starts here in Wales" and it is these stories that will be told to us. As such, we are invited to disregard our previous perceptions and refer to the original stories as what I have termed the "Ancient Function" is invoked: "what is certain is that the earliest of these 'Arthurs' are to be found in the Welsh tales known as the *Mabinogion*." Nevertheless, this challenge to the dominant myth appears to be only partially successful, as the parents on the boat fill in this particular story in greater detail for the benefit of their children.

The exhibits then proceed to relay tales from the *Mabinogion* in each cave respectively, with a constant emphasis on the Welsh origins of the myth either in the story themselves, or even in the props which often have waxworks holding something distinctively Welsh, such as the national flag. Finally, the tour finishes by telling us the well-known folk story of how, "once a long time ago ... there was a young man from west Wales who found the cave where King Arthur sleeps with all his knights, waiting for the day when he will awake and ride out to bring justice to a troubled world." By finishing on this note, the tour succeeds in linking the present experience with the past, and making it seem authentic. Arthur is found sleeping in a cave, we are currently in a cave. If the visitors wish to touch the walls they, much as those visiting the Roman remains at Caerleon make the view of the past presented at the site real, consequently making the Arthurian story "real" in its context in the labyrinth. Therefore the story allows a link between reality and fantasy to be made and as a result, "the otherworld penetrates momentarily into the everyday world" (Lindahl 17).

Why This Version of Arthur?

So is the presentation of a Welsh Arthur some noble effort on the part of the labyrinth to restore the Welsh Arthur to its rightful place as originator of the myth? I would beg to differ, and would suggest that, rather, it is more an opportunity to naturalize the commercial nature of the site. Alongside the labyrinth is the Corris Craft Centre, which according to the literature "is the starting point for King Arthur's Labyrinth," suggesting that this is the part of the site that motivates the labyrinth, rather than vice versa. As you walk round the center, each shop has a plaque on the wall which emphasises issues of craftsmanship, and how these ways of producing goods have been practiced for many centuries. The wood turning shop, for example, informs us that "wood turning is thought to have developed about 4000 years ago." Thus, the commercial element of making a living is indeed naturalized by use of the myth. If a Welsh Arthur holds authenticity, then this is reflected in the products sold. Moreover, an appeal to the royal connections of the craft is made, as we are given the information that "more than 12,000 wooden bowls were made for the coronation of Richard I." However, the use of the labyrinth serves to take away emphasis from the commercial nature of the site. Bourdieu suggests this effect can be achieved "simply by dissociating it from its economic and social raisons d'etre" (Bourdieu 178). With "this blending of past and future, [we see] one of the ways we attempt to convince ourselves that in a fragmented culture at least one part of our selves remains steady and unchanging" (Aden 55).

Naturally, although "visitors are invited to see at first hand the skills of the craft workers and displays of woodcraft, toymaking, pottery, jewellery, leatherwork and handmade candles," these "displays" are all carefully marked with price stickers, and situated within easy access to a cash till. This "traditional Welsh craftsmanship" also includes items such as "smoking Dragons" that are not unique to the center, but can be found in many Welsh or New Age tourist sites around the country. Arthur works as a type of cultural authority to create an artificial distinction in the product that otherwise would not be there and would be in danger of being viewed with distaste as cheap commercial fodder. It appears that although the labyrinth's "stance towards cultural tradition is one of irreverent pastiche, and its contrived depthlessness undermines all metaphysical solemnities" (Harvey 7), the actual effect of the presentation of Arthur is to construct an authenticity *experienced* by the visitors, which is as real to them as any presentation of the past to be found at Caerleon.

This approach, and appeal to an authentic Welsh culture, extends to the Y *Crochan* Restaurant on site, which is eager to point out that the food in the restaurant is made from "traditional Welsh recipes" wherever possible. Indeed, this approach extends as far as the toffees available for purchase as gifts, upon which is written "Made in Wales!"

In this way, King Arthur's Labyrinth uses a certain presentation of the myth not only to enable Welsh traditions to be reaffirmed, but also to persuade visitors to part with their cash. The visitor leaves the site poorer, but consoled by the fact that they themselves have played an active part in contributing to Welsh heritage and traditions, and ensuring they remain in place for the foreseeable future. By connecting past to present, the site has found a way to present traditional crafts as "authentic" tourist artefacts, and to naturalize their use as commercial entities. As we have seen, this is achieved by utilizing the cultural capital inherent within the myth of King Arthur. This cultural capital is channeled into particular cultural flows, managed by using intertextual elements such as the handbook and signage to close down readings of Arthur to one that uses the "Ancient Function" of the old Welsh folk tales to gain authority for a cultural site that previously had none. Places do not indeed have to be true to be true.

Notes

1. The authenticity of Tintagel as an Arthurian site is notwithstanding the fact that the current castle ruins were built by Richard, Earl of Cornwall, possibly to capitalize on the popularity of Geoffrey of Monmouth's *History of the Kings of Britain* and lend authority to his own power in the region by linking him to the great king (Thomas 15).

2. *The Independent's* interview with the author in 1999 dryly observed, "When the golden-haired queen yields to her king, Arthur, in a moon-soaked glade of wild honeysuckle, the novel quickly establishes itself as a top tip for the Literary Review's Bad Sex prize" (Stanford 12).

3. See Coupe's *Myth* and Segal's *Myth: A Very Short Introduction* for two of the best and most concise overviews of the many different forms that myth can take.

4. Cadw, who are responsible for running the Caerleon site, have the stated aims of "protecting, conserving, and *promoting* ancient monuments and historic buildings in *Wales*" (J. Knight, back cover, my emphasis).

5. Images can be found on http://www.caerllion.net/archive/prints/roundtable.htm.

6. See http://caerllion.net/archive/pcards/amphiwall.htm.

7. Witness the publicity surrounding the recent film *King Arthur*, where the publicity posters proudly privileged the fact it was "From the Producer of *Pearl Harbor.*"

Works Cited

Aden, Roger C. *Popular Stories and Promised Lands: Fan Cultures and Symbolic Pilgrimages.* Alabama: University of Alabama Press, 1999.

Barthes, Roland. *Image, Music, Text.* London: Fontana, 1977.

_____. *Mythologies.* London: Grant and Cutler, 1994.

Bennett, Tony. *The Birth of the Museum: History, Theory, Politics.* London; New York: Routledge, 1995.

Blake, Steve, and Scott Lloyd. *Pendragon: The origins of Arthur*. London: Rider, 2004.

Bourdieu, Pierre. *Distinction: A Social Critique of the Judgement of Taste*. Translated by Richard Nice. London: Routledge and Kegan Paul, 1984

Burke, Seán. *The Death and Return of the Author: Criticism and Subjectivity in Barthes, Foucault and Derrida*. Edinburgh: Edinburgh University Press, 1998

Coupe, Laurence. *Myth*. London; New York: Routledge, 1997.

Field, P.J.C. "Sir Thomas Malory's *Le Morte Darthur*." In *The Arthur of the English: The Arthurian Legend in Medieval English Life and Literature*, ed. W.R.J. Barron. Cardiff: University of Wales Press, 2001.

Foucault, Michel. "What is an author?" In *The Foucault Reader*, ed. Paul Rabinov. London: Penguin, 1991.

Hallam, Elizabeth, and Jenny Hockey. *Death, Memory and Material Culture*. Oxford; New York: Berg, 2001.

Harvey, David. *Justice, Nature and the Geography of Difference*. Cambridge, Mass.: Blackwell, 1996.

Higham, N.J. *King Arthur: Myth-making and History*. London; New York: Routledge, 2002.

Knight, Jeremey K. *Caerleon Roman Fortress*. Cardiff: Cadw Welsh Historic Monuments, 2003.

Knight, Stephen Thomas. *Arthurian Literature and Society*. London: Macmillan, 1983.

Lindahl, Carl. "Three Ways of Coming Back: Folkloric Perspectives on Arthur's Return." In *King Arthur's Modern Return*, ed. Debra Mancoff. New York: Garland, 1998.

Mcluhan, Marshall. *The Gutenbeg Galaxy*. Toronto: University of Toronto Press, 1962.

Mestrovic, Stjepan G. *Postemotional Society*. London; Thousand Oaks, Calif.: Sage, 1997.

Overing, Joanna. "The Role of Myth: An anthropological perspective or, 'the reality of the really made-up.'" In *Myths and Nationhood*, ed. Geoffrey Hosking and George Schöpflin. London: C. Hurst, 1997.

Parins, Marylyn, ed, *Sir Thomas Malory: The Critical Heritage*. London; New York: Routledge, 1995.

Relph, E.C. *Place and Placelessness*. London: Pion, 1976.

Rojek, Chris. *Ways of Escape: Modern Transformations in Leisure and Travel*. Basingstoke: Macmillan, 1993.

Segal, Robert. *Myth: A Very Short Introduction*. Oxford University Press, 2004.

Smith, Mark. *Culture: Reinventing the Social Sciences*. Buckingham: Open University Press, 2000.

Stanford, Peter. "The Books Interview: Rosalind Miles—A Feminist in Camelot." *The Independent*. May 1, 1999, 12.

Symonds, Roger. *King Arthur's Labyrinth*. Norwich: Jarrold, 2003.

Thomas, Charles. *English Heritage Book of Tintagel: Arthur and Archaeology*. London: Batsford, 1993.

Warner, Marina. *Managing Monsters: Six Myths of Our Time*. London: Vintage, 1994.

8 "Accident My Codlings"

Sitcom, Cinema and the Re-writing of History in The Blackadder[1]

KATHERINE J. LEWIS

On the 15th of June 1983 my mother observed to my father that Rowan Atkinson from *Not the Nine O'Clock News* had a new comedy series starting that evening, called *The Blackadder*, and suggested that it might be rather good. It was co-written by Atkinson and Richard Curtis (subsequently famous as the creator of a particular kind of British romantic comedy film). It purported to be the lost history of the reign of Richard IV (the younger of the two princes in the tower) spanning the years 1485–1498 and focusing on his ambitious, yet cringing and incompetent son Prince Edmund, aka the Blackadder. We duly watched and greatly enjoyed it, despite my thirteen-year-old self being secretly terrified by the ghost of Richard III. None of us would claim to have known that we were watching the birth of a comedy classic, but that is precisely what *Blackadder* was to become, of course, with four hugely popular and award winning series appearing on BBC1 from 1983 to 1989, as well as three stand alone episodes, featuring the same core character set in different periods of history.

The Blackadder won an international Emmy in the popular arts category in 1983, but is generally treated (even by those who made it) largely as an inferior trial run for its later, more successful counterparts. For reasons noted below the second, third and fourth series are linked by common features of characterisation, style and mode of expression which render them part of a coherent whole, whereas the first series is quite distinct in several ways. The first series is also arguably the most

113

interesting of the four because it is the one that makes the most sustained attempt at an authentic period setting, and also that makes the most explicit (albeit not serious) claims to be history. Despite the enormous popularity of the franchise, and the ways in which it has taken on the status of an alternative national history, there has, as yet, been very little scholarly analysis of *The Blackadder*, or indeed any of the other series. Only *Blackadder Goes Forth*, set in the trenches of World War One, is regularly discussed in relation to its use and representation of the past, specifically the ways in which the series is grounded in certain mythologies about war in general, and the First World War in particular (Badsey). Discussion generally focuses disapprovingly on the ways in which *Blackadder Goes Forth* has come to be popularly perceived as containing parodic or satirical "truths" about the First World War. The emphasis tends to be on pointing out its historical inaccuracies, without recognising or exploring the series' status as comedy. Conversely this chapter's focus is on the ways in which *The Blackadder* recreates late-fifteenth-century England in order to make it funny. As we shall see, this is a representation made up of tropes derived partly from certain ideas about the medieval past and the ways in which medieval history has been written, but which is also shaped by the conventions of sitcom and historical film. Given the nature of the audience at which it was aimed, consideration of *The Blackadder*'s version of the later Middle Ages can obviously tell us something about perceptions of the period. It sheds light in particular on approaches which regard it with a sense of superiority, condescension, and, crucially, as something intrinsically laughable, even before the jokes have started.

The Blackadder falls squarely within the genre of television situation comedy. It is a series with a limited number of episodes, lasting around thirty minutes, which were originally shown at the same time each week, and which focuses on the lives of a core set of characters, Blackadder and his side-kicks Baldrick (Tony Robinson) and Percy (Tim McInnery). The action largely occurs within the tightly defined parameters of certain settings (various rooms in the royal palace). While sitcoms remain under-explored in scholarly terms there has been discussion of the ways in which they are established upon a distinctive typology of characters, situations, relationships and antagonisms (Eaton; Neale and Krutnik; Casey et al.; Mills). The starting point for any week's plotline is the intervention of an external force or forces within the lives of the main characters and settings: Edmund being made the Archbishop of Canterbury at the beginning of episode 3, for example. But any disruption which this causes is only ever temporary. The narrative within individual episodes is almost always circular; the basic status quo is generally not interrupted in any profound way and the end of the episode brings closure and a return to the initial situation. In this case Edmund is excommunicated by all three popes and never allowed to be archbishop again, and we are back where we started. This is a formula with which the audience is familiar—humor and pleasure are derived not from suspense (there is never any real doubt as to the outcome and its ramifications, whether positive or negative) but rather from observing the various ways in which the protagonists characteristically try to deal with whatever has been thrown at them this week. Much scholarship about sitcoms focuses on the ways in which their content traditionally rests on the iteration and reiteration of a series of social and cultural stereotypes, both in the main and peripheral characters (Woollacott). In many cases these work to reinforce dominant ideological positions, while marginalizing or even ridiculing other groups who are seen to deviate from these norms.[2] This is one of the reasons why the term "sitcom" often has negative connotations, which, in turn, explains the lack of scholarly engagement with it. "Good" sitcoms, like the *Blackadder* series, are generally rescued from the charge of being "just" sitcoms (Mills 26–37).

Nonetheless, in many respects *The Blackadder* is clearly predicated on certain sitcom elements, and in some cases these are specific to the British tradition of the genre, perhaps most obviously here in the representation of its central character, for it has been said that, traditionally, British sitcom "centred on the lives of sullen, cynical men with frustrated ambitions and bleak dispositions" (Casey et al. 30). Prince Edmund's endless schemes to gain more power, or even to become king, are always doomed to come to nothing even before they begin. Thus he is clearly the heir to the similarly frustrated aspirant males around whom the action of such classic sitcoms as *Hancock's Half Hour* (BBC 1956–60), *Steptoe and Son* (BBC then BBC1 1962–74), and *Fawlty Towers* (BBC2 1975, 1979) are based. In this respect the traditional circular narrative acts as a negative force on their lives because no matter what they plan, dream, or attempt to improve their lot, things will never change for them, as the audience knows. Much of the comedy lies in the vast discrepancy between how such characters wish to be regarded by others, and how they actually appear; unlike American sitcoms in which, traditionally, the audience laughs with the central character, in the British version they laugh at him (Mills 41–2).[3] The crowning irony for Prince Edmund is that in the final episode of the series he does manage to achieve his ambition and become king, but only enjoys this triumph for a few seconds before dying of the same poisoned wine which killed the rest of the court and his family.

If we examine the action of an individual episode in more detail further parallels between *The Blackadder* and traditional sitcom emerge. The action of "The Queen of Spain's Beard" starts with Edmund being pushed off a rampart by a beautiful woman horrified at his ugliness, and then revolves around his increasingly desperate attempts to avoid an arranged marriage to the monstrous Infanta Maria of Spain: "in twenty four hours I'll be married to a walrus," he laments.[4] All of his plans fail (trying to marry someone else and thus become unavailable) or backfire (pretending to be gay—the Infanta is touched that he has dressed flamboyantly like her fellow countrymen).[5] In the end Blackadder escapes the marriage purely because of external intervention: international diplomacy takes a different turn necessitating his marriage to Princess Leia of Hungary instead, the punchline being that while the princess is very pretty, she is only a child, so Blackadder is right back where he started at the beginning of the episode.[6] This sort of scheming, plotting, pretence and disguise provide the mainstay of many sitcom plots, as does the central character's last minute reprieve and a double-bluff ending in which things don't really turn out as he had hoped. The series relies on these and various other synchronising motifs; partly provided by the theme tune and settings, but also by the specific qualities given to the central characters that serve to make them instantly recognisable to the audience. Sometimes this works in terms of conformity to wider character stereotypes such as the fat and sexually voracious Infanta, or Dougal MacAngus, the barbaric longhaired Scotsman. Behavioral motifs are also employed, such as Blackadder's constant attempts to get one over on his older brother, Harry, Prince of Wales, who is so clearly their father's favorite. Other characters are given their own individual motifs which are repeated throughout the series, such as the running joke that King Richard never gets Edmund's name right, calling him variously Edna, Osmund, Edward, Edwin, and Egbert, even announcing at one point, "I have two sons— Prince Harry and ... another one."

However, despite these affinities to traditional sitcom, *The Blackadder* also drew its inspiration from more contemporary developments in comedy writing and performance too. Curtis, Atkinson and the show's producer John Lloyd had all worked on the irreverent and sometimes controversial sketch show *Not the Nine O'Clock News* (BBC2 1979– 1982) before deciding to create *The Blackadder* as a solo vehicle for Atkinson. Moreover, in the series itself cameos were made by figures from the contemporary alternative comedy circuit such as Mark Arden and Stephen Frost (known at the time as the Oblivion Boys), who appear as the jailors in episode 5. Rik Mayall made two show-stopping appearances as Lord Flashheart in *Blackadder II* and *Blackadder Goes Forth*, but it is less often realised that he appeared in the first series too, as Mad Gerald in episode 6. Mayall had already co-written and starred in the first series of *The Young Ones* (BBC2 1982–84), an "alternative sitcom" that deliberately set out to subvert the generic conventions of the traditional format.[7] This was also the plan of the creators of *The Black-adder*. Curtis has said, for example, that a driving force behind *The Blackadder* was "the idea of getting away from *Terry and June* and plots about visiting vicars and having a real plot" (Richard Curtis interview). Much of the humor in Blackadder relies on intricately plotted farce and wordplay, in concert with Atkinson's famed "rubber face" qualities. And of course the historical setting means that some of the traditional sitcom stereotypes just aren't applicable, or at the very least have to be transposed. In fact, the adoption of a historical setting was the most deliberate way in which Atkinson and Curtis sought to produce something quite different from the norm, because the vast majority of sitcoms (with a few notable exceptions) are set in the present day. According to both, a key motivation here was what Atkinson has referred to as "the scourge of *Fawlty Towers*"; the awareness that anything they produced which was set in the present day would be immediately and unfavourably compared with it ("I Have a Cunning Plan").[8] In an interview for a program commemorating the twentieth anniversary of *Blackadder*, Atkinson explained that they chose 1485 to get as far away from *Fawlty Towers* as possible. He also says they weren't aware of anyone having done a period sitcom before. Given the huge popularity of World War Two sitcoms *Dad's Army* and *It Ain't Half Hot Mum* in the '70s and early '80s this may seem an odd thing to say, but presumably his point was that period sitcoms set in the distant past, rather than at the time of events which were still within living memory, were quite rare. These two classic British sitcoms were written by Jimmy Perry and David Croft, who also created *Hi-de-Hi* (BBC 1 1980–88), set in a seaside holiday camp of the 1950s. All three series drew on the experiences of the writers during the war and its aftermath, and owed part of their success to the nostalgia which they inspired in audience members of a similar age (Morgan-Russell). The shows presented an idealised, yet remembered and experienced past. Perhaps the only precursor for a far-off period setting was Frankie Howerd's *Up Pompeii* (BBC1 1969–70), which subsequently became a film (1971) and sequel (*Further Up Pompeii* 1975), and inspired a series of other films in which the same character was transposed to different historical settings, such as the Crusades in *Up the Chastity Belt* (1971) and the trenches in *Up the Front* (1972). Many commentators have noted that this is exactly the formula that the *Blackadder* series were to follow, but none of the creators cite Howerd's work as having been an influence upon them at the time.[9]

In fact rather than any existing sitcom, the chief influence which Atkinson cites is cinematic, for he has identified Golden Age Hollywood films and their colorful, thrilling version of the Middle Ages as a crucial model in the conception of *The Blackadder* ("I Have a Cunning Plan").

This also provided another way of distancing the series from the traditional sitcom. Atkinson stated that they wanted to do proper stories, which conveyed something of the heroic adventure of Errol Flynn's *Adventures of Robin Hood* (1938), for example; its darkness and excitement as well as its humor. They also wanted a title that sounded serious and adventurous—hence *The Blackadder* and his dramatic theme tune which in sound and lyrics (used over the closing credits) is designed to call to mind Flynnesque heroes. "The sound of hoof beats cross the glade / Good folk lock up your son and daughter / Beware the deadly flashing blade / Unless you want to end up shorter." This style obviously owes much to the famous theme for the 1950s television series *The Adventures of Robin Hood*: "Robin Hood, Robin Hood, Riding through the glen / Robin Hood, Robin Hood, with his merry men / Feared by the bad, loved by the good."[10] However, the joke is that Edmund Blackadder is entirely undeserving of such an introduction, especially as he originally chooses the name "The Black Vegetable" for himself and only changes it to "The Blackadder" on Baldrick's recommendation. The title credits of each episode instantly undercut any identification of him as a genuine hero, containing a montage of scenes (generally not drawn from the action of any of the episodes themselves) which show him as clumsy and inept—being thrown from his horse, falling into a hole in the ground and so on.

Nor was this the only cinematic influence upon the series. Another important way in which the audience was made to feel at home in this medieval setting was through the use of Shakespeare (who even gets an "additional dialogue provided by" credit in several of the episodes). In fact much of what is used starts off accurately, for example in episode 6 "The Black Seal": "We few, we happy few" (from *Henry V*), but ends rather less so: "We band of ruthless bastards!" There is also reference to certain classics of Shakespearean film, such as Peter Cook's portrayal of Richard III, which is in fact Peter Cook doing Laurence Olivier doing Richard III, in the 1955 film version. The scene in which Richard addresses the troops before the Battle of Bosworth in episode 1 is a pastiche of Olivier's delivery of the St. Crispin's day speech in *Henry V* (1944). Moreover the casting of various "serious" actors, such as Brian Blessed as Richard IV, Elspbeth Gray as the Queen, Frank Finlay as the Witchsmeller Pursuivant and Jim Broadbent as Don Speekingleesh, the Infanta's interpreter, lent both a recognition factor and gravitas to the whole project. It also helped to blur the boundaries between the series' status as sitcom and as "proper" historical drama, for its structure and content derived from both. Another cinematic influence worth mentioning is to be found in the structure of episode 6 in which Blackadder has finally had enough and goes in search of the seven most evil men in the land to help him take over the kingdom in a story line which owes an obvious debt to *The Seven Samurai* (1954) and *The Magnificent Seven* (1970).

In keeping with the desired "Hollywood" feel, the series was filmed in large cinematic sets and on location, rather than in front of a studio audience, as was usual for sitcoms at the time.[11] The BBC spent a million pounds on the series, visible in the lavish costumes and set-dressings, which also served to set it apart from any other sitcom it had ever made. The banner "Filmed in Glorious Television," which appears at the very end of the credits, served to underline its cinematic pretensions. However, the ambitious nature of the series was nearly its downfall, for although a million pounds was spent on it Atkinson has noted that it only looked like a million dollars ("I Have a Cunning Plan"). He believes that having Flynn's *Robin Hood* in mind meant that they concentrated too much on the setting, whereas a smaller *Fawlty Towers* style location would have helped them to focus on the jokes. Indeed, this is exactly what happened with the second series, which saw the introduction of Ben Elton as co-writer. He immediately wanted to do away with the "mini comic movie" style (as he termed it) and go back to a more contained gag-driven sitcom which should be filmed in front of a studio audience, so that the actors could adjust their pace and mood according to the reactions they got ("Timewarp: Blackadder II, Part 1 of 4").[12] This scaling down saved the second series from being cancelled by Michael Grade and also turned *Blackadder* into the huge success it was to become, catchphrases and all.

To return to *The Blackadder*, the final influence upon it to be considered is the idea of medieval history itself. This, filtered through the discourse of epic historical film, underpins the whole series, like sitcom providing a store of instantly recognisable motifs to the audience and acting as both background to and source for the humor. Indeed, there is a sense in some quarters that you need to know something about history in order to find the whole *Blackadder* oeuvre funny. Some of its fans, for example, claimed that this is why it came second in a 2004 BBC poll to find the nation's favourite sitcom, losing out to the less intellectual and more traditional *Only Fools and Horses* (BBC1 1981–91 and one-off specials) ("The Nation's Favourite Sitcom"). The idea of a link between Blackadder and history is also underlined by the BBC Blackadder Web site, which includes links to pages on the BBC history site which relate to people or events from all four series ("Blackadder: 1485–1917"). Interestingly, the never-broadcast pilot episode for *The Blackadder*, filmed in June 1982, was set not in 1485 (the start date of the eventual first episode), but "400 hundred years ago," and both this setting and Edmund's clever, crafty character are much more akin to those of the Elizabethan *Blackadder II*.[13] By the time the series proper came to be made, though, the setting had been put back 100 years, and, rather than the unidentified king and queen of the pilot, Atkinson and Curtis had created a specifically defined alternative history of later medieval England. The first episode sets up the series with the following voice over, accompanying scenes illustrative of its content:

> History has known many great liars. Copernicus. Goebbels. St. Ralph the Liar. But there have been none quite so vile as the Tudor king, Henry VII. It was he who rewrote history to portray his predecessor Richard III as a deformed maniac, who killed his nephews in the Tower. But the truth is that Richard was a kind and thoughtful man who cherished his young wards, in particular Richard, Duke of York, who grew up into a big strong boy. Henry also claimed that he won the Battle of Bosworth Field, and killed Richard III. Again, the truth is very different. For it was Richard, Duke of York, who became king after Bosworth field and reigned for thirteen glorious years. As for who really killed Richard III and how the defeated Henry Tudor escaped with his life, all is revealed in this, the first chapter of a history never before told: the History of ... the Blackadder.

This introduction may have been determined by a wish to provide recognisable events and actual historical characters as a starting point. Most people have heard of Richard III and the Princes in the Tower and many are also aware of the revisionist approach to Richard's character and career with which the opening aligns itself. By starting with two "real" characters the series itself and the stories it tells also have the appearance of being real.[14] In fact, the opening goes further and claims not only that the story is real but that it is true. The invention of King Richard IV and the idea that Henry VII personally expunged his reign from the record after the entire court die at the end of the last episode, is a way of creating an alternative space in history. The idea of the series as a lost chronicle is maintained throughout as each episode functions as a chapter, opening with a reeling text in "medieval script" introducing the action and fixing it in a particular year. For example episode 3 begins:

> England, November 1487. The battle between the Church and the Crown continues to rage and the Duke of Winchester, the greatest landowner in England, is dying.

This is, of course, a technique also employed in many historical films, intended to fix subsequent events in a particular context for the audience and also to lend veracity to the setting, especially if the action is claimed to be a dramatization of events that really happened (Chapman).[15]

There are, of course, all sorts of things we could say about the problems with *The Blackadder* as an accurate depiction of medieval history; although as this is a comedy it is surely not surprising to find the period and its people reduced to a series of amusing caricatures. For while this particular true history may never have been told before, it rests firmly on the recurring stock-in-trade medieval themes of plague, war, torture, crusades, chivalry, ignorance, corruption, stupidity, brutality, superstition, deformity, and oceans of mud. One online commentator judged: "Setting the comedy in late medieval times had other advantages. It was a time when life was nasty, brutish and short; the threat of extreme suffering or death gave comic set-ups an extra edge" (Bennett). This grim place is the Middle Ages which the audience expects to see. Their understandings and expectations of what the medieval past was like cannot be disrupted if they are to find the setting familiar.[16] This allows them to know what to expect of the show (e.g., all the peasants will be stupid and covered in shit). This, in turn, facilitates the jokes and saves the writers from having to provide excessive amounts of either verbal or visual set-up for them. Sometimes the humor derives from the weird otherness of the period; to take a very simple example, the tights and codpieces which Atkinson says they all thought were hilarious ("I Have a Cunning Plan"). Or the fact that the highlight of the St. Leonard's Day celebrations in episode 4, made up of morris dancers and a bear baiter, will be provided by the eunuchs. Unfortunately the eunuchs cancel so we never get to find out just how they would have entertained the audience, who are left to imagine something suitably bizarre for themselves. There is also a level of more knowing humor in which the audience is invited to feel superior to those it observes—indeed, in one of the few obvious pieces of anachronism in the series, Edmund is often seen to espouse a more informed and sceptical stance than those around him, and thus embodies an enlightened viewpoint with which the audience can identify. At the beginning of episode 3 we discover that the king has had another archbishop murdered, "the third this year," as Blackadder notes, but only he realises what is really going on. Prince Harry and Percy labor under the misapprehension that these were all tragic but bizarre accidents, such as "Archbishop Wilfred slipping and falling backwards onto the spire of Norwich Cathedral."

It is probably no coincidence, given the post–Reformation legacy of English attitudes to medieval Catholicism, that this approach is particularly marked in the two episodes dealing with religion and belief: "The Archbishop" and "Witchsmeller Pursuivant." Much of the humor in both episodes involves laughing at the superstitious backwardness of the period. In "Witchsmeller Pursuivant," in which Blackadder, Baldrick and Percy are tried and almost burned for witchcraft, despite being entirely innocent, we encounter many familiar tropes—the ludicrousness of the charge, the corruption of the authorities, the unfairness of the trial, the hysteria surrounding it, and the ultimate punishment of burning at the stake. The audience knows exactly what to expect from all of this, and the only aspect of it that is intended to make sense to the modern viewer is Edmund's attempts to mitigate the ridiculous beliefs of those around him: "Only last week a man with four heads was seen taking tea on the beach, and two women in Windsor claim to have been raped by a fish." Of course the problem here is that the picture of witchcraft and attitudes to it which *The Blackadder* so carefully constructs "is normally thought of as medieval" but really has no place in late fifteenth century England and in fact owes everything to the seventeenth century (Sharpe, *Instruments*, 5). Apart from a few high-profile, politically motivated cases (such as Eleanor Cobham), it seems that witchcraft was not of enormous concern in later medieval England and there was quite a divergence between England and the Continent in this respect. There are instances in church courts records involving people accused of using spells and incantations, but these were treated as fairly minor offences, involving recantation and penance, not burning at the stake. Witchcraft didn't become a felony (punishable by hanging, not burning) until 1542, and even then the later sixteenth century offers only patchy evidence for its prosecution (Sharpe, *Early Medieval England*, 136–7). The only instance of a proper witch-hunting craze in England comes from a very specific time (1645–7) and place (East Anglia). A large part of its inspiration was the personal interest and belief in witchcraft and demonology held by Matthew Hopkins, whose title and office of Witch Finder General was presumably the inspiration for the Witchsmeller Pursuivant. The other crucial factor in this outbreak of witch-hunting was the turmoil of the Civil War and its impact on social relations and local structures of authority (Sharpe, *Instruments*, 128–47). It has been argued that without this infamous case "there would be no English witch-craze to discuss" (Sharpe, *Early Medieval England*, 317). So, the post-medieval period that should have been more enlightened (by Whig standards of progressive history) evinces an episode which was actually far more intolerant and brutal in this respect. But according to the popular perceptions of the Middle Ages upon which *The Blackadder* is predicated, this really doesn't matter, because (by these standards) later medieval England was so nasty that it's the sort of place where they *would* have burned witches, even if they didn't in fact. Ironically, however, the scene in episode 3 in which Baldrick regales Blackadder and Percy with an account of the "holy relics" that he's made in order to "actually make a bit of money in this job" inadvertently reveals certain truths about the medieval period, despite its intention to mock superstition and unquestioning credulity. For there is plenty of evidence to show that people did not necessarily accept the teachings of the Church or the moral authority of its officials uncritically, and in the figure of the Pardoner Chaucer provided us with a very similar satirical commentary on the nature of the later medieval relic trade and the motivations of those involved in it.

Therefore the Middle Ages which Edmund Blackadder and the rest of the court inhabits and the medieval history which they produce may not be authentic by some standards, but it looks very real by others. Appropriately enough the same can be said of Alnwick castle, used in the opening credits and exterior shots of the series presumably because it looks just as a medieval castle should look. Whereas in fact most of what we see now comprises a nineteenth century rebuilding of an eighteenth century recreation of a medieval castle. Given the patchwork of themes and motifs upon which the medieval history of *The Blackadder* rests this is, however, a very appropriate setting. As a final observation, according to a survey of over 2000 visitors to Blenheim Palace conducted in 2004, 1 percent of people think that Edmund Blackadder was a real historical character. When the results of this survey were published there was much throwing up of hands in horror at the levels of ignorance people displayed about their history, the invidious effect of Hollywood films, etc. (*Daily Telegraph* 4/4/2004). However, if we look at the results more closely we find that the same percentage thought that Xena, Warrior Princess was real and that the defeat of humanity by the Cyborgs in *Battlestar Galactica* actually happened. It could be argued that this tells us not that people don't know the difference between fiction and reality when it comes to history but rather that at least 1 percent of those surveyed had a sense of humor about the past.

Notes

1. I am grateful to David Marshall for some insightful comments on an earlier draft of this essay. Many thanks also to Mad Gerald of blackadderhall.com for pointing me in the right direction for some of the factual background, and to P.H. Cullum for conversations about witchcraft. Graeme Neath provided invaluable technical support for versions of this essay that were delivered as papers, and John, Carol and Liz Lewis deserve a mention for helping to shape my early appreciation of *Blackadder*.

2. Some studies of sitcom have made claims for the ways in which reactionary stereotypes can be used within them in order to poke fun at the sort of people who espouse such views—perhaps the most famous example being the right-wing bigot Alf Garnett in *Til Death Do Us Part* (BBC1 1966–75; remade as *All in the Family* in the United States) and *In Sickness and in Health* (BBC1 1985–1992). The writer, Johnny Speight, held avowedly Socialist views, and controversy raged around the "proper" interpretation of Garnett's racist outbursts in particular. See also the progressive reading of *It Ain't Half Hot Mum* (BBC1 1974–1981) articulated by Morgan-Russell, but with an awareness that there can be a deep and problematic division between what writers intend and what audiences take from such representations.

3. Although the changing characterization of Blackadder after the first series, noted below, means that he subsequently becomes more laughed with than at.

4. The title of the episode is a play on the famous quotation "singeing the King of Spain's beard," Francis Drake's comment on destroying Spanish warships moored in Cadiz harbor in 1587.

5. Campness and suggestions of homosexuality are another staple of the British sitcom,

of course, as witness such figures as Mr. Humphries in *Are You Being Served* (BBC1 1972–1985) and Bombadier "Gloria" Beaumont in *It Ain't Half Hot Mum.*

6. This episode was originally shown second and still has the number "2" in the introductory credits, but in all subsequent showings and on the video and DVD of the series it has been switched with the original episode 4 "Born to Be King." This was presumably in order to provide narrative and chronological continuity because Princess Leia reappears in episode 5: "Witchsmeller Pursuivant."

7. Another co-writer on *The Young Ones* was Ben Elton, who would become the co-writer of *Blackadder* from the second series onwards.

8. *Fawlty Towers,* co-written by and starring John Cleese (of Monty Python's Flying Circus), received rave reviews at the time and continues to be a benchmark by which other British sitcoms are judged.

9. Curtis has cited the Flashman novels by George MacDonald Fraser as an influence for the way in which they depict the same fictional character participating in various historical events of the nineteenth century (Richard Curtis interview), but it's not clear whether this was in fact the plan for *Blackadder* from the beginning, especially as Atkinson has said that he originally thought the second series would be the last ("I Have a Cunning Plan").

10. *The Adventures of Robin Hood* (Sapphire Films Limited for ITC entertainment, 1955–60).

11. An audience was then shown the finished product in order to provide the laughter track, which was, until recently, a defining feature of the sitcom.

12. Elton's emphasis on the importance of a live audience undoubtedly derived in part from his own status as a stand-up comedian, as well as his experience of co-writing *The Young Ones*. Elton, who studied drama at university, is the nephew of the noted historian Sir Geoffrey Elton, but unfortunately I have been unable to discover the reaction of the latter to the variations incarnations of *Blackadder.*

13. A synopsis of the pilot can be found on the Blackadder Hall Web site, http://www.blackadderhall.com/specials/pilot_episode.shtml. In the past it has been available for download from the Web, but I have been unable to find a current Web site offering it.

14. Although of course Prince Richard, Duke of York, would not have been a middle aged man in 1485, he would have been eleven, and was almost certainly dead in any case.

15. The "lost history" idea of *Blackadder* has come to be a much wider and defining part of its mythos, as articulated, for example, in the linking sections of the script book (Atkinson, Curtis and Elton).

16. Mills 36–39 notes that scholarly commentators have tended to pay very little attention to the audience in analyses of sitcom, whether in relation to what they enjoy or find funny, or to what they know or expect, or the influence that this has in determining the nature of the content.

Works Cited

Atkinson, Rowan, Richard Curtis, and Ben Elton. *Blackadder: The Whole Damn Dynasty.* London: Michael Joseph, 1998.

Badsey, Stephen. *"Blackadder Goes Forth* and the 'Two Western Fronts' Debate." In *The Historian, Television and Television History,* ed. Graham Roberts and Philip M. Taylor, 113–26. Luton: University of Luton Press, 2001.

Casey, Bernadette, Neil Casey, Ben Calvert, Liam French, and Justin Lewis. *Television Studies: The Key Concepts.* London and New York: Routledge, 2002.

Chapman, James. *National Identity and the British Historical Film.* London and New York: I.B. Tauris, 2005.

Daily Telegraph 4/4/2004, http://www.telegraph.co.uk/news/main.jhtml?xml=/news/2004/04/04/nhitler04.xml&sSheet=/news/2004/04/04/ixhome.html. Accessed 1/6/06.

Eaton, Mick. "Television Situation Comedy." In *Popular Television and Film,* ed. Tony

Bennett, Susan Boyd-Bowman, Colin Mercer and Janet Woollacott, 26–52. London: British Film Institute Publishing, 1981.
Mills, Brett. *Television Sitcom*. London: British Film Institute Publishing, 2005.
Morgan-Russell, Simon. *Jimmy Perry and David Croft*. Manchester and New York: Manchester University Press, 2004.
Neale, Steve, and Frank Krutnick. *Popular Film and Television Comedy*. London and New York: Routledge, 1990.
Sharpe, James. *Instruments of Darkness: Witchcraft in England 1550–1750*. London: Hamish Hamilton, 1996.
Sharpe, J.A. *Early Medieval England: A Social History 1550–1760*. Second edition. London etc.: Arnold, 1997.
Woollacott, Janet. "Fictions and Ideologies: The Case of Situation Comedy." In *Popular Culture and Social Relations*, ed. Tony Bennett, Colin Mercer and Janet Woolacott. Buckingham and Philadelphia: Open University Press, 1986.

Web Sites

Bennett, Steve. "All Their Yesterdays ... 20 Years of the Blackadder." http://www.chortle.co.uk/TV/tvfeatures/blackadder.html. Accessed 1 June 2006.
"Blackadder: 1485–1917." http://www.bbc.co.uk/comedy/blackadder/. Accessed 1 June 2006.
"Blackadder: The Pilot Episode." http://www.blackadderhall.com/specials/pilot_episode.shtml. Accessed 1 June 2006.
"I Have a Cunning Plan." BBC Radio 4 documentary, originally broadcast 23 August 2003. Extracts can be found on the BBC Blackadder Web site. http://www.bbc.co.uk/comedy/blackadder/interviews/. Accessed 1 June 2006.
"The Nation's Favourite Sitcom." http://www.bbc.co.uk/sitcom/winner.shtml. Accessed 1 June 2006.
"Richard Curtis Interview." Blackadder Hall. http://www.blackadderhall.com/library/richard_interview.shtml. Accessed 1 June 2006.
"Timewarp: Blackadder II, Part 1 of 4." Blackadder Hall. http://www.blackadderhall.com/library/ba2_timewarp_1.shtml. Accessed 1 June 2006.

9 Medieval History and Cultural Forgetting

Oppositional Ethnography *in* The Templar Revelation

HANNAH R. JOHNSON

On a sunny midsummer day, the authors Lynn Picknett and Clive Prince are completing fieldwork in preparation for writing their book, *The Templar Revelation*. They are in Provence, waiting with the rest of the crowd on a busy, anonymous street for a glimpse of a golden reliquary alleged to contain the skull of Mary Magdalene. This trophy is carried in procession through the town of St. Maximin each year on the Sunday closest to the Magdalene's feast day on July 22. Picknett and Prince are impressed by the obvious devotion on display around them: "There did seem to be many genuinely fervent pilgrims among the throng," they remark, and "the sheer power of this festival gave us pause. This is indeed serious Mary Magdalene country" (58). But they quickly resume their distant, ethnographic point of view with a reminder of their skeptical position: "We had to remind ourselves ... that there are always pilgrims, always fervent believers, in any, or in every, thing, and that belief is in itself not a measure of historical authenticity" (58). *The Templar Revelation* is largely concerned with questions of historical authenticity, although Picknett and Prince tend to formulate such questions in terms that challenge our understanding of what is historical as well as what is authentic. Their work suggests that local practices are a repository of authentic historical knowledge, and history is a project capable of revealing the forgotten roots of Western culture to itself. The real source of the modern celebration in St. Maximin may have been forgotten, but for Picknett and Prince the gestures and signs of the

126

contemporary ritual encode crucial clues about Europe's origins in the ideological violence of early medieval history.

Beginning with this local relic, the authors of *The Templar Revelation* proceed to examine the historical basis of legendary stories about the Magdalene, and their narrative in this section of the book is a crucial index of the philosophy of history operative throughout their work. The *Revelation* itself is an "alternative history"—a work of speculative historical interpretation that is part revisionist narrative and part conspiracy theory, but also a philosophical meditation on the meaning of Western cultural paradigms. As one of the few alternative histories mentioned by name in the best-selling novel *The Da Vinci Code*, *The Templar Revelation* has recently received an increased measure of attention as a source of the novel's major themes, but I would like to suggest that the *Revelation*'s larger arguments about the trajectory and assumptions of our culture have inspired readers more than any specific revisionist claim advanced in the book.[1] The Middle Ages loom large in this work as the hyperreal source of modern traumas and yearnings, but Picknett and Prince also echo the concerns of contemporary academics who have sought to rethink the monolithic characterization of medieval Europe advanced in traditional historiographies. The turn toward social history within the academy over the past few decades has entailed a renewed interest in the lost or occluded experiences of religious minorities, women, heretics, and laborers, to name just a few. In the pages of *The Templar Revelation*, academic historiography's suspicion of too-easy representations of the European past explodes into a full-blown oppositional ethnography that deploys a skeptical reading of Christian legends and rituals in order to suggest that Europe has never been what it thinks it is.

The *Revelation*'s controversial central thesis is that Jesus and Mary Magdalene were married initiates in an Egyptian mystery cult, and were once disciples of John the Baptist. Jesus and Mary allegedly went on to attract new initiates (the twelve disciples) after a rivalry splintered the original religious group, but these new followers had not yet been fully initiated into the pagan sect when Jesus died. Picknett and Prince argue that after the Crucifixion, Mary Magdalene was ostracized by Jesus' new followers, and took the secrets of the mystery religion to Europe with her, where her beliefs flourished throughout the Middle Ages among heretics such as the Cathars and loosely affiliated groups like the Knights Templar. The ideas and practices of the Magdalene's vaguely-defined tradition were allegedly taken up by Renaissance occultists, and preserved down to the present by secret societies. While the book's theories are unconventional, to say the least, *The Templar Revelation* is similar to other texts of its genre, such as *Holy Blood, Holy Grail* or *The Woman with the Alabaster Jar*, in performing what Thomas McLaughlin has called "theory in the vernacular mode" (5), asking complex questions about the methods and aims of conventional historiography in the idiom of everyday language.[2] Such texts insist that medieval traumas and occlusions have not only played a foundational role in shaping the world of the present but continue to influence Western culture through unacknowledged repetitions and repressed longings which the culture has not yet managed to work through.

In their tour of Provence, Picknett and Prince set out to take the measure of local legends about Mary Magdalene, and they offer several hints that the origins of popular devotion to the saint may be misunderstood by modern worshippers. The authors begin to shift the ethnographic eye of Western knowledge back onto the West itself in order to suggest that European "natives" may be incapable of understanding the true origins of their own rituals and beliefs:

> Certainly there is extraordinary, even fanatical, devotion accorded to her [the Magdalene] in Provence.... Yet this is not merely another example of the pious continuation of Catholic tradition. We were struck by the pervasive feeling here that something much more significant lay under the surface. And it was precisely that submerged, *subterranean* vein of meaning that we were determined to uncover [59; emphasis theirs].

This "subterranean vein of meaning," which is surely "more significant" than a mere "pious continuation," lives on in local ritual, regional memory, and a certain indefinable authenticity. This "something more" is the residue of pagan practice that will be uncovered as *The Templar Revelation* progresses, living on in disguise as devotion to the orthodox female saint, Mary Magdalene. Picknett and Prince have adopted the familiar "two worlds" philosophy of history popularized in neopagan and occult works, in which an ancient European tradition of goddess worship was crippled by the rise of Christianity and its totalitarian vision of Western culture.[3] In spite of formidable Christian resistance, the authors argue, the pagan tradition was not only kept alive piecemeal by sympathetic individuals over the centuries, but was preserved deliberately by a "secret tradition" that protected its knowledge down to the present day. The modern worshippers and tourists who attend the procession in St. Maximin are largely unaware of any secret tradition, but Picknett and Prince suggest that they are nevertheless its heirs. We can recognize the true qualities of their devotion, its authenticity, by the fervor of the practice itself, which the authors emphasize several times within the space of a single page. We learn about "the devotion and pride of the local people," their "passion and devotion," and we are encouraged to wonder why the Magdalene "is not only revered, but *loved* with a curious passion," to ask how she became "the object of fervent, even passionate, devotion" (59).

This language of intense emotion—passion, devotion, *love*—appears to be foreign to the authors themselves, who make reference to their own cultural training as cool-headed Britons. There is a real sense in which both their wonder and their bafflement in the midst of this scene of devotion place them as moderns in a pre-modern setting. Passion and reverence, even worship, are attributes of a lost past, represented as anachronistic even in the "hot-blooded" world of contemporary European Catholicism (Picknett and Prince 59). The veneration of modern Frenchmen for this alleged relic of the Magdalene is figured as quasi-instinctive, meeting some deeply felt, archaic need of which the believers themselves are nearly unconscious. And yet this "curious" emotional response is nothing if not specific to its place: "Maybe the operative word here is 'local,' for it is the Provençal, not the French, flag that flies overhead, and this is taken to be very much a local saint" (Picknett and Prince 59). And it is here, in this subtle evocation of southern French nationalism, that the authenticity of the local, the purity of these acts of identification, becomes apparent. Picknett and Prince are reiterating a common refrain from alternative history as well as some academic accounts when they suggest that the world of southern France is a world sheltered from modernity.[4] They tell us that when this world remembers, even if its memories are imperfect, we would be wise to pay attention to what is being recalled. The authors' convictions about long-term structural continuities in Western history—what academics refer to as *longue durée*—are operative here. They are hinting at the survival of practices whose meanings have changed with time. The local people of southern France, who may or may not know what they do in the fullness of all its symbolic connotations, have nevertheless intuited "the truth about Mary Magdalene" (Picknett and Prince 59) through the veil of a Catholic veneration that has attempted to mask her connection to more ancient symbols.

Ultimately, the authors claim that the "real memory" of some crucial, lost, authentic devotion is as much at play in *The Last Temptation of Christ* as in modern Provençal processionals. And yet in its contemporary forms, this memory or intuition is only the faintest trace of a whole world of lost religious meaning. By interrogating recalcitrant sources like the orthodox Christian "script" of a ceremony involving the Magdalene's bones, Picknett and Prince suggest that we can recover the residues of a more ancient (pagan) practice. But they also understand that these traces may finally be available only in symbolic terms, in the overdetermination of certain metaphorical signs, obscure symbolic hints, and the occasional, significant historical event. Picknett and Prince present the Christian legend of Mary Magdalene's life after the Crucifixion as one historical account that once jostled among its competitors for a place of pre-eminence. In a crucial ethnographic gesture, they attempt to reconstruct the reality of the pagan world they say lost out in the battle for hearts and minds, a world conquered and rewritten by Christianity. In attempting to rescue what the modern world has nearly forgotten, the authors engage in what the anthropologist James Clifford famously called "salvage" ethnography ("On Ethnographic Allegory" 113), promising to preserve for us some cultural residue on the verge of extinction, one which will also tell us an allegorical story of redemptive meaning. This work of preservation depends upon their ability to salvage the traumatic history of Europe's colonization at the hands of Christian missionaries.

Picknett and Prince proceed to interrogate the medieval legends concerning the Magdalene's later life, preaching, death and veneration in the south of France. The details vary, "depend[ing] on which version of the story you read" (68), but the substance of the narrative is straightforward: the Magdalene sailed to the south of France following the Crucifixion, she preached to the unconverted, and finally became a hermit, repenting of her sins "for the implausible but biblically time-honoured period of forty years" before dying. But the authors suggest that "something else appears to be hinted at" (68) in this pious narrative of the Magdalene's travels. We are being asked to be suspicious of this legendary narrative, to demythologize this history and reveal its working ideological parts. Picknett and Prince are demonstrating a vernacular hermeneutics of suspicion in action, one that bears more than a passing similarity to certain historians' efforts to recapture the traces of a local world from suspect inquisitorial records, but alternative historians' methods manage to make this project look radically strange.[5] As with their claim that there is "something more" at work in modern rituals venerating the Magdalene, Picknett and Prince again suggest that "something else" is "hinted at" by the narrative's signs and symbols. In *The Templar Revelation*, this "something else" represents the residue, the trace of a heterogeneous world trampled by Christianity, and the narratives of the Magdalene's later life in Europe struggle to speak of this history hidden in the seams of the West's cultural narrative (Picknett and Prince 68–69).

It is only much later in the book that we will learn the nature of the Magdalene's true association with European paganism, according to Picknett and Prince—as a pagan priestess rather than a preacher of the Christian word. But for those readers who are adept at reading between the lines, readers who understand the "two worlds" philosophy of history, in which the lost voices of Christendom's margins must be reconstructed from hostile sources, it is already clear that the narrative hidden beneath the Christian legends involves the pagan history of Europe. The Magdalene was alleged to have lived as a hermit in a cave at Sainte-Baume, yet during this period "that very cave was a centre for the worship of the goddess Diana Lucifera," so that if the Magdalene had lived there, the authors tell us, "she would hardly have been alone" (68). Later, Picknett and Prince remark, "Local tradition has her preaching on the steps of an old temple of Diana" in Marseilles (71). While there is no record of these events, and no plaque to commemorate them, the alleged location of the pagan temple is a telling reminder of the "two worlds" that have always been in competition with one another: the long-vanished temple of Diana would have been located "in a tangle of streets roughly 200 metres away" from the foundation of Marseilles cathedral (71). Thus, face to face with its ideological competitor (at least in memory), the pagan temple can lay claim to the Christian saint honored in the local church. Meanwhile, the groundwork is being laid for an overdetermination of symbolic hints that will serve to ground the plausibility of this ulterior narrative. The Magdalene was alleged to have lived the life of a penitent in the midst of one pagan shrine, and is supposed to have preached on the steps of another: she is pagan by association.

The Christian veneer of local legends is thus alleged to hide a very different history—the Magdalene was not a Christian hero, but a pagan one, not a preacher of the word, but a pagan voice smothered by the ministrations of Christian monks. Picknett and Prince tell us that "undeniably, many of the details of the story of the French Magdalene are later accretions, but there are reasons to suspect that on the whole it is based on fact" (69). For one thing, they find the story of the Magdalene's travels geographically and chronologically plausible. For another, "she is explicitly depicted as a preacher" in these stories (69), a role they suggest medieval monks would have been unlikely to assign a woman were the tale merely invented wholesale.[6] Ruling out the possibility that this legend is simply the "invention of canny French publicists, eager to create a spurious biblical legacy for themselves," the authors suggest instead that "the story was based on a real memory, however embellished over the centuries, of the woman herself" (69–70). They claim that these "embellishments" are largely the result of efforts to Christianize the story and claim the Magdalene for the Church. Picknett and Prince remark that the surviving medieval legends portray the region as "a remote wilderness inhabited by pagan savages," when in actuality, "Provence was a major part of the Roman Empire," and suggest that this portrayal is a result of ideological shaping (68). As Christianity's religious empire expands, so the narrative goes, it subsumes the true character of local practices, rituals, and narratives and reshapes them to its own ideological image.

The result of this portrayal is a history more lost than found, a history that is occasionally exposed by the long life of local practices whose original meanings have been forgotten. Christianity stands in here for the very colonizing forces of European knowledge it will help to produce, and Europe itself becomes the scene of an originary crime that will be repeated over and over again as Western knowledge formations sweep out to encompass the globe, often covering over or dramatically altering the practices and self-understandings of non–Western peoples. In this view, Europe was a postcolonial society before it became a colonizing force in its own right. Although Picknett and Prince never speak of post-colonialism *per se*, they frequently suggest that Western culture was irreparably harmed by this early trauma and forced forgetting. Much later in the book, they consolidate their conclusions and explain the substance of hints they have provided along the way: "There have been other bitter harvests of this great mistake," they tell us, "of a Christian Church that has denied its true roots" (364). These "bitter harvests" include a Western tradition of misogyny, the historical persecution of non–Christian religious groups, and a modern spiritual tradition that the authors view as hollow and unsatisfactory.[7] In spite of the obvious methodological differences between *The Templar Revelation* and academic accounts, the historiographical project of the *Revelation* is reminiscent of recent projects within the academy seeking to propose a category of "postcolonial medievalism," employing a perspective that pays special attention to medieval Europe's troubled border zones, unstable national identities in formation, and the violent and differential relationships between Christianity and other faiths.[8] Picknett and Prince are asking questions that ought to be familiar to readers of contemporary academic historiography: Where are the voices of the subdominant? What is lost in the triumphal rhetoric of Western consolidation? What difference does the medieval make to our modern understanding of history, of culture, of ourselves?

Of course, the Magdalene is hardly alone in representing paganism in southern France, according to the authors. Picknett and Prince also describe what they see as a curious historical "coincidence" whereby shrines of so-called "Black Madonnas" appear in many churches founded during the Middle Ages that are also dedicated to Mary Magdalene, or else feature a chapel or altar dedicated to her. Like the Magdalene herself, they claim, these Black Madonnas "still evoke huge, passionate followings ... on a local scale," but they "are *never* recognized or supported by the Catholic Church" (75). Again, we encounter the "enormous local love and devotion" and the "rare and special passion" of the natives, both past and present, but this time their fervor is directed toward these dark-skinned statues of the Virgin Mary (76). After considering and dismissing a few of the theories meant to explain these images, including the suggestion that Crusaders brought them home from the

Middle East, Picknett and Prince go on to assert, "Black Madonnas are almost always associated with much more ancient *pagan* sites" (76). In contradistinction to the Catholic priest who is supposed to have told an inquiring researcher, "My son, she is black because she is black" (76), Picknett and Prince insist that the blackness of these virgins has a purpose, a symbolic resonance that devotees understand and intuit even when they know not what they do. Like the residents of St. Maximin, who "know" more about the Magdalene than they realize, the devotees of local Black Madonnas somehow understand that "the very blackness of these images suggests that they represent the continuation of pagan goddess worship that is dressed up as Christianity" (76). Furthermore, this great devotion suggests a motive for the Church's efforts to incorporate and domesticate these figures rather than remove them, according to the authors: "the fervour accorded to them makes such worship nigh on impossible to ban" (76).[9]

The authors' evident interest in those modern Christians who display "devotion" and "passion" for Black Madonnas as well as Mary Magdalene stems from their investment in a larger historical salvage operation and their conviction that this history can heal ancient signs of trauma in the present. What modern worshippers are really doing, according to *The Templar Revelation*, is worshipping an ancient archetype—the goddess—even if they have no other name for her than Mary. These intuitive Marians have tapped into some universal impulse, though they have managed to locate it within the Church rather than outside of it. Historically speaking, Picknett and Prince argue that this is no accident: "When the patriarchal Church came along," they tell us, "its first instinct was to eradicate pagan goddess worship. But the yearning for a goddess remained firm," and the Church fathers found themselves unable to uproot this ancient desire (78). So the Virgin Mary emerged as an institutionally approved, "bowdlerized version" of the ancient pagan goddess Isis, "a makeshift goddess created by misogynists for misogynists," and "resolutely unacquainted with the biological, emotional and spiritual imperatives of real women" (78). Enter the Magdalene—sinner, saint, and "companion" of the Lord. Together, the Virgin and the Magdalene made something like a "well-rounded Isis" (78), satisfying the deep yearning the Church could never quite eradicate, according to the authors. Picknett and Prince present their conclusion with a question that can only be rhetorical: "Could it be that the cult of Mary Magdalene, like that of the Black Madonna that is so despised by the Church, actually hides a much older and more complete idea of womanhood?" (78). Picknett and Prince are hardly the first authors to argue that portrayals of these Christian saints reveal a residue of pagan practice and point to a deep psychic need for a relatable female religious figure in the

West—indeed, such arguments have been relatively common among neo-pagans since at least the 1970s. *The Templar Revelation* replays a story that has taken on the quality of orthodoxy among some contemporary readers of alternative history, in which such hybrid "goddesses" as Mary Magdalene or the Virgin Madonna take on new significance as the representatives of the colonial enterprise of the Church, an enterprise whose basic assumptions and desires are understood to have prepared the way for much of the injustice visible in modern society.

Picknett and Prince argue that residues of an ancient pagan belief system have survived in modern rituals such as the procession at St. Maximin in part because such rituals speak to a universal spiritual need. The local acts of Marian devotion the authors locate in southern France stand for an intuition both global and sweeping: Mary Magdalene is "the woman believed to be at the heart of many ancient mysteries, and whose power extends to today's culture in a way we have not yet fully grasped" (59). What is more, her "continuing power is not imaginary: it has always existed and exerted a profound attraction throughout the centuries" (61). One need not be a Provençal villager to grasp the profound symbolic significance of Mary Magdalene, to decode subconsciously the true meaning of her story. Like many other alternative historians, Picknett and Prince reveal the traces of an outdated Jungianism here, with its emphasis on archetypes and instinctual desires. However, their fascinating critique of Christianity's installation of itself as the reigning Western religious paradigm suggests not only that cultural forms linger even after their meanings change, but also that certain aspects of human psychology remain fundamentally stable in spite of what the forces of social conditioning may demand. This is precisely the kind of claim contemporary historicism has largely shied away from in recent decades in favor of an emphasis on local practice and the ways in which culture and ideas of the self emerge through discourse rather than existing prior to language. Picknett and Prince approach the universal by means of the local, and their insistence on the importance of local knowledge to history ought to encourage us to re-examine the fruits of contemporary historicism's emphasis on the local, the limited, and the contingent. We might well ask whether microhistories such as Carlo Ginzburg's *Cheese and the Worms* or Mark Pegg's *Corruption of Angels* mask a similar appeal to universalism precisely at the heart of their recourse to the local.

From the Magdalene's appearance in *Jesus Christ Superstar* and *The Last Temptation of Christ* to her recent centrality in several popular studies, Picknett and Prince review the consistent modern fascination with this biblical figure. They go on to discuss her minimal role in the canonical gospel accounts, analyze references to her rivalry with Peter in the so-called "Gnostic Gospels," and present a short history of her reputation as a prostitute within the medieval Church (66–67). Historically, most believers have been unaware of all this, yet they have still been drawn to her by some inexplicable process: "Clearly her spell rests on something else, something elusive but not impossible to experience" (67). In this remark, as in the authors' earlier references to their own sensible British reserve, I hear the echo of a wistful alienation. Picknett and Prince may identify with history's outsiders, but they do not include themselves in the charmed circle of those who can experience the special magnetism. Instead, they are fact-finders, remedying historical injustice perhaps, but forever shut out from that "something elusive" that is in this case a variety of spiritual experience. Picknett and Prince claim for themselves a rhetorical position much like the one claimed by academic historians: implicitly, they are promising us that they will analyze the record without succumbing *too* much to partisan desire. More importantly, their position as analysts rather than believers signals their radical position as outsider ethnographers of the West, participant observers who have one foot in the culture and one foot outside it. There is an embedded irony in this position: even as the authors make a subtle argument for the universality of archetypal appeal, the universal does not appear to include them. What could be more academic than the claim to this kind of ultimate detachment?

While they are clearly interested in ideas of cultural memory, universal human desires, and even a kind of innate heretical orientation, Picknett and Prince also trace the existence of a literal chain of transmission, a secret genealogy of knowledge which they refer to as "the great heresy." The basic precepts of this heresy involve knowledge of Jesus' pagan origins, a theology involving sacramental sex and a balance of power between the sexes, and certain undefined notions about enlightenment and spiritual transformation. What past and present devotees of the Magdalene could only sense or suspect, the inner circle of the great heresy allegedly knows for a fact, as members of a transhistorical secret network. Clearly this notion of a well-defined body of secret knowledge operates in diametrical opposition to academic historicism's claims of the discrete quality of historical periods and unlikelihood of direct secret communications between them. I would argue that the "something more" that appears with such regularity as a kind of rhetorical tic in *The Templar Revelation* points to more than the presence of paganism within European history. This "something more" also signals that the oppositional identities the authors pick out across time, the proponents of "the great heresy" they claim to have discovered, are *intentional* historical actors. These individuals or groups are trying, often unsuccessfully, to convey a message of deep import to us. In advancing such a claim, Picknett and Prince literalize academic historiography's desire to recover the lost voices of the past. When the authors of *The Templar Revelation* invoke the capacity of historical actors to generate myths about and for their own historical moment, they are reading the body of Western history as a living organism capable of speaking back to the historian's ministrations, his interpretive work. Their attempts to speak for this past are problematic, yet their insistence on the idea that the past has an agency, even a diffuse consciousness, is a fascinating response to postmodern agonizing about history's fragility, its malleability in the hands of a skilled historian-narrator. Picknett and Prince believe that we can reconstruct subaltern historical experiences. But they go further by implying that history is a discrete reality even before the historian plays detective, and put pressure on the reigning theoretical maxim that history does not exist before it is constituted as narrative.[10] And whereas contemporary academic historians insist on the gap between past and present, asserting that the past cannot speak its experiences to us in any unmediated way,[11] Picknett and Prince argue that in spite of all we cannot know, the world of the past is still capable of delivering some of its messages to us. From the point of view of alternative history, the relics and documents of the past have real agency—the interpreter's work may enable or frustrate the designs of historical actors, but their messages will still lie waiting to be retrieved.

In *The Templar Revelation*, the subaltern figure of history is expressed through local memory, in the survival of peasant practices which speak of their original meaning only in symbolic terms. In this world there are also the occasional myth-makers, those who want to impart a deliberate structure to the remains they leave behind, such as the medieval monks who reshape legends about the Magdalene (74–75). And of course, there are martyrs here too, the lost Cathars, the dead Templars, the vanished pagans of a cave in St. Baume, a ruined temple of Diana in Marseilles. Alternative history's perspective is a historiographical one, in the sense that the authors hope to recover forgotten viewpoints from the past. It is also an ideological view, since alternative history affirms our ability to transform our cultural understanding, and gestures toward the desirability of asking again what our culture is really about, and demystifying its origins. But most powerfully, perhaps, alternative history's perspective turns the ethnographic eye of the West back on itself. Alternative histories take up the academic's championship of "other" histories of the West, and convey them straight into the heart of a volatile public sphere. These vernacular historians are modern-day ethnographers, having their revenge on all those bad old ethnographies that told us how Africans, or South Pacific islanders, or tribesmen in the Americas could not possibly understand what they were really doing or what their rituals really meant. Now that alienating lens is turned on modern-day Frenchmen and (via this proxy) all of Western civilization in order to upset the foundational narratives of the dominant world order. Not only have our history books lied, according to these writers, but Western history, Western culture, Western assumptions, have never been true as billed. At the very least it sounds like a job for a heretic, doesn't it?

Notes

1. I am currently working on an article about the reception of *The Da Vinci Code*, originally produced for Princeton's Center for Arts and Cultural Policy Studies, entitled "History's House Divided: *The Da Vinci Code*, Alternative History, and Some Popular Uses of the Past."

2. "Alternative history" is a term I have borrowed from a few alternative historians themselves; it is also a term that is replicated in some of the materials used to market their books. The claims of this genre are advanced as true—they are the claims of non-fiction. But these texts also have a well-known counterpart among fictional narratives: "alternate history" is a fictional genre that emerged into prominence after World War II. Often associated with science fiction, these stories and novels operate from the fictional premise that some actual historical event, sometimes major and sometimes minor, turned out quite differently than it did in fact. Some popular themes include the Nazis winning World War II, the South winning the American Civil War, or the American Revolution never taking place. For a useful overview of the claims of the fictional genre as well as the interest in counterfactual claims among historians and social scientists, see Hellekson; Rosenfeld 90–103. For a primer on the relation between causal explanation and counterfactual claims, see Bulhof 145–68, and T.D. Mey and E. Weber 28–38, especially 29.

3. For one example of the "two worlds" philosophy of history in action, see Barbara Walker's book *The Woman's Encyclopedia of Myths and Secrets,* a text frequently cited in *The Templar Revelation.* For the allure of what the anthropologist Sabina Magliocco has referred to as "the romance of subdominance," see her book *Witching Culture,* especially 185–204.

4. This is the same world that Baigent, Lincoln, and Leigh, the authors of another prominent alternative history *Holy Blood, Holy Grail,* described as being inhabited by a host of "peasants" in the later 1970s, a world of rootedness and changeless tradition. Also see scholar Mark Pegg's critique of quite similar assumptions about a pure, undiluted French agrarian heartland lurking within academic historians' accounts of an unchanging, and exceptionally long-lived, "medieval" countryside. See Pegg, "'Catharism,'" especially 259.

5. For some interesting commentaries on the historian's risk of complicity with the hostile sources he uses to advance his argument, see Clifford, "Naming Names"; Rosaldo; Sponsler; and Biddick, especially 105–134.

6. This is a rather broad generalization. In fact, medieval people were quite capable of imagining female preachers in the distant past. A number of early Christian women martyrs were supposed to have died as a result of their proselytizing efforts, and many of these narratives not only survived but were read with interest throughout the Middle Ages. For an extended discussion about the ways in which these stories were revived and recontextualized during the high Middle Ages, for example, see Wogan-Browne.

7. For another example of Lynn Picknett's argument for the explicit connections between medieval and modern modes of oppression, see her book *Mary Magdalene,* especially 1–14.

8. For two discussions see Holsinger and Cohen. Also see Bartlett, whose work prefigured the current discussion in important ways.

9. Ean Begg, author of *The Cult of the Black Virgin,* is the authors' primary source on this topic, and he makes much of some encounters with Catholic priests who claim not to

know anything about locally venerated Black Madonnas, as well as examples of local communities that changed or altered their existing cult figures. This is the trope of difficulty of access often apparent in alternative historical accounts, where ignorance, accident, or misprision is taken for deliberate obstructionism on the part of authority figures. Picknett and Prince employ this trope occasionally themselves, but it is usually difficult to be sure from textual accounts how many of these interactions can be chalked up to genuine obstructionism, and how many to miscommunications. Either way, these episodes reveal a great deal about alternative historians' acute awareness of a very real politics of knowledge, and their understanding of their own position in contemporary intellectual hierarchies.

10. See, for instance, Hayden White's essays in *The Content of the Form*, especially "The Question of Narrative in Contemporary Historical Theory" 26–57. Also see his earlier work on this topic in *Metahistory*, especially 1–42. Of particular interest for medievalists are Gabrielle Spiegel's incidental remarks on this topic in her well-known essay "History, Historicism in the Social Logic of the Text," especially 75.

11. The past itself is effectively figured as subaltern in this view. For one discussion of the ways in which the past is sometimes figured as a subaltern category, a move which goes hand in hand with portraying modern subalterns as subjects living in a Western cultural "past," see Ingham and Warren 1–7.

Works Cited

Baigent, Michael, Richard Leigh, and Henry Lincoln. *Holy Blood, Holy Grail*. New York: Dell, 1982; reprint 1983.

Bartlett, Robert. *The Making of Europe: Conquest, Colonization and Cultural Change, 950–1350*. Princeton: Princeton University Press, 1993.

Begg, Ean. *The Cult of the Black Virgin*. London: Arkana, 1985.

Biddick, Kathleen. *The Shock of Medievalism*. Durham and London: Duke University Press, 1998.

Bulhof. "'What If?' Modality and History." *History and Theory* 38:2 (May 1999): 145–68.

Clifford, James. "On Ethnographic Allegory." In *Writing Culture: the Poetics and Politics of Ethnography*, ed. James Clifford and George E. Marcus. Berkeley: University of California Press, 1986.

_____. "Naming Names." Review of *Montaillou: The Promised Land of Error*, by Emmanuel Le Roy Ladurie. *Canto* 3.1 (1980): 142–153.

Cohen, Jeffrey J., ed. *The Postcolonial Middle Ages*. New York: St. Martin's, 2000.

Hellekson, Karen. *The Alternate History: Refiguring Historical Time*. Kent: Kent State University Press, 2001.

Holsinger, Bruce. "Medieval Studies, Postcolonial Studies, and the Genealogies of Critique." *Speculum* 77 (2002): 1195–1227.

Ingham, Patricia Claire, and Michelle R. Warren. *Postcolonial Moves: Medieval through Modern*. New York: Palgrave Macmillan, 2003.

Magliocco, Sabina. *Witching Culture: Folklore and Neo-Paganism in America*. Philadelphia: University of Pennsylvania Press, 2004.

McLaughlin, Thomas. *Street Smarts and Critical Theory: Listening to the Vernacular*. Madison: University of Wisconsin Press, 1996.

Mey, T.D., and E. Weber. "Explanation and Thought Experiments in History." *History and Theory* 42.1 (Feb. 2003): 28–38.

Pegg, Mark. "'Catharism,' and the Study of Medieval Heresy." *New Medieval Literatures* 6 (2003): 249–69.

Picknett, Lynn. *Mary Magdalene: Christianity's Hidden Goddess*. New York: Carroll and Graf, 2003.

Picknett, Lynn, and Clive Prince. *The Templar Revelation: Secret Guardians of the True Identity of Christ*. New York: Simon and Schuster, 1997.

Rosaldo, Renato. "From the Door of His Tent: The Fieldworker and the Inquisitor." In

Writing Culture, ed. James Clifford, 77–97. Berkeley: California University Press, 1986.

Rosenfeld, Gavriel. "Why do we ask 'What if?': Reflections on the Function of Alternate History." *History and Theory* 41 (Dec. 2002): 90–103

Spiegel, Gabrielle. "History, Historicism in the Social Logic of the Text." *Speculum* 65 (1990): 59–86.

Sponsler, Claire. "Medieval Ethnography: Fieldwork in the European Past." *Assays: Critical Approaches to Medieval and Renaissance Texts* 7 (1992): 1–30.

Walker, Barbara G. *Woman's Encyclopedia of Myths and Secrets*. San Francisco: Harper and Row, 1983.

White, Hayden. *Metahistory: The Historical Imagination in Nineteenth-Century Europe*. Baltimore: Johns Hopkins University Press, 1973.

_____. "The Question of Narrative in Contemporary Historical Theory." In *The Content of the Form: Narrative Discourse and Historical Representation*, 26–57. Baltimore: Johns Hopkins University Press, 1987.

Wogan-Browne, Jocelyn. *Saints' Lives and Women's Literary Culture c. 1150–1300: Virginity and Its Authorizations*. Oxford: Oxford University Press, 2001.

10 Teaching the Middle Ages

Carl James Grindley

The difficulties of giving young students meaningful lessons about the Middle Ages—lessons that avoid romanticizing the era and offer at least a glimpse at the realities of the medieval world—are only a subset of the larger problems of teaching history in today's elementary and middle grades. The National Center for History in the Schools, seemingly in a moment of clearheaded pessimism, reported that many "have wondered if a national consensus could be forged concerning what all students should have opportunity to learn about our history as Americans, and of the peoples of all racial, religious, ethnic, and national backgrounds who have been a part of our story" (http://nchs.ucla.edu/standards.html). Regardless of the dangers of what the NCHS itself called the "contentious" nature of historical study, it went about its task with "enormous good will, and dogged determination ... [confident] in the inherent strength and capabilities of this nation to undertake the steps necessary for bringing to all students the benefits of an endeavor to raise the standards for learning history in our schools" (ibid.). Currently, at least 30 states have adopted their basic template, and the nation has moved towards standardized assessment. Indeed, with the reality of the No Child Left Behind Act of 2002, and its resulting "report cards," national standards are probably not going to go away anytime soon; but, as is well known, there are some troubling issues.

Two of the major problems with the implementation of any national standards for the teaching of social studies and history relate to their effective classroom application and assessment. Firstly, due to the time constraints inherent in a 180-day school year (http://nces.ed.gov/surveys/pss/tables/table_15.asp), social studies and history often enjoy only scant attention. For example, the typical grade 4 student receives "between 61 and 180 minutes per week" of social studies and history instruction (U.S. Dept. of Education, *Nation's Report Card* 90)—which works out to be somewhere between 36 and 72 hours in a given school year. Within that instructional framework, and provided a teacher adopts state guidelines— 60 per cent, on average, do (92)—very little time is spent discussing the medieval.

This small amount of potential instruction time seems to be split between a vague paucity of curricular hints at the lower end of the educational process and an impossibly specific set of learning objectives at the higher levels. In California, for example, it would be expected that grade seven social studies teachers would cover the following medieval topics:

7.6   Students analyze the geographic, political, economic, religious, and social structures of the civilizations of Medieval Europe.

1. Study the geography of the Europe and the Eurasian land mass, including its location, topography, waterways, vegetation, and climate and their relationship to ways of life in Medieval Europe.

2. Describe the spread of Christianity north of the Alps and the roles played by the early church and by monasteries in its diffusion after the fall of the western half of the Roman Empire.

3. Understand the development of feudalism, its role in the medieval European economy, the way in which it was influenced by physical geography (the role of the manor and the growth of towns), and how feudal relationships provided the foundation of political order.

4. Demonstrate an understanding of the conflict and cooperation between the Papacy and European monarchs (e.g., Charlemagne, Gregory VII, Emperor Henry IV).

5. Know the significance of developments in medieval English legal and constitutional practices and their importance in the rise of modern democratic thought and representative institutions (e.g., Magna Carta, parliament, development of habeas corpus, an independent judiciary in England).

6. Discuss the causes and course of the religious Crusades and their effects on the Christian, Muslim, and Jewish populations in Europe, with emphasis on the increasing contact by Europeans with cultures of the Eastern Mediterranean world.

7. Map the spread of the bubonic plague from Central Asia to China, the Middle East, and Europe and describe its impact on global population.

8. Understand the importance of the Catholic church as a political, intellectual, and aesthetic institution (e.g., founding of universities, political and spiritual roles of the clergy, creation of monastic and mendicant

religious orders, preservation of the Latin language and religious texts, St. Thomas Aquinas's synthesis of classical philosophy with Christian theology, and the concept of "natural law").

9. Know the history of the decline of Muslim rule in the Iberian Peninsula that culminated in the Reconquista and the rise of Spanish and Portuguese kingdoms [California State Board of Education, *History—Content Standards for California* 27–32].

What is surprising is that these particularly concrete learning objectives represent only one out of a total of eleven separate and equally detailed themes. Even if, for the sake of argument, each theme was studied with equal vigor (which may or may not be true), and to ignore the concept of holistic education, it would be unlikely that more than six hours or so of class time would be spent on the Middle Ages. Whereas it is unlikely that objective 4, a demonstration of "an understanding of the conflict and cooperation between the Papacy and the European monarchs," can be meaningfully assessed with anything shy of a Yale PhD in medieval political history.

On the other hand, despite the specificity of the middle school curriculum, medieval topics in elementary education are only vaguely identified. To remain with the example of California, its kindergarten to grade five curricula contain no specific content expectations other than a generalized call for students to "distinguish fact from fiction by comparing documentary sources on historical figures and events with fictionalized characters and events" (1). In addition, by grade one, students are expected to "recognize that some aspects of people, places, and things change over time while others stay the same" (6) while at the same time accepting "the role of individual choice in a free-market economy" (ibid.).

On a similar note, and as far as NCHS is concerned, between kindergarten and grade four, standards 7 (a) and 7 (b) of "Topic Four: The History of Peoples of Many Cultures Around the World" recommends that teachers should instruct students to:

- Investigate the ways historians learn about the past if there are no written records.
- Describe the effects geography has had on societies, including their development of urban centers, food, clothing, industry, agriculture, shelter, trade, and other aspects of culture.
- Compare and contrast various aspects of family life, structures, and roles in different cultures and in many eras with students' own family lives.
- Illustrate or retell the main ideas in folktales, legends, myths, and stories of heroism that disclose the history and traditions of various cultures around the world.
- Describe life in urban areas and communities of various cultures of the world at various times in their history.

- Describe significant historical achievements of various cultures of the world.
- Analyze the dance, music, and arts of various cultures around the world to draw conclusions about the history, daily life, and beliefs of the people in history.
- Explain the customs related to important holidays and ceremonies in various countries in the past.
- Trace on maps and explain the migrations of large groups, such as the movement of Native American ancestors across the Bering Strait land bridge, the Bantu migrations in Africa, the movement of Europeans and Africans to the Western Hemisphere, and the exodus of Vietnamese boat people, Haitians, and Cubans in recent decades.
- Draw upon historical narratives to identify early explorers and world travelers, such as Marco Polo, Zheng He, Eric the Red, and Christopher Columbus, and to describe the knowledge gained from their journeys.
- Draw upon historical narratives in order to identify European explorers of the 15th and 16th centuries, and explain their reasons for exploring, the information gained from their journeys, and what happened as a result of their travels.
- Gather data in order to explain the effects of the diffusion of food crops and animals between the Western and Eastern hemispheres after the voyages of Columbus (adapted from http://nchs.ucla.edu/standards/standardsk-4-4-7.html).

In the United States, these alternatively ambitious and vague curricula are currently assessed at grades four, seven and twelve by the National Assessment of Educational Progress. According to their data, at the grade four, seven and twelve levels, 13 percent, 3 percent and 1 percent of assessment time, respectively, is dedicated to medieval and Renaissance topics (U.S. Dept. of Education, *Nation's Report Card* 5). This is a typical question:

4. The voyages of Columbus changed life in Europe by:
   A) introducing new foods and spices to Europe
   B) showing Europeans a shorter route to Asia
   C) introducing the horse to Spain
   D) proving that the Earth was flat [http://nces.ed.gov/nationsreportcard/itmrls/itemdisplay.asp].

Distressingly enough, 53 percent of students tested could not obtain the correct answer (http://nces.ed.gov/nationsreportcard/itmrls/itemdisplay.asp). As a side note, at the grade four level, nearly 10 percent of students had no idea that quill pens were once used as writing implements (ibid.). So with alternatively over-complicated or barren curricula, assessed infrequently and poorly, it is no wonder that American students and their teachers face real challenges when approaching the Middle Ages and the Renaissance.

The work of SMART, Scientia Scholae and TEAMS notwithstanding, the majority of medieval content instructional moments are best characterized by inconsistency, and, indeed, some informally published lesson plans descend into the politically reprehensible. It is these lesson plans that interest me the most, as they reflect, perhaps, an unconscious agenda that leads not to Boorman but to Zucker.

In a 1999 survey of 700 Minnesota teachers, it was discovered that more than two thirds searched periodically for online lesson plans, but the sites most commonly notes as being favorites ranged greatly from the purely academic to the frighteningly populist:

> Common responses include, in no particular order, the Getty's ArtsEdNet, AskEric educational database, the Minneapolis Star Tribune, the MIA, ArtsConnectEd, NASA, Kathy Schrock's Scholastic Instructor, PBS, Smithsonian, Electronic Classroom, Scholastic News, National Geographic, Discover online, Wall Street Journal, MNHS, travel tracking, Yahooligans, Ask Jeeves for Kids, and the Library of Congress [Johnson].

Likewise, many educators have expressed an emotion somewhere between joy and despair at the prospect of evaluating online lesson plans:

> During my years as a seventh grade English teacher, I recall many late evenings spent searching the Internet for unique and creative ways to teach a concept or idea. The Internet became a territory of lost treasures waiting to be charted, and I assumed the role of a pirate searching and digging for these treasures. Search engines such as Yahoo and Google, served as my map; each link dictated the number of paces I had to take. Unfortunately, my maps did not always lead me down a straight and smooth path, for some of the links led me in the wrong direction. Others were dead ends. Many had nothing to do with what I wanted [Clark 292].

For the balance of this paper, I will provide some examples of the sorts of lesson plans that Clark inadvertently might have come across during her Google-based searches—and in the process attempt to explain why some seemingly innocent classroom games have unfortunate political messages. I shall then attempt to give some advice to educators, in the hopes that such lesson plans will become a thing of the past. All of the following lesson plans originate in American institutions, which is not to suggest that the motivations behind the early introduction of medieval political constructs are any different in other national cultures. It is simply that these lesson plans are the ones most often available online.

A popular, untitled and now unsupported lesson plan authored by Nancy Walker and Libbie Poole—fruitlessly indexed by a variety of subscription education sites including Lesson Planet, Education Planet, Archaeolink and over 150 other sites—claims that "students will explore the Middle Ages by focusing on castles, knights and dragons" (Walker and Poole). This set of lesson plans was designed for a grade three audience and the students are supposed to "discover the medieval world through the use of multi-disciplinary activities" (Walker and Poole). Walker and Poole's approach, featuring dragons, knights and castles, represents a relatively typical elementary school approach to the complexities of European culture from the ninth to fifteenth centuries.

Walker and Poole's learning unit includes a lengthy list of objectives:

1. Know the character's [sic] names and the roles they played in the Middle Ages. Twenty Vocabulary/Spelling words will be learned and mastered.

2. Know the geography of the Middle Ages.

3. Learn math skills through a "dragon math game."

4. Know the time frame of the Middle Ages and when major events in the Middle Ages occurred.

5. Know the art and music of the medieval world.

6. Use puppets in role playing characters of the Middle Ages.

7. Physically act out games such as jousting and ball & chain games.

8. Science of how castles were built.

9. Understand the importance of the tools and weaponry of the times.

10. Be able to make foods of the middle ages and understand what the society of the Middle Ages consisted of [Walker and Poole].

Perhaps the most politically revealing learning objectives are the first and the last, which call for students to know the "characters' names" and to understand the "society" of the Middle Ages, as if the subject related to mythological character types and play roles, rather than imposed and harsh realities. Indeed, the depiction of the Middle Ages as being harmless performance permeates this lesson plan in a way that would be utterly inappropriate if the subject was anything other than a time period that is routinely reduced to cartoonish stereotypes: unimaginable for a lesson plan on the Indian Wars, the Great Depression, the Holocaust, the Civil Rights Movement and so on. To carry this sort of teaching metaphor away from the Middle Ages and into any other time period would be distressing at best. Imagine a teacher separating children into Civil Rights Volunteers and Racists.

In order for pupils to gain an understanding of medieval cultural norms, one of the many areas Walker and Poole explore is chivalry. The teachers provide a basic list of what they consider knightly values, but do not suggest strategies for the acquisition of a more complete understanding of the historical truths behind those values, nor any recognition that those values were almost entirely the stuff of romance. Their knightly code reads as follows:

- Be always ready with your armor on, except when you are taking your rest at night.
- Defend the poor and help them that cannot defend themselves.
- Do nothing to hurt or offend anyone else.
- Be prepared to fight in the defense of your country.
- At whatever you are working, try to win honor and a name for honesty.
- Never break your promise.
- Maintain the honor of your country with your life. Rather die honestly then live shamelessly.
- Chivalry requireth that youth should be trained to perform the most laborious and humble offices with cheerfulness and grace; and do good unto others [Walker and Poole].

Walker and Poole then turn their focus to a discussion of the physical activities that children should perform in order to reinforce the noble values of their knightly code. The instructions read:

> Have children make cardboard swords with aluminum foil wrapped around them, them make shields, helmets, ball and chain (using knotted sashcord and old sock stuffed with rags). Then Let the Games begin! Play jousting/ball and chain games, and the girls can either participate or act like damsels (have costumes like old gowns/old dresses) [ibid.].

Before any objection is raised that offense has been taken where none was deliberately offered, it is important recognize that elementary education is a critical endeavor; it supports and fosters the next generation of citizens, and contributes not only to their social formation but also to their base knowledge. For many people, the world of the medieval stops in elementary school; this is something akin to having a knowledge of biology that starts and ends with unicorns. The California State standards for history, it should be remembered, included a mandate to enable students to distinguish fact from fiction.

The critical factor in an overall analysis of this lesson plan comes through the simple observation that the plan's audience is not Walker and Poole, nor a singular class of perhaps 25 grade three students, but comprises an indeterminate number of other grade three instructors, home-schooling parents and all the attached children. In many ways, the almost viral transmission of misinformation is understandable; lesson plans are extremely difficult, onerous and time-consuming to create. Some require years of specialized research, others a burdensome amount of sometimes outdated reading. In many cases, the adoption of tertiary resources presents an expedient solution to the contemporary realities of the education professional; many times, teachers who are parachuted into unfamiliar areas of teaching will be forced to consult their colleagues for class ideas, or will have to resort to adopting entire courses off the Internet or to photocopying old outlines from the departmental filing cabinets (during the research for this paper, it was not uncommon to find a great many Internet lesson plans silently "borrowing" from one another in such a convoluted manner as to obscure the original authorship). It is doubly understandable, therefore, that when the lesson plans of others are utilized, it is unlikely that any teacher can truly check everything. It is perhaps unfair to expect that an over-taxed elementary school teacher can digest a long and complex bibliography just to subject a one week lesson plan to anything approaching rigorous peer review. That such a lesson plan can fill an otherwise vacant Friday morning will probably be enough.

Walker and Poole's proposed outline spends a lot of classroom time on the pursuit of dragons, and, given the statistically small number of social studies instruction hours, it seems that class time should not focus on chivalry when students could be given a brief run down of some of the dark but true aspects of medieval society. It is akin to teaching elementary school science students that ether is necessary for the transmission of light, when they could be taught that without air they will die.

Although it might be argued that eight-year-old children should not be introduced to the real ambitions of medieval knighthood, or that such children are not capable of understanding the subtle interplay between literature and reality, between power and purpose, such a view is insupportable. Eight-year-old children are more than sophisticated enough to understand the realities of bigotry and prejudice, and are easily able to cope with the knowledge that the past was not always a just or romantic place, that dragons were not real. In California, for example, grade three students are supposed to learn about the lives of Harriet Tubman, Frederick Douglass and Martin Luther King Jr., so it seems generous to give them the benefit of the doubt regarding the Middle Ages (Calif. State Board of Ed., *Content Standards for California* 10).

Ruth Blanton, Shirley Finney and Becky Woodard's learning unit titled "Knight's Quest" is targeted to social studies classes from grades 3 to 8, and mostly concerns feudalism, a term that the authors gloss as "social class" (Blanton et al.). The ambition of Blanton et al. is to "allow intermediate elementary and middle school students to explore the wonders of the Middle Ages by concentration on three broad areas: castles, feudalism and famous people" (ibid.).

In the lesson plan, Blanton et al. suggest that educators should:

Teach children to play chess. Give a short explanation of the game, its origins and purpose. Show and explain the pieces and their moves. Relate the pieces to their social class and their responsibilities: King, Queen, Knight and Rook, (Nobility); Bishop (the Church); Pawn (the peasant class). The moves, rules, restrictions and importance of each piece are very structured, much like the social system of the time period. A demonstration can be done as a group using a video data projector or LCD panel [Blanton et al.].

Although Blanton et al.'s salient model eloquently suggests why Richard II was so easily deposed—he could only move one square at a time—it fails to address the assassination of Saint Thomas à Becket, who could have easily avoided death at Canterbury by sliding diagonally all the way to Palermo in one fluid motion. Likening the medieval estates to chess, though, only serves to sterilize and deproblematize a complicated system that middle school students should be able to understand. Their lesson plan reveals one of the fundamental difficulties of sharing resources online: different states have different mandated learning objectives, and seemingly similar learning objectives may be taught at different grade points in different states.

Carla Kinnard's lesson plan titled "Knighthood and Chivalry," targeted to literature students from grades 9 to 12, is designed to teach students "that young men must complete certain steps in order to become knights" (Kinnard)—omitting the quite obvious step of being born to the appropriate social class or with an equivalent access to capital.

Kinnard's exploration of knighthood asserts "that Medieval knights often participated in quests, or long journeys, in search of some goal," and requires that students "write about the quest for knowledge, love, a certain career, or excellence" (Kinnard). Successful students, Kinnard writes, will "participate in a knighting or dubbing ceremony," just as long as they "bathe [on] the day of the ceremony" and "wear their school colors" (ibid.). Kinnard suggests that students should "stay awake all day long at the school on the day of the ceremony" (ibid.). As intriguing as it is to make basic hygiene and consciousness part of the official requirements of a high school credit course—and these features *are* graded components of the lesson plan's fourth section—what is more intriguing is that the needs and roles of female students are not addressed other than to suggest that the knighthood ceremony include the dubbing of a "Lady."

In Trudy Driskell's "Life Inside Castle Walls," directed at Texan middle school students in grades 7 and 8, the instructor claims her lesson plan is "filled with icons that the students are familiar with such as castles, knights, dragons, carousels and coats of arms." Driskell's lesson plan ends "with a feast," and features a description of the types of people who lived in castles:

> In Medieval times there were knights and lords but also many others who lived in and around the castles. There was a clerk who kept the castle accounts, a steward who was in charge of the household, a priest who guarded everyone's souls, reeves and bailiffs who collected rent from the serfs who farmed the lord's land and lived under his protection, archers and cross bowman [sic] who protected the fortress, traveling jugglers, jesters, and musicians who entertained at large banquets. Servants kept the household running, cooks, meat carvers, and cupbearers prepared and served the

food and drink. Often there was a taster who sampled all food before it was served, checking for poison. Spinners and weavers made clothing for the household, servants cleaned the castle, grew food, kept the buildings and grounds in good repair and cared for the lord's horses and other animals. After studying this period and learning more about life in the castle, ask each student to assume the identify of a castle dweller. Students might draw a job identity. Students will write an illustrated story about their life and job in the middle ages using ClarisWorks word process and by accessing the tool box to draw onto the word processing document. The students could be encouraged to use factual information with their own creative ideas of what it would be like to be a knight, food taster, weaver or musician in the medieval castle [Driskell].

This plan illustrates, perhaps, one of the most interesting notions that get presented in the more commonplace online lesson plans: the fundamentally lucky democracy of feudal hierarchies and their completely balanced structure. Students randomly determine their social condition through a sort of lottery, with each individual estate and each individual societal position being represented more or less equally—for every weaver there is a king, for every reeve, a juggler. Driskell's focus on life in a castle, for example, excludes "serfs."

Kaye Branch, Faye Boyd, Wanda Buice, Diane Meyer, Frances Mosher, Carla Sisk, and Carol Trusty from Midway Elementary School in Alpharetta, Georgia, created a lesson plan, "Europe in the Middle Ages," that calls for students to "develop an awareness of time and place; develop an understanding of the complex nature of a given culture; and develop an understanding of real and mythical characters."

In their outline's second lesson, Branch et al. reduce feudalism to twelve essential concepts:

   a. Feudalism—a system of life in the Middle Ages in Europe
   b. Lord—one who offered protection in return for loyal service
   c. Vassal—one who gave loyal service
   d. Knight—a soldier on horseback
   e. Manor—the lord's land and possessions
   f. Mill—building for grinding grain into flour
   g. Smithy—building for shaping iron objects
   h. Serfs—peasant farmers who stayed on a given manor
   i. Freedmen—peasant farmers who could move from the manor
   j. Fallow—unused (as in fields)
   k. Moat—water surrounding a castle
   l. Tapestries—a picture of a story woven on cloth, hung on castle walls for decoration and warmth [ibid.].

In keeping with so many other Internet sources, Branch et al. focus on creating some distance from the negative aspects of feudalism, which is surprising given the amount of time grade four students have spent discussing slavery. In the following lesson, Branch et al. discuss chivalry, and include a contemporary "Code of Chivalry," suggesting that teachers should discuss how "knights would treat the ladies, write poems of love, and perform courageous acts of rescue."

Brad Verrell and Brent Johnson's "Medieval Life" addresses the question "what was it like to live in the Middle Ages?" by taking students to the Annual Medieval Fair at the Santa Barbara Fairgrounds. During Verrell and Johnson's 8-day unit, students concentrate on "what it was like to be a knight" and will challenge "antiquated information." Verrell and Johnson, although suggesting that teachers lecture on "the social makeup of the period," limit their questioning of the social order to an exploration of the idea that "who had more money ... was more esteemed." Nowhere do the instructors suggest that students question the validity of the feudal social order, nor do they discuss the inherent class and gender inequities, and the only content specifically related to women is embodied by a solitary reference to "costume."

There are, of course, more enlightened exceptions to the troubling norms. Nancy Twilley's "Black Death: Then and Now," for example, presents a very clear picture of the bubonic plague in fourteenth century Europe, and goes far to refrain from depicting the Middle Ages as being overly ignorant. Twilley's site can be faulted, however, when it immediately attributes sources for contemporary plagues to notions of terrorist attack, including, as one of its examples, Yankee Stadium. Likewise, Kirsten Rooks' work on Discovery Education, "The Middle Ages," goes out of its way to show that the Middle Ages were a time of gross inequalities. In the lesson plan, Rooks explains: "the majority of the people who lived in the Middle Ages were peasants—poor, uneducated laborers who farmed the lord's land and had to give him much of the food. Under the system of feudalism, they belonged to the lord and were not free to leave the land," but almost immediately, Rooks sabotages her good intentions by requiring that students "list the good and bad aspects of this system and discuss how this system could have been changed to be fairer to the peasants."

The lesson plans in this essay are by no means the only ones posted on-line. There are hundreds and hundreds of such creations, geared to all sorts of different levels of education, and generated by a myriad of diverse teachers from across the United States. The ones selected were by no means the most bizarre or badly focused, and unfortunately, represented an utterly random sample, albeit one that has a certain basic sheen of sameness. Most, for example, had something to say about feudalism, but that what they all said basically neglected to mention a few horrible truths is odd.

Ironically, nearly all of these outlines were authored by women, and yet in no syllabus is any mention made of the savage and unequal relationship between men and women that was seen during what was arguably the patriarchy's high water mark. For the most part, these educators romance their young charges with the ever-present image of the knight in shining armor who comes to rescue the damsel in distress and woo her with his cleverly rhyming ballads. Instead of perpetuating a historical falsehood, more teachers should be informing their nine-year-old girls that if this was the Middle Ages, they would not only be denied an education, but would be, in fact, getting ready for a miserable life of servitude, forced marriage and a painful and unnecessary death through multiple childbirths, or that they would be lucky to see their thirtieth birthday. As far as the delicate arts of embroidery and such are concerned, how many nobles would there be in a typical class of 25 eight-year-olds? Probably none.

Why, when the instructors suggested that their students could be divided into social estates, could they not have bleakly looked out at those eager little faces and despairingly informed each and every one that due to the class system everyone in grade four was a peasant. They could have added, in a matter of fact sort of way, that the only child in school who would have had any sort of privileges was perhaps little Timmy in grade six, whose father owned a manor and, by definition, all of the rest of the children in the school.

Today, teachers are under amazing pressure from NCLB, and should be expected to search the Internet for additional materials to use in their classes; but the danger of reproducing inaccurate material is ever present. Entire legions of children are being brought up with a skewed and potentially harmful view of the Middle Ages, one that centers on a flapping dragon being harassed by a little boy wielding a cardboard sword. The seemingly ubiquitous curricular presence of lesson plans introducing the Middle Ages could have presented an ideal opportunity to address some of the wrongs in society that have existed for some time. American students learn about slavery, but how many "white" children understand that their ancestors in many and perhaps most cases were also slaves?

In searching for accurate and meaningful material, teachers should rely first and foremost on academic sources. Most teaching professionals should have access to the EBSCO databases, for example, and should limit their searches to refereed, full-text documents. The best way to teach a child about medieval trade between the Far East and Europe is to read a few academic articles and condense the material into a form appropriate to a given grade level. Google and other popular search engines should be viewed with suspicion and, if possible, entirely avoided. If the World Wide Web is to be consulted at all, the best sites are those maintained by practicing medievalists, sites such as Luminarium, the Medieval Sourcebook, and the Medieval Labyrinth. In the Minnesota survey, for example, one of the findings was that few teachers used discussion boards, and yet, those too, especially those where there are eager graduate students to be found, could be exceptionally useful resources. Another thing teachers could do to make the process of creating a detailed and accurate lesson plan in an essentially alien subject is to educate themselves regarding safe searching strategies. Many teachers, even at this late date, are new to using the World Wide Web, and could benefit from some basic courses in online research. These few steps could perhaps represent a way forward, offering some progress toward a new teaching goal: a treatment of the Middle Ages that, while necessarily incomplete, is at least intelligent.

Works Cited

California State Board of Education. *History–Social Science Content Standards for California Public Schools, Kindergarten Through Grade Twelve.* Ed. Bob Klingensmith, Greg Geeting, and Gregory F. McGinity. Sacramento, Calif.: 2000. http://www.cde.ca.gov/re/pn/fd/documents/histsocsci-stnd.pdf. Accessed on July 24, 2006.

U.S. Department of Education. Office of Educational Research and Improvement. National Center for Education Statistics. *The Nation's Report Card: U.S. History 2001, NCES 2002–483.* Ed. M.S. Lapp, W.S. Grigg, and B.S.-H. Tay-Lim. Washington, D.C.: 2002. http://nces.ed.gov/nationsreportcard/pdf/main2001/2002483.pdf. Accessed on July 24, 2006.

U.S. Department of Education, National Center for Education Statistics, Private School Universe Survey (PSS), 2001–2002. http://nces.ed.gov/surveys/pss/tables/table_15.asp. Accessed on July 24, 2006.

U.S. Department of Education. Institute of Education Sciences, National Center for Education Statistics. "NAEP Questions." Accessed on July 24, 2006.

Blanton, Ruth, Shirley Finney and Becky Woodard. "Knight's Quest." *Nashville Schools.* Available at http://www.nashville-schools.davidson.k12.tn.us/CurriculumAwards/knightsquest/knightsquest.htm. Accessed December 1, 2005.

Branch, Kay, Faye Boyd, Wanda Buice, Dianne Meyer, Frances Mosher, Carla Sisk and Carol Trusty. "Europe in the Middle Ages." *Core Knowledge.* Available at http://www.core-knowledge.org/CK/resrcs/lessons/498EuropeMidAges.htm. Accessed December 1, 2005.

Clark, Shanetia P. "Watch Out for the Fool's Gold! Searching for Internet Treasures for Teachers." *The Clearing House* 76.6 (July/August 2003): 292–294.

Driskell, Trudy. "Life Inside Castle Walls." Available at http://pt3.d.uh.edu/lessonplan/lessonplansee2.cfm?ID=55. Accessed December 1, 2005.

Hughes, Sherick A. "Some canaries left behind? Evaluating a state-endorsed lesson plan database and its social construction of who and what counts." *International Journal of Inclusive Education* 9.2 (April–June 2005): 105–138.

Johnson, Diana. "From the Horse's Mouth: How Our Teachers Are Using the Internet." *Museums and the Web 2000.* http://www.archimuse.com/mw2000/papers/johnsond/johnsond.html. Accessed on July 24, 2006.

Kinnard, Carla. "Knighthood and Chivalry." *Education World.* Available at http://www.-education-world.com/a_tsl/archives/01–1/lesson0020.shtml. Accessed December 1, 2005.

Rooks, Kirsten. "The Middle Ages." *Discovery Education: Discoveryschool.com.* Available at http://school.discovery.com/lessonplans/programs/timesmedieval/. Accessed December 1, 2005.

Twilley, Nancy. "Black Death: Then and Now." *SuccessLink*. Available at http://www.successlink.org/gti/gti_lesson.asp?lid=4156. Accessed December 1, 2005.

Verrell, Brad, and Brent Johnson. "Medieval Life." *Education Planet*. Available at http://www.educationplanet.com/extension/Medieval.html. Accessed December 1, 2005.

Walker, Nancy. and Libbie Poole. "Untitled." Available through the *Internet Archive* at http://web.archive.org/web/20021212231349/http://www.libsci.sc.edu/miller/Midage.htm. Accessed December 1, 2005.

11 Virtually Medieval

The Age of Kings *Interprets the Middle Ages*

DANIEL T. KLINE

To begin, an anecdote. I walked into my office at home to check my e-mail a few years ago and was met with the following scene: one of my sons sat at the computer, playing an online game and chatting with other players via the embedded chat function. At the same time, he cradled the phone receiver between his ear and shoulder to give another friend tips for playing a different game. How old was he? Seven.

Having had access to computer technology and digital media throughout their educational careers, these are the kids who are beginning to enter our college classrooms, and to whom text-messaging, video gaming, and multi-media composition come naturally. As Cynthia Selfe and Gail Hawisher have shown, new technological literacies create new forms of expression, and as James Gee has demonstrated, playing computer video games instills into players complex forms of technological literacy and new varieties of sociality. In fact, this cultural moment marks the first time that younger generations know more than their elders about the new media.

In other words, computer and video games are teaching tools, and rather than decry them as inconsequential "kid stuff" or sniff at their profligate anachronisms, academics should rather understand video games and account for them in their teaching. As a medievalist, I argue in this essay that medieval-themed video games reveal a constellation of related ideas that influence a game player's understanding of the Middle Ages, some consciously articulated as part of the game world, others less consciously facilitated by the implicit and ideological dimensions of the game design and playing process. So, in the same way movies are often seen as a contemporary expressions of "medievalism"—the modern appropriation of the themes, tropes, characters, stories, and images characteristic of the Middle Ages—so too computer games provide a privileged avenue of entry into current representations (and contemporary understandings) of the medieval period.[1] In this essay I examine the *Age of Empires II: The Age of Kings* (*AOE2*), a 1999 Ensemble Studios–Microsoft computer game that focuses explicitly upon "the Middle Ages," as an implicit argument about the nature of history itself and as a pedagogical tool that imbues players with a specific historical sensibility concerning the medieval period.[2] As I analyze *AOE2* game play, I will outline the historical ideas and cultural implications central to the game and pertinent in the classroom, even when academically suspect.

Although, to the uninitiated, the acronym laden world of videogaming can seem dense and impenetrable, knowing the terminology is essential to understanding game formats and objectives. Real time strategy (RTS) games, like the *Age of Empires* (*AOE*) series or *Warcraft*, pit player against player(s) or computer AI (artificial intelligence) in a struggle to develop a superior civilization or to defeat the opposition in battle. In RTS games, all players operate simultaneously in real time. In contrast, turn based strategy (TBS) games, like *Medieval Total War* or *Civilization*, set player against player (or AI), except that players take turns making decisions and thus react to each other's strategic and tactical choices in sequence. Role playing games (RPGs) like *Baldur's Gate* and *Fable*, allow the player to build a character (or "avatar") by exploring terrain, defeating enemies, solving puzzles, forging alliances, and developing skills like spellcasting or diplomacy, or purchasing goods like food, weaponry, and armor. In first person shooters (FPSs), the often ultra-violent "shoot 'em ups" like *Doom*, *Quake*, *Half-Life*, and *Halo*, the player interacts with the gaming world through the avatar's first person perspective. In a third person shooter (TPS) or action-adventure (AA) game, like *Grand Theft Auto*, the player maneuvers a computer-generated figure within the game world, as in an RPG. TPSs and AAs, like FPSs, are some of the most violent games and garner the most media attention. Massively multiplayer online role playing games (MMORPGs), like the hugely popular *World of Warcraft*, *EverQuest*, *The Sims*, or *Diablo II*, put thousand of players from across the world into different "realms" where they interact with one another's characters and create online communities (often called "guilds") based upon their character "classes" or "races." RTS and TBS games differ from most RPG, MMORPG, and FPS games in that the player controls an entire culture in the former but most often a single character in the latter. Like *AOE*, many FPS, RPG, RTS, and TBS games can be played online against a number of opponents or in single-player mode against the computer AI.

The *Age of Empires* series itself now boasts five titles, each building upon the previous one, chronologically and technically. *Age of Empires* (1997) covers the "stone age" Ancient Near East; *Age of Empires: The Rise of Rome* (1998) depicts the classical world centered in the Mediterranean basin; *Age of Empires II: The Age of Kings* (1999), the focus of this paper, portrays the medieval epoch across Eurasia; *Age of Empires II: The Conquerors Expansion* (2000) represents the early modern period and the Atlantic expansion; and most recently, *Age of Empires III* (2005) dramatizes the colonial era in North America.[3] The games all follow a similar trajectory: players develop their chosen civilizations from "simpler" into more "complex" forms by progressing through developmental stages while competing against other players or the game AI. In the *Age of Empires* series, each stage of development requires a balance of economic growth (gathering resources), strategic planning (developing offensive and defensive military forces or fostering diplomatic ties with other cultures), and technological progress (building new types of structures and acquiring new technologies). In turn, each historical stage allows the civilization access to more advanced technologies ("upgrades" earned by payment in resources like wood, food, gold, and stone) that supplement the civilization's structures, units, and capabilities in a race to defeat the other civilizations. So, in the same way that "history" is indelibly shaped by the basic presuppositions informing any investigation, so too *AOE2*, like the other *AOE* games, posits a simple, single overarching supposition that effects all other aspects of the game and provides the first historical lesson: *(1) History is understood as a narrative with a definable origin and explicit destiny, and cultures prosper through territorial expansion and by exploiting natural resources.* As a product of 20th century global capitalism, *AOE2* reflects the culture that created it.

Age of Empires II: Age of Kings
Opening Gambits

AOE2 depicts the medieval period and challenges a player to build a civilization from the "Dark Age" to the "post–Imperial Age"; to strike a productive balance between economic necessity, cultural development, and military power; and to defend that culture against competing cultures. *AOE2*'s opening screen, figuratively placing the player on a cobblestone street into the medieval world, confronts a player with the first of many choices that decide game play. Players can choose the learning scenario, single player mode, a multiplayer (online) game, the custom map editor, and the brief historical write-ups describing *AOE2*'s medieval topics and game play scenarios. The opening screen does not yet reveal the different civilizations available to the player. Rather, as indicated in the right hand column, *AOE2* presents four game types (in addition to player designed campaigns and scenarios). A *Historical Campaign* enacts a series of events related to an important historical personality like William Wallace, Joan of Arc, Frederick Barbarossa, Ghengis Khan, or Saladin, each of whom is described in the brief, competent essays under "History." A *Death Match* begins with huge reserves of wood, food, gold, and stone so that players get right into battle and do not have to gather resources to build a civilization from scratch. In a *Regicide* game, the object is to kill the opposition's king. In a *Random Map*, the standard *AOE2* game type, players choose one of thirteen civilizations and win the game by destroying all enemies (military conquest), accumulating the highest total score (social advancement), or building a wonder or holding all the relics on the map for 300 game years (cultural achievement). Herein lies the second lesson of *AOE2*, even before a player initiates a game: *(2) History can be viewed from different perspectives, and cultural development can be motivated by different forces.* *AOE2* implicitly embodies different historiographical conceptions in these game types—"history" might be seen as a unified narrative (as in a Historical Campaign) or as the chaotic totality of events at a particular locale (as in a Random Map), while cultural development can be motivated by different forces like the life and death of a powerful monarch (as in a Regicide) or acquisition of overwhelming economic and military superiority (as in a Death Match).

After choosing the game type, players can also control other game factors, and at this point players can select one of thirteen medieval civilizations, each of which is described in a brief essay in the *AOE2* manual:

AOE2's Thirteen Civilizations

1. Britons	6. Goths	11. Teutons
2. Byzantines	7. Japanese	12. Turks
3. Celts	8. Mongols	13. Vikings
4. Chinese	9. Persians	
5. Franks	10. Saracens	

With the choice of civilizations, *AOE2* teaches a third lesson: *(3) History occurs in places other than contemporary Europe, and cultures are not isolated entities.* Although the Vikings and Mongols probably never interacted as depicted in the game, and the Saracens, Persians, and Byzantines actually describe the same region at different times, *AOE2* describes medieval history as a Eurasian, rather than Western European, phenomenon, giving it a greater cultural breadth than is depicted in many classrooms. Likewise, although the game does not highlight religious conflict *per se*, it does depict Islamic as well as Christian (and Far Eastern) civilizations.

In addition to being able select from thirteen different civilizations, the trick to "replayability" is to provide a number of player-controlled variables, which allow *AOE2* to be customized, altered, and otherwise varied according to the player's preferences. In *AOE2*, players can select one of five difficulty settings, include up to seven different players, designate thirteen different map types in six different sizes, specify the civilization's population limit from 25 to 200 units (in increments of 25), designate three different map conditions, specify one of six starting periods, and select one of four victory scenarios. Players can also establish up to four teams, allow their civilization access to all game technologies, and record the game play for later replay and analysis. In the normal gameworld display, all territories but the player's own are blacked out, and the territory is revealed only when it is explored by the player's units.

For all but the Historical Campaigns, whose maps loosely mimic actual terrain, *AOE2* random map designs range from *Arabia* (desert plateaus with little wood) and *Continental* (a large land mass surrounded by water), to the *Black Forest* (dense forest with small clearings) and *Small Islands* (small archipelagos surrounded by water), or the *Fortress* (a pre-fab walled enclosure) and *Gold Rush* (central stores of gold).[4] These topographical options convey the fourth lesson of *AOE2*: *(4) History occurs differentially in particular places, and cultures are indelibly shaped by their physical environment and geographical placement.* The most important variable in *AOE2* is its physical positioning in the gameworld, for the proportion of forest versus open vista; the distribution of resources like wood, food, gold, and stone; the severity or simplicity of topographical gradients; and the presence or absence of oceans and rivers determines the immediate priorities for developing a civilization. Therefore, different civilizations experience their own distinct histories at the same time other cultures experience theirs. So, for example, while Japan's development during the medieval period differed from the Britons', their commonality as maritime societies creates a point of contact amidst their profound differences, and the presence of navigable waterways determines the necessity for building docks, harvesting fish, developing a navy, and defending the coastline, while a landlocked map presents a smaller set of tactical difficulties.

AOE2 Game Play: Civilization Building

The goal of *AOE2* game play is to develop chosen civilizations through four distinct eras:

Table 1: *AOE2* Historical Stages

Period	*AOE2 Description*
1. The Dark Age	Following the fall of Rome, western Europe entered what has been called the Dark Ages. This name was applied partially because so much of the Roman civilization was destroyed and replaced by a more barbaric culture. The name was used also because so little written history survived from the period that sheds light on the events that took place.
2. The Feudal Age	The predominant economic and political structure of the Middle Ages was feudalism. This system evolved in response to a breakdown in central authority and a rise in social chaos following the end of Roman rule. A hierarchy of strongmen in allegiance replaced the Roman system of emperor, senate, province, city, and town.
3. The Castle Age	Beginning in the ninth century, local strongmen began dotting the landscape of Europe with castles. These were first of simple design and construction but evolved into stone strongholds. Many of these belonged to kings or the vassals of kings, but the majority appear to have been built out of self-interest by local nobles....
4. The Imperial Age	The rise of the great kings and their quest for empire brought about the final segment of the Middle Ages that can be called the Imperial Age. The feudal system was being replaced by kings at the head of nations in England, France, Spain, and Scandinavia. Trade was booming and cities were growing in size and power.... Technology and learning surpassed that of the ancient world. Firearms and other innovations brought an end to the military dominance of knights and castles. Events marking the end of the period include the fall of Constantinople in 1453, the first use of the printing press in 1456, the European discovery of the Americas in 1492, the Protestant Reformation, triggered by Martin Luther in 1517, and the flowering of the arts in Italy.[6]

Although I am not aware of any academic schema that matches *AOE2*'s periodization, nor are the periods identified according to a consistent principle of classification, a basic assumption remains consistent— that history progresses through stages. Here is then the fifth essential lesson of *AOE2*: *(5) History moves through explicitly differentiated periods, and cultures develop in distinctive ways during the same historical moment.* Players simultaneously develop their cultures in a race for cultural, technological, and social superiority.

In a typical *AOE2* Random Map game, the basic *AOE2* game type, players begin in the Dark Age with three villagers, a town center, a mounted scout, and a modicum of resources (200 units of wood, 200 food, 100 gold, and 200 stone).[7] Villagers, like the civilization's other units, speak what seem to be snippets of the original language, and these peasant figures build lumber camps, mining camps, and mills to collect wood, gold, stone and food respectively. The villagers also build all the necessary structures that allow the civilization to move into the next era. In the Dark Age, villagers fashion a barracks, wooden palisade walls, and elevated outposts for defense. They also can fashion a dock, from which fishing boats net fish and will yield trade and combat vessels in later ages. The constant accumulation of resources and a strong peasant population is absolutely necessary for further development. This is the basis of the sixth lesson: *(6) Historical development requires an extensive, compliant labor force, and cultural development requires an economic base that provides the raw material for further progress.* It might not be too much to say that the extensive use of villagers in *AOE2* creates the opening for a Marxist analysis of both videogaming and medieval culture.

The three categories of buildings in the Dark Age also denote the three primary cultural spheres in the *AOE* series—the social (town center), the economic (resource camps), and the military (barracks)—again, all built by villagers. In *AOE2*, players immediately have to balance each of these cultural demands as they develop their strategy. For example, generating a villager at the town center (who can also gather more resources and build other structures) requires 50 units of food; a house that sustains 5 units of population requires 50 units of wood; a barracks that creates infantry needs 175 units of wood; a dock that can generate fishing boats (and later warships) needs 150 units of wood. In a Random Map game, villagers can pick berries, hunt deer or boar, and gather fish; alternatively, an aggressive player can develop a small army of militia at this early stage to knock out an opponent, so it is also important to have a few infantry for defense as well. This forms the seventh lesson: *(7) History is shaped by the interaction of cultural, social, and military forces, and cultures must balance economic, social, and military priorities to survive long term. Short-term overinvestment in any one area spells defeat.*

After building two Dark Age structures (a barracks; a house, mill, and/or dock) and gathering 500 units of food, players advance into the Feudal Age, where new social, economic, and military options become available. Players can add a blacksmith, an archery range, and a stable to their military structures; upgrade their militia to men-at-arms (the basic swordsman) and add skirmishers (spear-throwing militia) to their military. They can also construct stone walls and gates; build trade cogs, small transports, and military galleys at the docks; and add farms to their mills or town centers. Adding a blacksmith enables players to create different grades of armor (improving defense), fletching for projectiles (raising accuracy), and advance smelting techniques (upgrading weapons' strength and efficiency). Town center upgrades enable villagers to use wheelbarrows and thereby increase their productivity.

In the Feudal Age, players must continue to husband resources and balance social needs (villagers gathering wood, food, gold, and stone and building houses for every 5 units of population) against military contingencies (whether to opt for a defensive or offensive strategy and spend resources on military units) and trading opportunities. Players might advance quickly from the Dark to the Feudal Age but have drawn their resources too thin and be vulnerable to attack. Players might likewise stay in the Dark Age a little longer to be in a better economic position (that is, accumulate more resources) once they advance into the Feudal Age, but may fall behind technologically. Significantly, however, only villagers are depicted as both male and female in *AOE2* (other than in the Historical Campaigns), so the "lower classes" are the only strata of society to display gender differentiation. This simple distinction betrays the eighth lesson: (8) *History is conducted primarily by males, but cultural advancement depends upon the labor contributions of both males and females. History might be made "from above" but requires those "from below."*

The Feudal Age also enables players to build a market through which they can buy and sell wood, food, and stone. The technological upgrades associated with the market, such as building trade carts and researching cartography and coinage, also allow players to create diplomatic alliances. These upgrades allow players to notify their allies when attacked or to ask when they need additional resources. A player can also convey tribute to another player via the "diplomacy" screen. Clever players can also turn a neutral or even an enemy player toward their side with massive resource donations—economic bribes, as it were. After building a market, players can then improve their civilizations through peaceful trading rather than military conquest alone. So, while the term "Feudal" might be rather inaccurately applied to this stage, *AOE2* does introduce the possibility of political alliance based upon tribute, trade, and treaty at a relatively realistic stage of social development. The ninth historical lesson emerges here: (9) *Although history is a teleological narrative based upon technological (particularly military) progress, cultures may use trade and diplomacy to improve their particular situations.*

After building two Feudal Age buildings and gathering at least 800 units of food and 200 of gold, players then advance to the Castle Age. At this point, the military technologies available to the civilizations broaden considerably. As the name implies, the primary achievement of the Castle Age is to build a castle. Because castles are resource intensive (requiring 650 stone), the reward for building one is equally high, for a castle supports 25 units (villagers, soldiers, ships, and siege weapons) and it is well-defended. More importantly, the castle is the home of the trebuchet, *AOE2*'s ballistic missile, and is the source of a civilization's unique military unit. The full repertoire of unique units for *AOE2* is as follows:

Table 2: Each Civilization's Unique Military Units

Civilization	Unique Unit	Medieval Historical Parallel
Britons	Longbowman (ranged infantry)	Famed archers in the Hundred Years' War
Franks	Throwing Axeman (ranged infantry)	Frankish axe-bearing infantry
Goths	Huskarl (armored infantry)	Germanic chieftain's personal retinue
Teutons	Teutonic Knight (powerful infantry)	Knights of the crusading orders
Celts	Woad Raider (speedy infantry)	William Wallace's troops
Vikings	Berserker (self-healing infantry)	Viking warriors in hand-to-hand combat
	Longboat (fleet & maneuverable boats)	Viking raids in shallow-draft vessels
Byzantines	Cataphract (heavy cavalry)	Ancient & medieval mounted infantry
Turks	Janissary (ranged infantry)	Islamic hand-cannoneers
Saracens	Mameluke (ranged cavalry)	Camel-mounted Arabic cavalry
Persians	War Elephant (powerful infantry)	None—Reminiscent of Hannibal
Mongols	Mangudai (ranged cavalry)	Mongolian mounted warriors
Chinese	Chu Ko Nu (ranged infantry)	Chinese repeating crossbow
Japanese	Samurai (bladed infantry)	Traditional Japanese warrior class

Adding to the military possibilities, the Castle Ages also allows players to build a siege works, which creates different grades of battering ram, catapult, scorpion (large crossbow), and eventually, in the Imperial Age, bombard cannons. Players who thrive into the Castle Age often have many villagers gathering resources, a variety of military units (including bladed, horsed, and bowed weapons), at least a few siege weapons (especially trebuchets for long range attack and defense), suitable defensive fortifications (particularly walls and guard towers), and a number of technological upgrades that keep all the units productive and efficient.

The Castle Age also enables the building of the university and the monastery, both potent sources of social, cultural, and technological advancement. The university, home of scientific thinking in the *AOE2* gameworld, provides for advanced building techniques (upgrading wall and building strength) and ballistic innovations (making more accurate, longer, and more damaging siege weapons and watch towers), while the monastery, site of literary technologies, creates only one unit, the highly upgradeable monk (with seven additional upgradeable skills available). The monk can heal injured troops and convert enemy units and buildings. Perhaps most importantly, and with a realistic nod toward the medieval traffic in saints and relics, when a monk returns a relic to his home monastery, it generates gold automatically, and seizing all the relics on a map triggers a cultural win within 400 game-years.

Advancing from the Castle to the Imperial Age additionally entails collecting 1000 food, 800 gold, and building at least one castle or two Castle Age buildings. However, the Imperial Age offers no new structures except a "wonder" (a civilization's unique historical structure). The strength of the Imperial Age is in advancing the technologies developed in previous periods. For example, chemistry, researched at the university, allows for gunpowder units and explosives; illumination and block printing, researched at the monastery, upgrade the monk's abilities. The secret behind the system of upgrading and advancement in *AOE2* is the "technology tree." It describes the buildings, units, and technologies available to each civilization. For example, the lowly logging camp, a staple of the Dark Age, is upgraded through the addition of the double bit axe in the Feudal Age, the bow saw in the Castle Age, and finally the two man hand saw in the Imperial Age. The rapid acquisition of additional upgraded units assists players in their move toward victory, whether in a timed, point-based game; a relic or wonder victory; a trade and diplomatic strategy; or the ever-popular military conquest scenario.

The trick to "balancing" the game is to allocate each building, unit, and technology relative strengths and weaknesses and to assign each civilization a unique military unit. For example, the Vikings exclusively have extra quick longboats in addition to the normal complement of vessels available to the other cultures, but they lack cavalry units. The Goths, with their unique huskarl, lack gates, walls, and towers but have increased resource gathering abilities. The Japanese have the samurai and extra powerful archers, but lack some of the advanced siege weapons. Unique units, created at the castle (except for Viking longboats), are upgradeable to even more powerful elite units. *AOE2*'s attention to the unique military unit conveys the tenth historical lesson: *(10) The engine of the historical process is military advancement, and cultural clashes via military conflict are essentially unavoidable.* The strengths and vulnerabilities of every unit in *AOE2* are precisely calculated. Each unit has a total number of hit points, as reckoned against the unit's attack points, armor rating, range, speed, and special attack bonus. For example, the elite hurskarl's attributes are as follows: 70 HP / 12 Attack / 0–6 Armor / 0 Range / S Speed + Bonus vs. buildings and archers. In essence, all *AOE2* civilizations begin at the same point, with only slight differences in developmental possibilities and culturally unique units. Thus, the necessity for balancing the game ideologically reproduces distinctly contemporary American notions of equality (Hayot and Wesp, "Reading" para. 27).

AOE2 *Architecture: A Medieval Mash Up*

AOE2 therefore also incorporates a contemporary multicultural element into gameplay, for each civilization has distinctive attributes that facilitate its success against other civilizations in the race for dominance. For example, all cultures begin with identical Dark Age structures (a simple town center, fabric dwellings, wooden barracks, mule-powered mill, and so on), but four different regional architectures emerge as the civilizations advance: Far Eastern architecture features pagoda-like structures, Near Eastern offers Islamic stylizations, Northern European creates crenellated parapets, and Western European offers Romanesque- and Tudor-inspired buildings. These four regional architectures then branch out into each civilization's unique "wonder," the epitome of cultural development which can be built only in the Imperial Age. For the most part, each wonder has a recognizable affinity to its historical culture, and coincident to its name, a wonder is the most valuable structure a culture can build (requiring 1000 units each of wood, food, gold, and stone). The Japanese (representative of the Far Eastern style) feature a monumental pagoda; the Turks (Middle Eastern) sport a grand mosque with four minarets; the Vikings (Northern European) in a nice touch display a striking stave church; and the Franks (Western European) display a Chartres-like cathedral's west façade and nave. The tension between military advancement (in the unique military unit) and cultural attainment (in the wonder) leads to the eleventh historical lesson: *(11) "Culture" (understood as social attainment) is subservient to, and dependent upon, "History" (understood as technological progress) in the same way that an* AOE2 *wonder can be constructed only after some degree of military success.*

What is most likely to drive medievalists to distraction is the historical nature of the synchronic game play. One might be able to accept the notion of historical stages but there's no way the Mongols should be on the same screen as the Vikings, at least as they are each depicted in *AOE2*. However, this synchronic blending of different cultures, themes, and media is commonplace in contemporary popular culture, where movies like *The Matrix* easily intermingle disparate mythological motifs and contemporary philosophy, where amateur technophiles remix popular music on their home computers, where youthful videographers document their own lives at media Web sites like myspace.com, and where gamers collaborate with others around the globe in MMORPGs like *World of Warcraft*. Despite its many historical flaws, *AOE2* gives a more accurate sense of the inherent "messiness" of history, its irreducible clutter and jumble, than the tidy stories told in many textbooks. In this sense, even the postmodern pastiche of the Briton's wonder in *AOE2* is a defiant exemplar of what is both exactly wrong and exactly right about *AOE2*. Although this *AOE2* wonder is not the representation of a real building, it references a number of English cathedrals in a postmodern hybrid structure: the tower, topped by four small spires, recalls Blackburn, Canterbury, and Derby; the single spire atop the tower cites Sheffield, Salisbury, and Norwich; the gothic choir section, with hints of stained glass windows and flying buttresses, resembles Lincoln, Winchester, and Worcester; while the dome references St. Paul's (not strictly a medieval structure).[8] At the same time, the Briton's *AOE2* wonder represents something essential about many medieval structures, which were often constructed over centuries and incorporate widely different architectural styles. The best example might be Mont St. Michel, the popular pilgrimage site just off the coast of Normandy, with its combination Romanesque nave, Gothic choir, and dramatic central spire. The "mash-up" is not simply a contemporary phenomenon.

Temporal and Spatial Complexity in AOE2

While *AOE2* essentializes the idea of historical periodization, the game itself also represents a "period" in a different real-world chronological sequence. From its first release, the *AOE* series has become increasingly sophisticated in game play and has required increasingly powerful technology. For example, the 1997 *Age of Empires* requires a Pentium 90, 16 MB RAM, a CD-ROM drive, and 74 MB of hard drive storage (187 MB including pre-game cinematics). The 1999 *AOE2* requires, at a minimum, a Pentium 166, 32 MB RAM, 4X CD-ROM, 300 MB space, Win 95/98, and a 2Mb video card.[9] These increasingly demanding technological requirements embody another important historical lesson—technology drives innovation, innovation advances game play, advanced game play demonstrates advanced culture. So, the release history of *AOE* parallels the historical ideology embodied in the game itself, for the progress of history is dependent upon technological innovation.

Within this technological history, it is perhaps easiest to visualize the complex temporality of *AOE2* in terms of a three dimensional x, y, and z coordinate field. The x-axis indicates the diachronic progress of a civilization in the gameworld through historical stages from the Dark Age to the Imperial Age. The y-axis represents the synchronic development of the civilization within each developmental period within the game. The z-axis demarks those temporal dimensions "outside the box" and often under control of the player. These can include *game duration* (whether the game itself can be completed in months or years [long], days or weeks [medium], or hours [short]); *absorption rate* refers to how quickly a player "gets into the game"; *play rate* indicates how quickly game elements proceed or proliferate; and *advancement rate* names how quickly the game play progresses.[10] For *AOE2*, the play and advancement rates are tied to *game speed* (which can be set to slow, normal, or fast at the opening screen). Players can increase or decrease the speed at which the game is played and create easier or more difficult game play. Thus, the experience of passing time within the game world can be manipulated according to the player's preferences—a fluidity not unlike that experienced, depending upon the exigencies of the moment, in the "real world." Of course, in *AOE2* victory and defeat are also objective, measurable outcomes to be mapped against the segmentation of time, and in the manner of an ergonomic time-work efficiency study, victory and defeat can be parsed six different ways. Over and against the more ambiguous reality of defining victory in cultural or military conflict, *AOE2* allows a post-mortem examination of the game play. Players can analyze the total score, military stats, economy stats, technology stats, and society stats. Each of these are mapped against each civilization's total population (divided between villagers and military units) and each culture's relative achievement of the four historical stages.

The experience of time and the calculation of victory in *AOE2* is equally tied to the appropriation of space. One of the primary ideological effects *AOE2* enacts, as in other strategy games like the *Civilization* series, is that the land upon which the game civilizations develop is always previously undeveloped and uninhabited. Like the American myth of Manifest Destiny, the land in *AOE2* is "empty" and invites settlement and expansion. Simultaneously, *AOE2* collapses under the term "civilization" a number of historical and cultural differences and attenuates historical specificity. It also accentuates the idea of historical contingency; that is, history might have, could have, and may indeed really be other than what we think it was, for each historical choice occurs within a range of alternate possibilities.[11] It is only in retrospect that such choices seem necessary. At the same time, *AOE2* naturalizes perhaps the most contrived and artificial thing we academics "do to history," and that is to divide it up artificially into segments that seem to be coherent, on the basis of an arbitrary conceptual principle. In *The Postmodern Condition* (28), Fredric Jameson is correct, I think, in his assessment of the crisis in periodization:

> The larger issue is that of the representation [of] History itself. There is in other words a synchronic version of the problem: that of the status of an individual "period" in which everything becomes so seamlessly interrelated that we confront either a total system or an idealistic "concept" of a period: and a diachronic one, in which history is seen in some "linear" way as the succession of such periods, stages, or moments.[12]

Yet because *AOE2* naturalizes *and* operationalizes the crisis of periodization both synchronically and diachronically in a form alien to academics, *AOE2* also creates the possibility for questioning the notion of periodization itself both within the gameworld and in the classroom. So, the replayability of games like *AOE2*, while "unrealistic," does present the opportunity to rethink "history."

Valorizing the Visual

By way of conclusion, another anecdote. During a class discussion concerning affective piety and religious devotion in the Middle Ages, I asked if anyone knew what an "icon" was. There was one of those rather long silences, until a student raised her hand tentatively and said, "It's one of those little pictures on the computer screen that you click to make something happen." Initially chagrined, I was then struck by the pertinence of the analogy between the religious and technological definitions of "icon," and as a class we began to chart out the correspondences: both are gateways into a kind of invisible, even metaphysical realm; both require a specialized knowledge to understand and properly implement; both are "overdetermined" in that they pack an entire history into a rather simple image; both enable, to the uninitiated, a kind of power, or even magic.

The data compressed into the spatial field of the *AOE2* gameworld provides a living, contemporary analogue to any program of medieval stained glass, statuary, or iconography. As a simple glance at the game demonstrates, the *AOE2* game screen is separated into three separate planes of information: an upper statistical border, the large central playing screen, and a lower informational region. In the upper region, the icons to the left indicate the amount of wood, food, gold, and stone available to the player and the civilization's population; the icons to the right denote game objectives, the civilization's tech tree, a chat channel, the diplomacy screen, and the main menu. The central screen provides a close-up view of the gameworld, and it is here that the player develops the civilization. The lower plane, the most informationally dense region of the interface, itself is partitioned into three sections. The leftmost icons indicate the options and upgrades available to a selected unit or building; the central icons specify the number and type of the selected units, and the rightmost icons encircle a miniature gameworld map.

The miniature gameworld map is in itself another complex iconographic representation: The central diamond depicts the entire gameworld, and the central screen view is indicated by a rectangle outline. The mini-map is surrounded by eight additional icons: (on the upper side from left to right) a signal allies icon; statistics, help, and advanced command icons; and (on the lower side from left to right) an idle villager icon, and specific mini-map designations for all units, combat units, and economic units. I detail these aspects of the *AOE2* screen not so much to belabor the obvious as to make the point that players learn these icons and their functions as second nature as they become more experienced. To reflect upon the *AOE2* game screen—or any video game screen—as a technological image to be read, interpreted, understood, and operated much like a religious icon is to see an essential point of contact between the medieval and contemporary periods, and to recognize that contemporary gamers operate within this complex iconographic environment with an ease that would be the envy of many art historians is to grant to the gaming generation a complex literacy that can and should be harnessed in our classrooms to the benefit of medieval studies.

The title of this essay thus reflects my pedagogical approach to medieval videogaming: Medieval-themed video games are *virtually medieval* in that (1) they are *nearly but not quite* accurate representations of the Middle Ages. At the same time, (2) they are *in fact* or *to all intents and purposes* stimulating and provocative representations of the Middle Ages; and simultaneously (3) they are virtual representations, or more specifically, *digital simulacra* of *a* Middle Ages. Instead of the scholar's ideal—the laconic image of a real Middle Ages that existed in some place and at some time—video game representations of the medieval period are Baudrillardian *simulacrum*: the copy of an original that never existed.[13] Even so, these digital simulacra of the Middle Ages create persistent effects in the real world as they influence gamers' ideas about the medieval period. Rather than demonstrating to me how terribly popular culture gets history "wrong," these games remind me that even the most extensively researched, closely argued, and academically nuanced rendering of the expanse of time we call "the Middle Ages" is, in its own way, simply a different kind of discursive account prone to its own ideological investments and material deficiencies.[14] Medieval video games can teach medieval specialists as well as gamers.

Notes

1. See, for example, Kevin J. Harty's *The Reel Middle Ages* (Jefferson, N.C.: McFarland, 1999).

2. I will generally cite games by their generic or series titles. Likewise, although console games (which use a controller to connect the player to the gaming platform), video games (which utilize a video display), and computer games (which can be video or text based and played on a computer through the keyboard and/or mouse) are technically different, I will use the general terms "video game" or "computer game" in reference to the *Age of Empires* games.

3. The *Age of Empires* series features two additional titles: *The Age of Mythology* (2002) and the *Age of Mythology: The Titans Expansion* (2003). These games, which offer the deities and mythological creatures of the Greco-Roman, Egyptian, Norse, and (with the expansion pack) Atlantean civilizations, are outside the chronology of the historical *Age of Empires* games. Eric Hayot and Edward Wesp, in "Strategy and Mimesis," 407, confuse *Age of Empires II: The Age of Kings* (1999) with the next release in the series, *Age of Empires II: The Conquerors Expansion* (2000).

4. *AOE2*'s map types include Arabia, Archipelago, Baltic, Black Forest, Coastal, Continental, Fortress, Gold Rush, Highland, Islands, Mediterranean, Rivers, Team Islands, and Random.

5. The descriptions are taken from the in-game descriptions under the History link on the opening screen. The *Age of Empires II: Age of Kings* manual (Redmond, Wash.: Microsoft, 2000), provides more detailed write-ups (pp. 31–32).

6. The *AOE2* in-game note on "The Middle Ages" helpfully also states that "historic periods in Asia and the Middle East do not fit easily into the concept of a European Middle Age. China evolved gradually from prehistoric times up to the advent of Western modern history without the great disruptions that befell Europe. China passed under the control of several dynasties and suffered from invasion, but the basic culture progressed steadily. Japan progressed steadily, as well, and was left largely alone. The history of the Middle East fits together more closely with the European Middle Ages because these two regions were adjacent and shared many interactions."

7. From a medievalist's perspective, it is important to note that the term "the Dark Ages" is not applied to the medieval period in general, and the *AOE2* manual (like the brief historical write-ups available from the opening screen) correctly denotes that the "Dark Ages" refers more to the paucity of information available concerning the several centuries after the Fall of Rome than a *de facto* primitive civilization.

8. To review a range of English cathedrals, see "English Cathedrals in Music and Photographs," http://www.english-cathedrals.freewebspace.com/.

9. In contrast, the 2005 release of *Age of Empires III* needs Windows XP, 256 MB RAM, a high-speed CD-ROM, 2 GB of hard drive space (not including the extensive cinematics), and a 3-D accelerator card.

10. For my z-axis, I have slightly revised the terms from Wood et al., p. 3.

11. Here I am reacting to Christopher Douglas's analysis of the TBS game *Civilization III*, para. 23: "In this view, computer games could be understood to set the rules of play wherein the human player navigates through particular ideological or social contradictions; as rules, importantly, they naturalize certain historical and cultural contingencies." However, Douglas overextends his argument by claiming that "in this way, historical specificity is forgotten ... [and because] these ideas are coded into the game rules they appear as inevitable historical rules."

12. Cited in Orr, "Modernism and the Issue of Periodization."

13. The classic statement is Baudrillard's "The Precession of Simulacra."

14. My thanks go to Sam Holley-Kline, who co-presented an earlier version of this essay with me to the 2005 Pacific Rim Conference on Literature and Rhetoric at the University of Alaska Anchorage, and to Jacob Holley-Kline, for their criticism of the final draft of this essay. It goes without saying that any errors in fact, judgment, or gameplay strategy that remain are their dad's, not theirs.

Works Cited

Baudrillard, Jean. "The Precession of Simulacra." *Art & Text* 11 (1983): 3–47.

Douglas, Christopher. "'You Have Unleashed a Horde of Barbarians!': Fighting Indians, Playing Games, Forming Disciplines." *Postmodern Culture* 13.1 (2002).

Gee, James Paul. *What Video Games Have to Teach Us about Learning and Literacy*. New York: Palgrave-Macmillan, 2004.

Harty, Kevin J. *The Reel Middle Ages*. Jefferson, N.C.: McFarland, 1999.

Hayot, Eric, and Edward Wesp. "Reading Game/Text: EverQuest, Alienation, and Digital Communities." *Postmodern Culture* 14.2 (2004).

_____, and _____. "Style: Strategy and Mimesis in Ergodic Literature." *Comparative Literature Studies* 41.3 (2004): 404–23.

Manual to *Age of Empires II: Age of Kings*. Redmond, Wash.: Microsoft, 2000.

Orr, Leonard. "Modernism and the Issue of Periodization." *CLCWeb: Comparative Literature and Culture* 7.1 (March 2005). http://clcwebjournal.lib.purdue.edu/clcweb05–1/orr05.html. Accessed 20 March 2006.

Selfe, Cynthia L., and Gail E. Hawisher. *Literate Lives in the Information Age: Narratives on Literacy from the United States*. Mahwah, N.J.: Lawrence Erlbaum, 2004.

Wood, Richard T.A., Mark D. Griffiths, Darren Chappell, and Mark N.O. Davies. "The Structural Characteristics of Video Games: A Psycho-Structural Analysis." *Cyberpsychology and Behavior* 7.1 (2004): 1–11.

12 A World unto Itself

Autopoietic Systems and Secondary Worlds in Dungeons & Dragons

DAVID W. MARSHALL

The medieval aesthetic of *Dungeons & Dragons* features armor-clad knights wandering through ruined castles alongside fur-wearing barbarians, wily thieves, and sage wizards, often encountering orcs, giants, and the occasional displacer beast.[1] The game's creators, initially under TSR, Inc., then Wizards of the Coast,[2] define "medieval," here, as ranging from late antique to early modern, so characters typed as centurions, Vikings, knights, and cavaliers can all make appearances, and as the global economy has opened up greater awareness of different cultures, the game has been quick to incorporate near– and far–Eastern elements, so that samurai or Persian warriors join forces with those European heroes to thwart the plots of monstrous evils. Creating an even more peculiar sense of the medieval, however, are elements like the displacer beast, which disrupts the roughly period atmosphere of the game. Two contradictory impressions of these Middle Ages strike the casual observer: that the Middle Ages still thrive and that no time ever looked quite like this recent vision of them.

Role-playing requires a convincing imaginary space in which characters or personas can interact without the illusion of their space being violated. The success of the role-players in performing their characters, then, is largely dependent on the creation of what J.R.R. Tolkien called "Secondary Worlds." In his 1947 lecture "On Fairy-Stories," Tolkien argued that the success of fantasy or "fairy stories" depends upon an act of "sub-creation" that generates a believable world. He explained that the sub-creator "makes a Secondary World which your mind can enter.

Inside, what he relates is 'true': it accords with the laws of that world" (70).[3] This concept has become foundational within the fantasy genre, but the principle is also essential to the generation of a context in which to deploy game characters and to perform their personas. Narrative drives the game as players collaborate in the writing of a story. For the participants playing characters, vivid settings facilitate that process, and the gaming materials promote secondary world creation by offering the components for defining settings, or in some cases, even by providing fully described worlds, such as Greyhawk or the new Eberron campaign setting.

To construct these fundamental secondary worlds for player-characters, *D&D*'s creators and revisers seem to use the Middle Ages as an ingredient repository, but that direct connection deceives. The relationship between the Middle Ages and the secondary world generated by the *D&D* apparatus began perhaps with the iconic images of knights and castles, but the development of the secondary world took its impetus from the fantasy genre, which predisposed the game towards becoming an independent closed system, separate from fantasy itself. In subsequent editions of the game materials, that closure deforms historical influences to maintain the integrity of the fantastical secondary world. With the release of the third and most recent edition of the game by Wizards of the Coast, the system's closure reaches a new level. In effect, as the game evolved into a highly expansive and complex organism, it moved away from its fantasy origins and its adoption of medieval influences to become an autopoietic system that generates its evolving secondary world out of its own elements, most profoundly, its system of quantification.

In *Autopoiesis and Cognition*, Humberto Maturana and Francisco Varela explain that an autopoietic system reproduces itself in a closed loop in order to maintain its own distinctive existence. The idea is this: any given entity distinguishes itself from the external environment to preserve its own distinctiveness, responding to external stimuli by self-referentially redefining the boundaries between self and environment based on its own needs and perceptions of that relationship.[4] As Richard Halpern explains:

> Self-reference is, essentially, the recursive process in which relations of production create the components by which they are in turn produced.... As a result of their recursive functioning, autopoietic machines are informationally closed systems: they do not receive or process input from their environments, nor do they produce output of any kind, nor do they admit of heteronomy [52].

The given entity, then, can be said to produce the components for its own existence by constructing a sense of the external environment that conforms to its own needs. Because the entity continually responds to external stimuli, it repeatedly adjusts itself, making it dynamic, redefining the precise nature of the boundary between self and environment with each new stimulus. But note that communication is not conceived of as exchange; rather, it is understood as external stimuli to which an entity is sensitized, perturbing the way it constructs itself. The theory argues that communication is a self-determined interpretation by the organism that suits its own needs.

Niklas Luhmann has extended the theories of Maturana and Varela into General Systems Theory, using it to rethink law, romanticism, and art, and arguing that social systems are rooted in distinct modes of communication that are self-perpetuating by the recursive use of the system's own self-determined terms. Recently, Niels Werber has shifted this theory to the realm of literature.[5] Werber suggests that genres exist as systems in feudal relationships to other literary categories. Fiction, as a large category of literature, emerges as a system, defining itself by making the distinction fiction/not fiction through repeated dependence upon its own established conventions. Fiction, however, subdivides into "realism" and "fantasy," for example. While "realism" and "fantasy" share aspects of fiction's mode of communication, each draws a distinction between itself and what is not itself.

As a system, fantasy conventionally employs the secondary world, continually redeploying the principle to distinguish itself against realism, which declines use of secondary worlds. Fantasy as a genre, therefore, repeatedly defines itself as its own distinct system by recursive dependence upon its own distinct idioms, those that distinguish it from realism. When talking about a genre as established as fantasy, this idea takes special importance. The catalogues of publishers like Daw, Eos, and Tor, have largely established what counts as fantasy that can be sold under that generic publishing label. The conventions that these publishers have established in order to define the genre constitute the recursive terms to which authors consistently return in order to perpetuate the existence of the genre. As I will demonstrate, *D&D* grows from this generic system. The preponderance of medieval imagery in the game enters by way of the surge of fantasy fiction in the 1960s, and as a result, exists in that feudal relationship as a system emergent from fantasy.

A theory that explains the self-preservational functioning of an organism within its environment seems particularly relevant to this topic, given that the revisers of the *Dungeon Master's Guide* state, "We consider D&D to be a living game" (3rd ed. 4). The fantasy organism of the *D&D* game apparatus, consisting of rule books and supplemental materials, exists as an autopoietic system, self-referentially preserving its own fantasy milieu and expressing it in its own unique terms. That apparatus, growing out of fantasy, does not accept input from what we might term a "real middle ages," though segments of the game's environment, history or current events, for example, perturb the game apparatus in each new edition. The fantasy realms of *D&D* are produced by the component parts of fantasy literature, which may in themselves refer back to a "real middle ages." If fantasy literature is a form of medievalism, then *D&D*, as an outgrowth of fantasy, is a separate system of medievalism-ism.

Dungeons & Dragons' *Fantasy Roots*

Dungeons & Dragons grew out of table-top war-gaming groups in Wisconsin in the late sixties and early seventies who became bored in the medieval campaigns, which offered fewer challenges than the war games set in periods of mechanized warfare. Contrary to war gaming, which sees players moving armies over sand-table terrains, this innovation had players develop individual characters whom they controlled in small party engagements in medieval settings. That initial scenario led Gary Gygax and Dave Arneson to a more complex system in which one player, called the dungeon master (DM) constructs a fantasy world (Rausch screen 2). The other players create characters around basic traits by rolling dice to determine six attributes: strength, dexterity, intelligence, wisdom, constitution, and charisma. The players perform these characters to interact with non-player characters (created by the DM), to battle monsters and to amass treasure, all of which will increase character abilities. The outcome of each adventure is determined by dice rolls, so players are not guaranteed success and character death is a real possibility. As a gaming session develops, the DM and players collaborate on constructing a narrative of another world in which archetypal figures pursue ongoing adventures.

Not coincidentally, *D&D* emerged in the gaming world within a ten year window that saw the first surge of fantasy genre publishing. As L. Sprague de Camp explains, the mid-sixties witnessed a "publishing phenomenon" (3–5). While American fantasy had been popular in the pulps, such as *The Thrill Book*, initiated in 1919, *Weird Tales* (1923), which published the stories of Robert E. Howard and H.P. Lovecraft, and the fantasy partner to *Amazing Stories*, *Unknown Worlds* (1939), by 1945 this market had dried up. Fantasy remained a lifeless area until Tolkien's opus was published in the fifties, and it remained listless until a surge in the sixties. Then, in 1965–1966, two fantasy series became bestsellers: first, two rival publishing houses released editions of Tolkien's *Lord of the Rings*; second, Lancer Books published re-edited editions of Howard's Conan stories, which, even if it did not match Tolkien's sales, did sell millions of copies. Alongside these successes, the sixties produced other now standard fantasy tales, including Fritz Leiber's stories of Fafhrd and the Gray Mouser, Ursula Le Guin's *A Wizard of Earthsea*, Jack Vance's *The Dying Earth*, and Michael Moorcock's *Stealer of Souls* and *Stormbringer*. These now classic texts are largely responsible for defining the conventions that established fantasy as a genre. Its character types people Robert Jordan's *Eye of the World*, while its other-worldly creatures animate Anne McAffrey's *Pern* novels, and its magic moves the popular *Shannara* books of Terry Brooks.

In this climate of resurgent fantasy Gary Gygax and Dave Arneson fleshed out the rules for *D&D*, and Gygax, for one, was clear about his literary influences. In the forward to the original edition of the game, Gygax writes,

> Those wargamers who lack imagination, those who don't care for Burroughs' Martian adventures where John Carter is groping through black pits, who feel no thrill upon reading Howard's Conan saga, who do not enjoy the de Camp & Pratt fantasies or Fritz Leiber's Fafhrd and the Gray Mouser pitting their swords against evil sorceries will not be likely to find dungeons & dragons their taste [3].

Gygax's warning to tabletop war gamers points not just to influences in developing the *Dungeons & Dragons* apparatus, but to the inherent participation of the game in fantasy as a defining genre. Gygax told readers in a 2004 interview that, in an attempt to reenergize his gaming friends, he began to include fantasy elements drawn from the authors he cites above as well as Jack Vance (screen 2). Gygax's process, then, may have been just to cobble together a world drawn from literary sources, but the result was the construction of a simple system that perpetually creates a secondary world by a recursive dependence on the generic conventions of fantasy. Fantasy, as a parent to the game, thereby becomes a part of the game's environment to which it is highly sensitized.

The scope of the *D&D* apparatus is immense. Rules, depending on what edition you look at, detail not just a system of magic, but dozens of individual spells categorized in multiple ways; not just a handful of basic character types, but more than a score of possible sub-types and "prestige classes," and hundreds of races and monsters that can come in more than one variety (all of which is quantified in die rolls, of which more will be said below). For that reason, this essay cannot offer a source study for all game elements, but will isolate several components to demonstrate the ultimate indebtedness to the fantasy works that get reiterated. Much must be left out, including individual appropriations, such as Michael Moorcock's soul stealing sword, Fritz Leiber's Thieves' Guild, and a host of other specific borrowings.

As I have said, the impetus of *D&D* is towards the creation of narrative, but that narrative typically comes in episodic bursts directed by the individual goal of each game session's adventure. Adventures are the means for "leveling up" of characters, which is done by amassing combat or skill experience and treasure, and which drives players in the game. That episodic structure of role-playing narrative, however, can be tied to the origins of American fantasy fiction, which grew out of the pulps as serial fiction, such as Burroughs's *A Princess of Mars*, which appeared in twenty-eight chapters of not more than a handful of pages in *All-Story Magazine* in 1912. While Burroughs's tale of John Carter has something like an overarching plot, Leiber's adventures of Fafhrd and the Gray Mouser function more as isolated short stories, though often linked under a broad heading, such as those collected in *Swords against Death*, which sees the two heroes coming and going from the city of Lankhmar having adventures along the way. To read an episode of Burroughs's or Leiber's stories is to read a *D&D* adventure. The heroes—we might think of them as player characters—journey into ruined towers, as in Leiber's "The Jewels in the Forest," in search of treasure. In the process they nearly always encounter magic, a wizard, an enchanted gem, or a charmed room. When they overcome the magic and obtain their reward or find that it does not exist, they exit and move on to the next adventure. Leiber's work seems to set the parameters for the game by defining what characters do when they adventure—seek treasure. The treasure quest promotes the episodic, single adventure–based format of the game experience. And even though most gamers move their characters through an extended narrative, called a campaign, the over-arching structure of the DM's campaign remains episodic, with each game session dedicated to one chapter of the story marked by a clearly delineated beginning and end. These extended adventure arcs come to resemble *A Princess of Mars*, in which each serial episode could be read either as part of the overall work or as a stand-alone adventure in an other-worldly place.

Gygax and Arneson seem to have adapted the organizing cosmological structure of Michael Moorcock's *Elric* saga in order to direct the behavior of characters within those treasure quests. Once players have "rolled up" the attribute scores of their characters, they imagine identities for them, and as part of that process, they choose an "alignment," or the character's outlook in relation to moral structures. The rule books categorize morality into two intersecting binaries: law vs. chaos and good vs. evil, with neutrality existing in between each. While the recent third edition of the game rules foreground good/evil, the original rules invert that emphasis, relegating good/evil to a function of law/chaos: "characters may be lawful (good or evil), neutral, or chaotic (good or evil)" (*Dungeons* 8). Character morality, then, is a function of the character's adherence to principles of order or entropy, just as in Moorcock's Age of the Young Kingdoms, in which Elric lives. In "While the Gods Laugh," Elric pursues an ancient tome from which he hopes to learn what power controls the forces of his world. "Know you not," explains Elric to his comrade, Moonglum,

> that two forces govern the world—fighting an eternal battle? ... Law and Chaos. The upholders of Chaos state that in such a world as they rule, all things are possible. Opponents of Chaos—those who ally themselves with the forces of Law—say that without Law *nothing* material is possible. Some stand apart, believing that a balance between the two is the proper state of things" [58].

In his first full length Elric novel, *Stormbringer*, Moorcock develops this theme, with the forces of chaos disrupting the normal functioning of the natural world to the peril of all who live in it. In Moorcock, Gygax and Arneson found rival philosophies of collective will versus individual volition that can be used to create myriad ethical schemes, all of which define the positions of game characters in relation to organized structures of social control and management.

Jack Vance's wizards of *The Dying Earth*, such as Turjan and Mazirian, provide the foundation for the game's magical system, although magic in the game owes less of a debt to a single author. In Vance's science fiction–fantasy hybrid, old books preserve a small remnant of the spells once in existence. The power of the incantations bars a wizard from remembering more than four or five at any given time, and when a spell is cast, the energy inherent in the remembered incantation vanishes from the memory in what has come to be called "fire and forget." Gygax's rules adopted this system nearly in entirety. As the original rules explain it, magic requires words and sometimes physical substances, and concentration is required. Once the spellcaster casts a spell, it fades from memory and must be relearned (*Dungeons & Dragons* 13). The thirst for more magic that marks Vance's wizards becomes the motivation for the *D&D* character class to embark upon adventure.

Expanding on that system and version of the wizard, Le Guin constructs a background for wizardry in which magically inclined youth apprentice themselves to wizards to learn the craft, and wizards often serve communities, helping with needed weather changes, mending objects, and defending villages from attack. In *D&D*, wizards "for hire are useful to the military as firepower ... or a wizard can serve the community as a well-paid troubleshooter—someone able to rid the town of vermin, stop the levee from bursting, or foretell the future" (*Guide* 3rd ed. 132). Le Guin's twist is that the power of magic incantations is dependent upon knowing the "true" names of things. Knowing the true name allows the wizard to call upon whatever s/he wishes. When Ged is first taught the true name of the falcon, "he found that the wild falcons stooped down to him from the wind when he summoned them by name" (5). *D&D*, thus, includes in its spell lists a series of "Summon" spells, which allow magic-using characters to call upon various types of creatures, as well as other fantasy-inspired spells, like Gandalf's light spells and offensive spells modeled after Vance's "Excellent Prismatic Spray."

Vance and Le Guin share an emphasis on the power of language and words or names in their worlds of magic, a key feature in defining the dragons in the secondary world of the game. As *The Classic Dungeons & Dragons Game* describes the talking varieties, "these are intelligent.... Only talking dragons can use magic-user spells" (78). While the dragons in the game certainly trace their lineage back to Tolkien's Smaug, particularly their jealous guardianship of treasure hoards, Le Guin (who also hearkens back to Tolkien's feared beast) inspires the magical dragons of *D&D*. While not all dragons in the game possess magic, all are linked to hoarding treasure. Similarly, Le Guin's dragons start young and immature, capable only of flying and using their fire-breath, but these mature into speaking creatures. The dragon of Pendor, for example, after failing to lure Ged with images of his treasure horde, offers Ged power over the shadow creature that haunts the young wizard, tempting him: "If you could name it you could master it, maybe, little wizard. Maybe I could tell you its name, when I see it close by" (90). While Le Guin does not render the dragon explicitly magical, the Old Language by which wizards perform their magic is the language of dragons, making the creatures inherently magical. While Fafnir and Beowulf's *wyrm* are clear precursors to the dragons of the gaming world, they are at a remove from the game, and their heirs provide the raw materials for Gygax.

Aside from magic, wizards, and dragons, the barbarian fighter may be one of the most iconic elements of *D&D*, and of fantasy as a genre. Resonating of Anglo-Saxon raiders or harrying Vikings, the barbarian is a warrior clad in skins and fond of over-large weapons, popularly imagined by artists like Frank Frazzetta. We owe this image to Howard, who in his 1930s Conan stories defined the type. In "The Tower of the Elephant" (1933), Howard tells us Conan "had discarded his torn tunic, and walked through the night naked except for a loin-cloth and his high-strapped sandals. He moved with the supple ease of a great tiger, his steely muscles rippling under his brown skin" (64). While in fantasy as a genre barbarians have ravaged landscapes for decades, *D&D*'s barbarian has appeared as a character class only recently, in the third edition. As the *Player's Handbook* describes it, "Barbarians are never lawful. They may be honorable, but at heart they are wild. This wildness is their strength, and it could not live in a lawful soul" (3rd ed. 24). The description is a typical one in which the barbarian nature emerges in comparison to animalistic ideas of wildness, such as the tiger's ease of Conan and as marked by savagery in battle. Little sets the character class apart from Howard's above-cited lines, save the loincloth.

As Gygax's forward to the original rules suggests, and as this handful of cases demonstrates, the resemblance in *D&D* to the medieval is not a direct one. While table top war games like Chainmail may have offered an initial medieval setting, the fantasy rules of the 1974 edition of *D&D* indicates that fantasy provided the European-type context for the early form of the game and accounts for the "loosely" with which Gary Alan Fine qualifies his statement that "Dungeons & Dragons is based loosely on the European Middle Ages" ("Legendary Creatures" 13). That being said, we must consider the extent to which the game's makers do draw on aspects of the medieval lifted from period texts.

Deforming the Past

The 1980 supplemental book *Deities and Demigods* details the various gods and heroes of (but not limited to) early medieval Europe, including Celtic, Finnish, and Norse. Referencing Malory's *Le Morte d'Arthur*, it even devotes a chapter to Merlin, Arthur, and the knights of the round table. While such appropriation might suggest that the genre-based system I have argued for is not closed, but rather open to non-fantasy, there are two points that suggest otherwise. First, and most simply, *Dungeons & Dragons* does not adopt medieval forms as much as it includes those fantastic components that appear in the medieval's equivalent of fantasy as a genre. Thus, returning to magic, the sleep spells that appear in the game's descriptions of magic resemble the spell that Malory's Merlin casts upon King Pellinor (I.24), but these magical elements of romance are only "medieval" inasmuch as romance is a medieval form. Fantasy, or the fantastic, is a component of literature that dates back to our earliest written texts, such as *Gilgamesh* and *The Odyssey*. There is nothing particularly medieval, in other words, in Merlin's magical spells.

Secondly, the theory of autopoiesis can account for what appears to be input into a closed system, revealing the limited extent to which the medieval can actually make inroads into the apparatus of *D&D*. The dynamic processes by which a system continues to create itself are not totally insulated from the outside environment. Environmental influences can cause an autopoietic system to deform as the environment perturbs the system and causes it to re-distinguish itself, as I have described above. Similar to an author's meaning being deformed by the reader in Bakhtin's idea of the utterance, the autopoietic entity is perturbed by the external stimuli to which it is sensitized, and a deformation in the components of the entity occurs. In terms of the game, outside events or sources can be drawn into the apparatus, but as they are deformed to fit the game, they cause a deformation of the game.

In terms of the game's subject matter, perhaps the best example of this principle in recent manifestations of the game is the adventure module "Fallen Angel" published in *Dungeon* magazine (December 2004), which sends characters to a ruined section of Sharn, an imagined city in the new game setting of Eberron. The provided background explains that a group wished to harness for evil purposes the magic that kept the tower suspended in air, but as they initiated their rite, they disrupted the magic and brought the tower crashing to the ground. The parallel to the terrorist attack on the World Trade Center on September 11th should be rather obvious: the floating tower in a city of towers standing in for New York's twin towers, evil magicians serving as terrorists in airplane missiles, and the collapse of impossible structures. Whether a conscious or unconscious response, the world-changing events of 9/11 confront the game and cause a shift—a deformation or perturbing—that results in a new form of a standard game component. The standard labyrinthine ruins of a wizard's tower so common in Leiber's stories of Fafhrd and the Gray Mouser become the shattered wastes of a fallen tower of magic. While the game scenario rings true, the lens of fantasy disrupts the similarity and world events are forced into the generic requirements of the game. Technology disappears in favor of magic, political causes are replaced by cosmological ones, and subsequent efforts to restore order, in the adventure module, are re-imagined in the post-apocalyptic mode that defines a whole subset of fantasy and science fiction. Simultaneously, the game's secondary world deforms with the addition of that new input: there must be evil people who wish to use the floating tower for their own dark ends and the unbelievable structure becomes profoundly vulnerable. In a double-move, as the "real world" input is deformed in the game's secondary world logic, the secondary world is deformed in a response to the "real world" stimulus as it attempts to maintain its own definition of itself in its environment.

This principle of deformation works on two levels to explain how the system can maintain closure despite the presence of medieval cultural products referenced in the second edition of the *Player's Handbook*. To start with the surface level, the *Handbook* describes the cleric in terms of real historical precursors: "The cleric class is similar to certain religious orders of knighthood of the Middle Ages: the Teutonic Knights, the Knights Templars, and the Hospitalers. These orders combined military and religious training with a code of protection and service" (33). In the secondary world of *D&D*, the cleric does devote him/herself to serving a deity as a holy warrior, but the game maintains its systematic closure by introducing holy magic to the class. Clerics perform designated spells, often such acts as purifying food and water, casting a holy light, healing the sick or wounded, and detecting or turning away evil or undead creatures. While bearing some semblance to the medieval saint *cum* channel for divine miracles, and while collapsing that medieval image into the warrior monks of the fighting orders, the cleric class seems inspired by the sword wielding sorcerer Elric, from Moorcock's sagas of the Eternal Champion. Though Elric at times serves only himself, Moorcock fused the magic-using adventurer with the determined warrior in a hybrid form often pitted against the forces of chaos and evil. With the fighting mage (we might also include Gandalf in this category) as a fantasy trope, the closed game system is able to absorb the historical precedent of the Teutons, Templars, and Hospitalers. Those historical organizations influence the image of the cleric, but autopoietic closure is maintained by reconstituting them in the game's own language of fantasy. The game effectively works in analogy rather than influence.

The second way in which deformation preserves the distinction between game and environment is in the quantification by which the game operates—and if we are going to read this game as autopoietic (or any role-playing game for that matter), this is the crux of the issue. While the cleric may appear to be related to medieval Knights Templar or Moorcock's sorcerer-warrior, at its core the cleric is a bundle of numbers. Despite the qualitative description of the class, the game functions based on probabilities and die rolls. The *Player's Handbook*, therefore, offers key information in the form numeric data and tables. For a cleric character, players should have high numbers for the wisdom, constitution, and charisma ability scores that define the character class's basic form (3rd edition 31). The way the class functions in the game is similarly expressed in numbers—First level: +0 attack bonus, +2 Fortitude Saving Throw, +0 Reflex Saving Throw, +2 Will Saving Throw (31).[6] These numbers differ from those of a rogue, for example—First level: +0 attack bonus, +0 Fortitude Save, +2 Reflex Save, +0 Will Save (49). Each character class, therefore, is expressed in terms of a unique set of numeric bonuses or penalties applied to the die rolls for any given action in order to affect the probability of the character succeeding in his or her attempts to meet die-rolling goals. The same is true for magic, which becomes either a weapon or a means of temporarily adjusting characters' ability scores. For example, the spell Magic Missile causes "a missile of magical energy darts ... dealing 1d4+1 points of force damage" (*Handbook* 3rd ed. 251). The spell mimics the rules for attacking with the game's described dart in that the attack results in a decrease of an enemy's hit points.[7]

Expressions of a weapon's or spell's potential effect, such as "1d4+1," constitute the fundamental communicative element of the game. The cleric, therefore, is not "a master of divine magic and a capable warrior as well" (*Handbook* 3rd ed. 21), but rather wisdom >12, attack +0, fort +0, ref +0, will +2. Although the medieval idea of the cleric may exist as a stimulus that perturbs the game's self-distinction, the game reconceives that stimulus in its own fundamental communicative element—numeric qualifiers for probabilities based on die rolls. In other words, the rules are a response to the existence of the qualities of the cleric in the environment (history and fantasy), but the rules express the idea of cleric in a self-determined way, in the only way they can—as a function of numbers and probabilities.[8] Those same expressions of probability can be draped in the guise of cleric, an interstellar being, or even an anthropomorphized banana. For the game's purposes, the way the class functions is dependant on the numeric expression and the garb is largely arbitrary.

While *D&D* shows clear affiliation with common images of the Middle Ages, both the game's dependence on fantasy (on a surface level) and the game's basic mode of communication through numbers (at its core) limit the extent to which medieval tropes exist within the secondary world of the game. The "medieval" subject matter of the game, however, becomes even more distanced from the medieval with the rise of *D&D* fantasy novels.

Conclusion: The System Fully Closes

While the first edition rules include the medieval heroes of *Deities & Demigods* and the second edition of the *Players' Handbook* incorporate medieval Templar knights, the third edition rules discard anything that is not firmly *Dungeons & Dragons* brand fantasy, which has so internalized Tolkien's orcs and halflings, the versions of magic offered by Le Guin and Vance, and the cosmology of Moorcock, that they have become elemental to the recursive structure of the game's existence. No direct reference to the Middle Ages appears in the game, unless we put undue emphasis on the presence of armor and weapons. Instead of mythologically derived pantheons, Wizards of the Coast has substituted its own invented pantheon of deities, and clerics are freed from needless historical precedent.

On the level of subject matter (as opposed to the quantifying rules), the system seems to reach full closure with the increased success of fantasy fiction publishing by TSR and now Wizards of the Coast. With the *Dragonlance* series, TSR began to archive the secondary world that defines it against the medieval analogues or the other versions of fantasy realms. The *Forgotten Realms* series, initiated in the early 1990s, perpetuates that shift to full self-reliance, with authors such as R.A. Salvatore creating novels out of the components supplied in the *D&D* game apparatus. Those *D&D* novels supplant the external fantasy works from which Gary Gygax and Dave Arneson drew their original inspiration for the game while supplying a clear source of the specific conventions necessary for the recursive articulation of the constituting elements that define the secondary world of the game.

Salvatore, for example, is best known for his creation of the character Drizzt Do'Urden, a Drow elf whom many of his more than twenty novels follow.[9] While the black-skinned, white-haired Drow originated within *D&D*, Salvatore has developed a thoroughly imagined world that has allowed game and adventure developers to elaborate on the basic description offered in the *Monster Manual*. Players crafting a campaign or adventure from within the *D&D* apparatus are able to utilize those elements of the game on which the game depends for its unique identity by becoming conversant with them through the novels as well as the rule books.

The fantasy publishing of the game's creators and developers effectively trains consumers in the system's proper mode of communication, in the conventions out of which the game recursively defines itself, preserving the closure of the system. And because the success of the game, the convincingness of the secondary world and its characters, depends upon preserving the integrity of the secondary world, players jeopardize the coherence of the imaginary realm by deviating from the components in the game apparatus. If my cleric brandishes a machine gun, the illusion dies with the displacer beast.

Notes

My thanks to John Blandford and William Rasch for reviewing drafts of this essay. Extra thanks to Dr. Rasch for assisting me with groping my way through Systems Theory. Any errors in my use of the approach are entirely my own.

1. This creature resembles a large black panther but features tendrils that allow it to appear to be other than where it is.

2. Allen Rausch explains that poor management of TSR led to the company's financial decline and ultimate sale to Wizards of the Coast, developers of the popular card game Magik: The Gathering.

3. W.R. Irwin has argued that use of secondary worlds in fantasy literature should be understood as part of a game in which the rules stipulate that an author will develop a fully imagined alternative space and the reader will accept that world—just as long as the author does not disrupt that illusion. See Irwin 11–32.

4. For lucid explanation of the theory and its developmental history, see Hayles 131–59.

5. Werber develops the idea of literature as a system, perhaps most significantly in *Literatur als System: Zur Ausdifferenzierung literarisher Kommunikation*.

6. "Attack bonus" refers to the number that a player adds to die rolls determining the success of attacking a monster. "Saving throws" are die rolls made to avoid the effects of attacks, which are expressed in numbers as a result of die rolls. Thus, if a sorcerer attempts to magically charm a cleric, that cleric rolls a "Will Save" to see if he can resist that attempt. The sorcerer's proficiency is measured in a number that the cleric must beat by the die roll.

7. "Hit Points" quantify a character's or monster's life. In this case, the attacking player-character rolls a 4-sided die and adds 1 to the result. That total is subtracted from the defending player-character's hit points. When a player's character loses all hit points, the result is character death.

8. Luhmann explains that communication is autopoietic, with a communicative system always articulating its response to environmental stimuli in its own terms. See "What Is Communication?" especially 156–161.

9. Salvatore's Drizzt Do'Urden is most often read in *The Dark Elf Trilogy*, which includes the novels *Homeland* (1990), *Exile* (1990), and *Sojourn* (1991).

Works Cited

Baker, Keith. "Fallen Angel." *Dungeon Magazine* 117 (December 2004): 43–51.
Brooks, Terry. *Sword of Shannara*. New York: Random House, 1983.
Burroughs, Edgar Rice. *A Princess of Mars*. New York: Random House, 2003.
de Camp, L. Sprague. *Literary Swords and Swordsmen*. Sauk City, Wisc.: Arkham House, 1976.
Dungeons & Dragons. Lake Geneva, Wisc.: TSR, 1973.
Dungeon Master's Guide 3rd Edition. Renton, Wash.: Wizards of the Coast, 2003.
Fine, Gary Allen. "Legendary Creatures and Small Game Playing Cultures: Medieval Lore in Contemporary Role-Playing Games." *Keystone Folklore* n.s. 1.1 (1982): 11–27.
Gygax, Gary. *Dungeon Master's Guide*. 1st ed. Lake Geneva, Wisc.: TSR, 1979.
_____. "Gary Gygax Interview: Part I." Interview with Allen Rausch. *Gamespy*, 15 August 2004. http://pc.gamespy.com/articles/538/538817p1.html.
Halpern, Richard. "The Lyric in the Field of Information: Autopoesis and History in Donne's Songs and Sonnets." *Yale Journal of Criticism* 6 (1993): 185–216.
Hayles, Katherine. *How We Became Post-Human: Virtual Bodies in Cybernetics, Literature, and Informatics*. Chicago: University of Chicago Press, 1999.
Howard, Robert E. "The Tower of the Elephant." In *The Coming of Conan the Cimmerian*, 59–82. New York: Del Rey Books, 2003.
Irwin, W.R. *The Game of the Impossible: A Rhetoric of Fantasy*. Urbana: University of Illinois Press, 1976.
Jordan, Robert. *The Eye of the World*. New York: Tor Books, 1990.
Le Guin, Ursula. *A Wizard of Earthsea*. New York: Bantam Dell, 1968.
Leiber, Fritz. *Swords Against Death*. New York: ibooks, 1995.
Luhman, Niklas. *Social Systems*. Trans. John Bednarz Jr. with Dirk Baecker. Stanford: Stanford University Press, 1995.
_____. "What Is Communication?" In *Theories of Distinction: Redescribing the Descriptions of Modernity*, ed. William Rasch, 155–168. Stanford: Stanford University Press, 2002.
Maturna, Humberto R., and Francisco J. Varela. *Autopoiesis and Cognition: The Realization of the Living*. Dordrecht: D. Reidel, 1980.
McAffrey, Anne. *Dragonriders of Pern*. New York: Del Rey Books, 1988.
Moorcock, Michael. *Stormbringer*. 1977. Reprinted in *Elric*, Fantasy Masterworks Series. London: Gollancz, 2003.
_____. "While the Gods Laugh." 1968. Reprinted in *Elric*, Fantasy Masterworks Series. London: Gollancz, 2003.
Player's Handbook 2nd Edition. Lake Geneva, Wisc.: TSR, 1989.
Player's Handbook, 3rd Edition. Renton, Wash.: Wizards of the Coast, 2003.

Rausch, Allen. "Magic & Memories: The Complete History of Dungeons & Dragons." *Gamespy*, 16 August 2004. http://pc.gamespy.com/articles/538/538262p1.html.

Salvatore, R.A. *The Dark Elf Trilogy*. Renton, Wash.: Wizards of the Coast, 2000.

The Classic Dungeons & Dragons Game. Lake Geneva, Wisc.: TSR, 1994.

Tolkien, J.R.R. "On Fairy-Stories." In *The Tolkien Reader*. New York: Del Rey, 1966.

_____. *The Lord of the Rings*. Boston: Houghton Mifflin, 1982.

Vance, Jack. *The Dying Earth*. New York: Tom Doherty Associates, 1978.

Ward, James M., with Robert J. Kuntz. *Deities and Demigods*. Lake Geneva, Wisc.: TSR, Inc., 1980.

Werber, Niels. *Literatur als System: Zur Ausdifferenzierung literarischer Kommunikation*. Wiesbaden: VS Verlag für Sozialwissenschaften, 1992.

13 Anything Different Is Good

Incremental Repetition, Courtly Love, and Purgatory in Groundhog Day

WILLIAM RACICOT

The Harold Ramis film *Groundhog Day* seldom comes up in discussions of the intersection of the medieval and the modern. It does not take place in the Middle Ages; it does not feature King Arthur or Robin Hood; it has no wizards and no dragons. It nevertheless functions in much the same way a medieval romance does. The film depicts boorish weatherman Phil Connors enduring the same Groundhog Day in a loop of trial and error. Every morning he awakes at 6:00 A.M. to Sonny and Cher's "I've Got You, Babe," only to live the same day all over again. On each recurrence, he negotiates the challenges and responsibilities inherent in that one day until the day ends. Although the same day repeats, with Phil attending the same Groundhog Day festivities and encountering the same Punxsutawney locals, each repetition builds on the previous one. Phil's actions change slightly each time, allowing repeated images and events to accumulate thematic significance. The repetitions in *Groundhog Day* are incremental, much like the incremental repetitions that organize, for instance, the lais of Marie de France and Chretien's *Conte du Graal*.

The movie, like Chretien's romance, uses incremental repetition to explore what makes a knight worthy of his lady. The sequence of repeated days documents Phil's increasing emotional maturity and sense of social responsibility, primarily by way of his attitude toward Rita. Initially scornful and then self-interested, Phil learns to appreciate her without expecting reward. He learns new skills and behaviors, all of them parallel to those delineated in the courtly love tradition. But the courtly love aspects of this film serve to explore yet another medieval motif, Purgatory. Considered in parallel to the cleansing torments of Purgatory, Phil's permanent residence in Groundhog Day offers him the opportunity to be cleansed, purged of sin—to become a man worthy of Paradise, represented by life with Rita. By allowing the incremental repetitions of Phil's experience to depict the slow process by which he makes the painful transition from boor to hero, from wicked soul to virtuous, the film develops a contemporary image of Purgatory, in which the torments of Groundhog Day purge Phil Connors of his failures of personality.

Medievalism and the Non-Medieval

Although most medievalist film scholarship focuses on movies with explicit medieval settings or subjects (12th century Britain, Robin Hood, King Arthur, etc.), it can be valuable to apply medievalist critical techniques to movies without such motifs. Despite the enormous differences between medieval and current modes of thinking and behavior, our attitudes and conventions have grown out of theirs. Space opera, for example, has well-established roots in medieval romance, and King Arthur is a popular subject in film. Just as we retain the descendents of medieval genres and subjects, our literature and art make use of medieval structuring devices and develop themes of medieval origin. These themes and devices appear in unexpected places—even in a movie like *Groundhog Day*. Considering their effects and implications enhances understanding of the relationship not only between the viewer and the film, but also between contemporary and medieval modes of thinking. While the two periods are undeniably different, indeed bordering on alien, it is nevertheless valuable to explore the similarities, to see the medieval origins of contemporary ideas, images, and strategies.

In *A Knight at the Movies*, John Aberth points to medievalism as studying "the many ways in which modern society influences and is influenced by the actual history of the Middle Ages," and exploring "how history is 'written,' by historians and others" (ix). He notes several films that he considers to succeed "by reveling in the differences between those times and our own and by drawing us into another world in order to better understand and appreciate those differences" (viii). He stresses "how both medieval and modern chroniclers of the past have viewed the historical events or characters being portrayed" and celebrates "the revealing window they provide onto the medieval mind" (x). "Medieval" movies should help viewers understand the medieval mindset by reducing the distance between it and modern modes of thought. Although he focuses on differences, he implicitly calls for those differences to help us see similarities. In fact, he explicitly suggests that such movies can "capture the spirit of the times" (ix). Harty suggests something similar when he cites Eco's comment that "people seem to like the Middle Ages" and when he himself asserts that "we see in the medieval a world at once distant from yet related to our own" (7).

This is a dangerous project, of course, with its inherent risk that viewers will lose sight of the vast gulf between medieval and modern thinking,[1] since "in making a film, the filmmaker, sometimes with the historian acting as a consultant, invariably reflects the current mode of how society wishes to remember its ancestors" (Aberth ix). How can medieval ideas be brought to the screen without being made modern? In his survey of "medieval" films, Harty discusses the "search for a true cinematic translation of the Arthurian myth" and worries that "we may never get a definitive screen version" (29).

The value of medievalism supersedes such concerns, if it does not actually make benefits of them. Medievalism can be "the attempt as old as the birth of the early modern or Renaissance period to revisit or reinvent the medieval world for contemporary purposes" (Harty 7). Lacy notes "the power cinema has to remake even our most profoundly held myths" (42). That is, medievalism need not achieve accurate representation of the medieval mindset; by striving to a greater or lesser degree toward that goal, medievalism can provide us with a better understanding of ourselves. DeWeever, for instance, estimates that Morgan leFay "makes her most dramatic and important appearances" in film, citing film's "need for contrasting characters to represent good and evil" (54). Furthermore, medieval material in movies can help us retain our cultural heritage by encouraging interest in the past. For instance, Lacy suggests that "only constant renewal can ensure the continued vitality of the Arthurian story" (41). And such retention is useful, because that heritage is itself useful. Harty notes "the continuing vitality of the Arthurian legend, especially in terms of its ability to heal" (29).

Perhaps for these reasons, most medievalist film criticism focuses on movies with medieval settings and/or subjects. It's tempting to assess the usefulness of anachronism, for instance, in *A Knight's Tale*—even though the tournament audience could not possibly have known Queen's "We Will Rock You," perhaps having them chant it and pound the railings to the beat does provide a reasonable contemporary analogue to help us understand what a tournament might have been like. The later scene at the ball, in which the medieval dance becomes a rock and roll production number, functions in a similar way, providing a modern audience with a useful frame of reference, bridging the gap between the medieval experience and our own. We still share social events parallel to the tournament and the formal court ball, despite cosmetic changes to those events.

Analysis of films without medieval settings or subjects is rare, but it does exist. Lacy, for instance, in a footnote recognizes that *The Natural* uses the story of Perceval as its underlying structure (42). Lupack goes further, exploring clear and intentional parallels between the movie and the legend, announced through names and images: "Pop Fisher," a name that explicitly recalls the Fisher King, is the coach of a ball team called the Knights; The film's hero, Roy (French for "king") suffers a groin wound, again pointing explicitly to the legend of the Fisher King, whose infertility causes a drought throughout his kingdom. Notice here that the movie explicitly calls for comparison to medieval material. Similarly, Harty traces Arthurian themes in the modern setting of *The Sixth Sense*. This film, too, explicitly calls for medievalist analysis by including the Arthurian plotline directly in Cole's school play (28–29). Martin Shichtman looks to *Apocalypse Now*, which seems a less obvious choice, but he compares it to *Excalibur*. Similarly, Lupack discusses *Invasion of the Body Snatchers*, but does so in comparison to *The Black Knight*. In "*Tortilla Flat* and the Arthurian View," Kleis actually attacks the notion that the film is parallel to the Arthurian legend despite Steinbeck's explicit claim that such parallels exist for the novel on which it is based. In a footnote, he points to other Steinbeck novels he considers more likely to fit the Arthurian model. The body of the essay, however, discusses the text that he believes does not (78n).

If medievalist assessment is valuable in "medieval" films, surely it is similarly valuable in films that don't explicitly demand such assessment. Surely understanding what we as a modern culture have chosen, perhaps even unconsciously, to do with medieval tropes—surely that helps us understand ourselves better in relation to those tropes and to the artifacts in which we use them. Why not apply the techniques and conventions of medievalism to other movies?

Incremental Repetition and Groundhog Day

The Harold Ramis film *Groundhog Day* uses incremental repetition, a structuring device crucial in medieval texts such as Chretien's *Conte du Graal* and Marie de France's lai *Guigemar*, to explore the process by which the hero becomes worthy of his lady. Rather than revisiting similar or analogous situations as the medieval texts do—*Guigemar*, for instance, revisits the act of refusing love to explore what makes love real;

and the *Conte du Graal* revisits Perceval's failure to comprehend instructions to demonstrate the qualities that make a worthy knight—*Groundhog Day* actually repeats the same day, the same events, to explore the qualities that make Phil Connors, analogous to the knight in a romance or lai, initially unworthy and later worthy of Rita, a lady of quality.

In Chretien's *Conte du Graal*, the knight receives advice several times, each time misunderstanding some crucial element of the advice. His mother says he may accept a ring, food, and a kiss from a lady who offers them. He takes these things by force from the woman in the tent, and her knight accuses her of infidelity. Kay tells Perceval sarcastically that Arthur has already granted him the red knight's arms, and, failing to recognize Kay's sarcasm, Perceval proceeds to claim them by killing the red knight with a spear through the eye—a breach of knightly protocol. A different knight advises him to ask fewer questions, so Perceval stops asking any questions at all, and thereby fails to fulfill the ritual of the grail. Each incremental repetition of advice and misinterpretation highlights a different facet of Perceval's primary challenge: naivete. He just doesn't get it.

Only after he begins learning what is expected of a knight socially, only after he begins attending sincerely to social ritual, does he learn his name. He goes without identity, without substance as a person; in a sense he is no one until he develops the skills and traits that make a worthy knight. He must learn the rituals and customs appropriate to religion and spirituality, the court, knightly combat, and appreciation of women. This romance uses the incremental repetition of two related situations—Perceval receives advice, and Perceval makes a mistake—to claim that worthiness as an individual, demonstrated by attention to the demands of one's situation and the ability to make good decisions based on those demands, requires a long process of learning and personal growth.

In its own idiosyncratic way, *Groundhog Day* uses incremental repetition to explore a similar theme: human worthiness as a result of hard-earned personal growth. Incremental repetitions of Groundhog Day fall into a few stages related to Phil's maturity: he progresses by increments from childishness in the first stage, through a period of adolescent behavior in the second, into a state of sincere emotional maturity in the final stage. The original day demonstrates Phil's character as explored in the first sequence of repetitions. This sequence depicts him as self-centered and cynical, as childish. In accordance with the formal expectations of incremental repetition, this period in the film establishes a base-line for his behavior against which his behavior in later repetitions can be measured. During this sequence, he views Rita as a necessary obstacle, possibly useful but not inherently interesting. During this set of repetitions he explores the freedom and power of his situation by stealing money from an armored truck and seducing other women by creating the illusion that he cares for them. Incrementally repeating these events and their analogues develops a very unsympathetic portrait of Phil.

The stage of iterations between these depicts his doomed attempts to bed Rita, not because she is inherently desirable, but because she is unavailable. Like Guigemar at the beginning of Marie's lai, Phil pursues Rita for the sheer gratification of the hunt. Taking his original attitudes a step further, he perfects his cynicism by treating her as prey—to be wounded for his pleasure through the calculated illusion that he is worth her time. These seductions differ from those in the first sequence because they are characterized by failure, frustration of his empty desire. If his initial state is childish, and his final state is mature, here he is adolescent, wielding unaccustomed power in pursuit of immediate personal gratification without concern for the consequences his actions might have on those around him, and in the end forbidden to succeed because certain privileges are reserved for adults.

Repetition and the Purgatory Theme

In fact, *Groundhog Day* develops this essentially medieval motif, parallel to the ideals of knightly behavior developed in the courtly love tradition, to explore images of Purgatory, establishing the moral implications of Phil's growth. Purgatory, the smelter in which fiery torment burns the impurity from the souls of those departed Christians who have not been virtuous enough to go directly to Heaven or wicked enough for Hell, figures prominently in the medieval mind. Although the influence of Calvinist thinking and a reduced emphasis even in the Roman church have made Purgatory less prominent in the twenty-first century mind, images of moral and spiritual cleansing persist even today: Consider the film *Scrooged*, based on the Dickens *Christmas Carol*, which follows a wicked man's painful journey to virtue.

Groundhog Day depicts a similar journey. Phil's futile attempts to commit suicide upon realizing that Rita cannot be seduced, which occur during the adolescent sequence of incremental repetitions, display a self-centered disregard for the effects his actions have on the people around him, on the community—and they do not, as he hopes they will, allow him release from what passes as fiery torment in the bitter cold of a Punxsutawney winter. Phil Connors must repeat Groundhog Day until its torments burn the sin from his soul making him worthy of release into Heaven—in this case into life with Rita.

At the beginning of the movie, Phil is directly analogous to Chretien's Perceval: as an emotional child, he does not yet truly understand the qualities, the social requirements, that make a worthy man. Metaphorically, he is a sinful soul bound for Purgatory. Each time he repeats Groundhog Day, he comes to understand slightly more—the cleansing fires burn him gradually closer to virtue. He begins the movie as a coarse, self-centered, ignorant, unambitious, pretentious man. He is childish. Rita, on the other hand, is kind, gentle, generous, intelligent, sophisticated, and largely unavailable to an oaf like Phil.

Initially, like Perceval, Phil learns facts and misuses them. He learns a few details about Nancy, a woman he sees in the café and at the Groundhog Day festivities. He asks her name, the name of her high school English teacher, etc., in order to take advantage of her, knowing there can be no consequences, because when the day repeats she will return to her original condition. She will not realize that what she foolishly interpreted as sincere affection was in fact a one-night stand, the result of Phil's cynical manipulation of information she does not remember giving him. She will not realize it, because for her it will not have happened. He later uses intimate information he gained while seducing her ("She makes chipmunk sounds when she gets really excited") to support his claim of godhood. He abuses the power that goes along with repeating the same day forever, using it frivolously to achieve empty carnal satisfaction by deceiving foolish women. He is wicked.

Unaware that he resides in a Purgatorial state, he tries to make the best of a situation he finds painful. Repetitions of his seduction incrementally demonstrate first his mastery of the situation (like Perceval, who is able to kill a knight with a spear through the eye, he is powerful in unworthy ways) and then demonstrate his powerlessness. He attempts over a sequence of Groundhog Days to apply the technique to Rita, learning facts about her life but not from a sincere interest in her as a person—that is, not really recognizing her worth—only to discover that she cannot be seduced. The film emphasizes his failure with a montage of moments in which she repeatedly slaps his face. Rita is his ultimate reward, his Heaven, and so far he remains in Purgatory because he is not yet worthy. If he was childish at the film's outset, through this period he is sophomoric, adolescent.

Throughout this sequence he sees the pain that realizing she has been tricked causes Rita, but throughout the sequence he nevertheless repeats and refines his attempts to trick her. For instance, when in a fit of self-blame she says "I even ate fudge! Yuck!" he mumbles "No white chocolate, no fudge." He treats her pain coldly, as purely objective, a source of data, of intelligence, that allows him to refine his strategy. The reason he fails, the reason he is unworthy, is that his interest in her is not sincere. He learns about her not out of affection or respect, but in order to seduce her. She describes the situation as "a big setup." Like an adolescent, he explores how much he can get away with.

When he finally realizes the boundaries of his situation, realizes Rita's value as a person, and recognizes that she cannot be seduced and will therefore never be available to love a man like him, he understands himself to be trapped, to reside in Purgatory. Despite his previous belief to the contrary, he is not the master of his perpetually repeating environment; he is a prisoner. Although he understands himself to be unworthy, he does not yet acknowledge his ability to become worthy. That is, he doesn't yet perceive his own responsibility, that the trap is himself. Instead, he seeks to escape the trap by killing himself. He attempts to leave Purgatory prematurely.

Repetitions of his suicide change incrementally as well. In the first one, he kidnaps Punxsutawney Phil, the groundhog, and drives off a cliff into a strip mine, asserting that the groundhog "must be stopped"—here he seeks outside himself both for blame and for release from the trap. He electrocutes himself in his bathroom, knocking out the lights all over his bed and breakfast and leaving the other guests in darkness. He leaps from a building onto a populated street. He stands in front of a speeding truck, involving its driver in his death. These incremental repetitions of suicide differ widely in method and location. Despite wild variation in detail, they all fail. Phil cannot escape Groundhog Day through suicide. Although some cases are less public than others, all of them inconvenience the community, which underlines his continuing irresponsibility. He remains, metaphorically, too wicked for Heaven and not enough for Hell.

Paradoxically, though, these suicide attempts represent progress of a sort, because they derive from hope rather than despair. They are explicitly identified as attempts to break the cycle of repeating days, which indicates that he believes the cycle can be broken. Despair is the defining quality of Hell. The hopeful fires of Purgatory are meant to cleanse, but hellfire recognizes no such goal. Phil is not in Hell. He is burning, but his continued attempts to escape, however misguided and irresponsible, foreshadow his eventual release—his torment is designed to cleanse, not to punish. His numerous deaths do not result in release from Groundhog Day because, in Purgatorial terms, torment has not yet burned the imperfections from his soul. As long as he persists in being inconsiderate, a burden on the community rather than a contributing member, he remains unworthy of release into Heaven.

His suicide attempts also identify a key aspect of what he must learn: the worthy man is a constructive member of his community. Just as Perceval's ignorance of social ritual and his neglect of his mother cause him to fail in the grail castle, extending the plight of the Fisher King and his kingdom, Phil's suicides become a public problem caused by the failure to understand his responsibilities as a member of the community and his consequent failure to fulfill those responsibilities. Phil overcomes this ignorance in the final sequence of repetitions by seeking advice from the one member of the community he knows to be wise: Rita. He approaches her out of respect, out of recognition of her worth as a person. This is an important moment, because, despite framing his problem as analogous to godhood, he recognizes his own helplessness and acknowledges Rita's superiority. He now understands not only what Rita, a woman of quality, a great lady, deserves, but also that he does not measure up. He sees that he does not belong in Heaven.

Just as Perceval's meditation on his lady, inspired by red spots in the snow, marks the beginning of his maturity as a knight, this repetition of Groundhog Day marks the beginning of Phil's maturity as a man. Rita learns that he has been using his eternal Groundhog Day to perfect the art of tossing cards into a hat and as part of her advice to him observes, "This is what you do with eternity?" He has wasted countless opportunities to be a useful, generous member of the community, but it is not too late.

As she falls asleep, he whispers praise to her, noting in particular her kindness and generosity to others. This represents quite a change in his attitude. For example, while driving to Punxsutawney, Rita makes a groundhog face and gesture and offers a sympathetic interpretation of the Groundhog Day tradition, saying "I think it's nice. People like it." He responds with sarcasm and a comment about blood sausage being evidence that "people are stupid." Kindness and generosity, qualities that in the original iteration of Groundhog Day he not only lacked but scorned, are, by the end of the film, the qualities that he values most in Rita. That she is asleep when he praises her indicates he seeks no reward for the speech. He is sincere. Nevertheless, he awakens the next day to discover it is once again Groundhog Day. While he understands her worth, he remains himself unworthy. But now he knows what qualities he must develop.

The final sequence of repetitions shows Phil improving himself and trying to help as many people as he can. He learns French. He studies poetry. He becomes an accomplished jazz pianist. He even learns some medicine. He learns the limitations of his own personal power, and by extension his place in what serves for the great chain of being in Punxsutawney, Pennsylvania. He cannot save the elderly homeless man, but he *can* change a tire, perform the Heimlich maneuver on a choking man, and offer marital advice to a hesitant bride. He does all of these things without hope of reward, because he believes himself unworthy of reward. Instead he performs these good deeds because they are good. In fact, he explicitly postpones a date with Rita in order to be on time to catch a boy falling from a tree. He highlights the issue of social ritual by his

good-natured complaint that "you've never thanked me!" By performing good deeds without regard for reward, he proves that, despite (or
perhaps as a result of) his own opinion that he is not worthy of reward,
he is now worthy, his soul purged of its imperfections.

The final iteration of this sequence culminates with Rita selecting
him as a lover. Rita overhears the thanks that members of the community lavish on him, and observes first hand his surprising talent and his
unexpected modesty. She witnesses him playing virtuoso jazz piano, not
in an attempt to impress her (she was out of the room for the largest
portion of his performance), but from the sheer joy of music-making and
to please the celebrating community. Rita spends the contents of her
checkbook, accurate to the penny, to purchase him at the Punxsutawney
bachelor auction, and they spend the evening together.

That Phil and Rita do not make love at the end of that evening is
crucial. By waiting, he demonstrates that his interest in her is no longer
primarily carnal, that he seeks her company. His worthiness is further
demonstrated by the structure of the film when the next morning he
awakens to discover that Rita remains by his side and that Groundhog
Day is over. He has been released. Rita is not his prize; her presence here
is by her choice, a choice that demonstrates he is now worthy of her. During his cynical attempts to learn how to seduce her, Phil solicited a list
of qualities Rita seeks in a man. He must be humble, intelligent, sup-
portive, funny, romantic, courageous, fit, modest, kind, sensitive, and
gentle. He must love his mother and play an instrument. During that
period, Phil attempted to create the illusion that he possessed many of
these qualities. At the end of the film, he has actually developed them,
not out of a desire for reward but because he has learned that they are
objectively valuable. He demonstrates the purity of his motives when,
after his beautiful speech about Chekov, he declines Rita's invitation to
coffee. His soul has been purged of its former cynicism.

The Purgatorial aspects of the film are implicit in its imagery as well.
The morning after his first suicide, the one where he drives off a cliff, the
film superimposes the flames of his burning truck over the clock that
delimits one Groundhog Day from the next. Phil is condemned to burn
until the sin has been burned from him. In fact, Phil's situation is analogous to confession, which must be motivated by a sincere desire for forgiveness. Confessions motivated by fear of damnation do not earn
absolution. In the same way, Phil cannot escape his Purgatory until he
stops seeing escape as his goal. Until his desire to love Rita and to be a
better person are sincere, he achieves neither. When they are sincere, he
earns release.

Although incremental repetition is a structuring device primarily
prominent in medieval literature and Purgatory a primarily medieval

motif, contemporary authors have inherited and retained them both. Similarly, contemporary authors persist in exploring the prominent medieval topic of knightly worthiness. In *Groundhog Day* as in the *Conte du Graal*, the hero experiences profound personal growth on the way to achieving the full privileges of a worthy man. *Groundhog Day* demonstrates the persistent relevance of these medieval motifs in the cinema. While not explicitly medievalist in costume or setting, this film *is* self-consciously medieval in its argument and in its structure. Consider Phil's dialogue when Punxsutawney teens engage him and Rita in a snowball fight: "Assassins! I'll protect you your highness!" The knight offers the protection due to a lady of quality.

In the director's commentary on the *Groundhog Day* DVD, Harold Ramis marvels at the sheer volume of letters he received about the movie, letters that claimed it as a rallying cry for everything from Buddhism to 12 step programs. Although given the volume and variety of letters he received he might not be surprised by medievalist analysis, he does not at any point mention medieval parallels in the film. Whether Ramis opted to use medieval tropes and themes intentionally[2] or simply inherited them through the ethereal process of intertextual influence, medievalist analysis can and does here provide a richer understanding of the film and how it functions both independently and in relation to its viewers.[3] Even though the medieval parallels in *Groundhog Day* are not explicit, indeed even if they are not a conscious part of the film at all, nevertheless those parallels are present, not just due to our fascination with King Arthur, but due to the fact that—for all the incredible differences between our culture and that of the medievals—our culture develops from theirs.

Notes

1. Aberth cites David Herlihy, who questions the value of film as a teaching tool. "Herlihy's main objection is that movies create a make-believe world where viewers are required to suspend their critical judgment" (viii). To defend film as pedagogical tool, Aberth names the medium "a powerful tool for demonstrating the connections to be made between the medieval and the modern" (ix).

2. Despite his silence on the matter, at least one of his other films has striking medieval parallels: *Ghostbusters* features characters who amount to knights errant protecting their people from corrupt rulers and pernicious supernatural figures.

3. Although most articles about *Groundhog Day* are reviews, one analyzes it in terms of the hero's journey and descent into hell (Sanchez-Escalonilla). Although the classicists have apparently caught on that their scholarly conventions can offer insight about unexpected texts, medievalist assessment of the movie provides additional insights: Since Phil does eventually emerge from his lengthy cycle of Groundhog Days, his situation is Purgatorial—that is, since Hell is not for purification, Phil is not in Hell: he is in Purgatory. This distinction likely reflects a Calvinist bias in English-language scholarship, a useful insight into the modern mindset.

Works Cited

Aberth, John. *A Knight at the Movies: Medieval History on Film*. New York: Routledge, 2003.

DeWeever, Jacqueline. "Morgan and the Problem of Incest." In *Cinema Arthuriana: Twenty Essays*, ed. Kevin J. Harty, 54–63. Jefferson, N.C.: McFarland, 2002.

Hanning, Robert, and Joan Ferrante, trans. *The Lais of Marie de France*. Durham, N.C.: The Labyrinth Press, 1982.

Harty, Kevin J. "Cinema Arthuriana: An Overview." In *Cinema Arthuriana: Twenty Essays*, ed. Kevin J. Harty, 7–33. Jefferson, N.C.: McFarland, 2002.

Kleis, John Christopher. "*Tortilla Flat* and the Arthurian View." In *Cinema Arthuriana: Twenty Essays*, ed. Kevin J. Harty, 71–79. Jefferson, N.C.: McFarland, 2002.

Lacy, Norris J. "Mythopeia in *Excalibur*." In *Cinema Arthuriana: Twenty Essays*, ed. Kevin J. Harty, 34–43. Jefferson, N.C.: McFarland, 2002.

Lupack, Alan. "An Enemy in Our Midst: *The Black Knight* and the American Dream." In *Cinema Arthuriana: Twenty Essays*, ed. Kevin J. Harty, 64–70. Jefferson, N.C.: McFarland, 2002.

Lupack, Barbara Tepa. "The Retreat from Camelot: Adapting Bernard Malamud's *The Natural* to Film." In *Cinema Arthuriana: Twenty Essays*, ed. Kevin J. Harty, 80–95. Jefferson, N.C.: McFarland, 2002.

Owen, D.D.R., trans. *Chretien de Troyes: Arthurian Romances Including Perceval*. Rutland, Vt.: Everyman's Library, 1991.

Sanchez-Escalonilla, Antonio. "The Hero as a Visitor in Hell: The Descent into Death in Film Structure." ProQuest Information and Learning. Available at http://gateway.proquest.com.

About the Contributors

Benjamin Earl is a PhD candidate in the School of Journalism, Media and Cultural Studies, Cardiff University and is completing his thesis titled "Sites of Arthur: Mythic quests for cultural identity and value."

Carl James Grindley, assistant professor of English at Eugenio María de Hostos Community College of CUNY, writes and speaks on the Middle Ages in popular culture, but also takes an interest in pedagogy. He has delivered papers on teaching Dante in American high schools and on the benefits of an asynchronous approach to medieval studies, and has published on pedagogy in *Scientia Scholae.*

Paul Hardwick is a senior lecturer in English at Trinity and All Saints, Leeds (UK). He has published widely on twentieth century medievalism and on the marginal arts of the late Middle Ages. As Oz Hardwick, he has published two poetry collections, *The Kind Ghosts* (bluechrome, 2004) and *Carrying Fire* (bluechrome, 2006).

Kevin J. Harty, professor and chair of English at La Salle University in Philadelphia, has previously published essays on Chaucer, Boccaccio, *The Chester Mystery Cycle*, Henryson, Ionesco, cinematic responses to the AIDS pandemic, and King Arthur, Robin Hood and Joan of Arc on film. He is, in addition, the author or editor of eleven books including *Cinema Arthuriana: Twenty Essays; The Reel Middle Ages: American, Western and Eastern European, Middle Eastern and Asian Films About Medieval Europe; King Arthur on Film: New Essays on Arthurian Cinema; The Chester Mystery Cycle: A Casebook;* and *Cinema Arthuriana: Essays on Arthurian Film.*

Lesley Jacobs is a graduate of Brown University completing her PhD in English at Indiana University, where she studies the languages and literatures of the medieval British Islands and Scandanavia. She has presented papers on topics such as Cynewulf's runic signatures and incest and violence in Volsunga saga.

Hannah R. Johnson has recently completed her doctorate at Princeton University and is currently working as an assistant professor at the University of Pittsburgh, where she is completing a manuscript titled *The Medieval Limit: Historiography, Ethics, Culture.*

Daniel T. Kline, associate professor of English at the University of Alaska in Anchorage, specializes in Middle English literature and culture, Chaucer, and medieval drama; literary and cultural theory; religion and literature; and digital medievalism. He has published in *Chaucer Review*, *Philological Quarterly*, *College Literature*, *Literary and Linguistic Computing*, and *Comparative Drama* and has a chapter in the *Cambridge Companion to Medieval Women*. He edited *Medieval Children's Literature* (Routledge, 2003), and his current research investigates the problem of sacrifice in the representation of children and childhood in late-medieval England.

Katherine J. Lewis is a senior lecturer in history at the University of Huddersfield. She has published widely on aspects of the cult of saints in the later Middle Ages and is currently working on aspects of kingly and monastic masculinity in fourteenth and fifteenth century England.

David W. Marshall recently completed his PhD at Indiana University and currently works as an assisstant professor of English at California State University in San Bernardino. He has published on John Ball's letters and is working on the *Beowulf* story as it has been used in popular media in the twentieth century.

Aleks Pluskowski, a junior research fellow in medieval archaeology at Clare College, Cambridge, and a fellow at the McDonald Institute for Archaeological Research, studies human-animal relations in medieval Europe. He is finishing a pan–European survey of responses to animals in social and environmental contexts. His research interests include theories of hyper-reality, neo-medievalism and digital presentations of the historical past.

William Racicot is completing his PhD in English at Duquesne University. His research addresses the use of Middle English dream poetry in later periods.

Simon Trafford is based at the University of London's Institute of Historical Research and specializes in early medieval migrations, in particular the Scandinavian settlement of England. He is currently engaged in a study of gender and ethnic identities in the Danelaw.

Alison Tara Walker is completing her PhD in UCLA's English Department. Her interests include 15th century literature, the history of the book, medievalism, and new media.

Stephen Yandell, assistant professor of English at Xavier University, maintains research interests in medieval political prophecy and apocalypticism, which led him to co-edit the *Prophet Margins: The Medieval Vatic Impulse and Social Stability*. He has also published on the Middle Welsh *Mabinogi* tales and on Oxford's Inklings.

Index